Two Dianas in Alaska

AGNES HERBERT IN NATIVE PARKA DRESS

SISTERS OF THE HUNT

Two Dianas in Alaska

AGNES HERBERT
AND A SHIKÁRI

FOREWORD BY MARY ZEISS STANGE

STACKPOLE
BOOKS

Published by
STACKPOLE BOOKS
5067 Ritter Road
Mechanicsburg, PA 17055
www.stackpolebooks.com

Printed in the United States

First edition

10 9 8 7 6 5 4 3 2 1

Cover design by Tracy Patterson

Library of Congress Cataloging-in-Publication Data

Herbert, Agnes.
    Two Dianas in Alaska / Agnes Herbert and a shikári ; foreword by Mary Zeiss Stange.
        p. cm. — (Sisters of the hunt)
    Originally published: London : Lane Co., 1909.
    ISBN 0-8117-3131-6 (alk. paper)
    1. Hunting—Alaska. 2. Alaska—Description and travel. I. Title. II. Series.

SK49.H5 2004
799.29798—dc22
                                                                                2003067455

FOREWORD

*What wonder of civilization can compare with the mysteri-
ous fascination of the wild? The weird enchantment, the
silence, the space, the intangible something of everything.
Ah, it is living indeed.*

—*Agnes Herbert,*
Two Dianas in Alaska

Little is known of Agnes Herbert's early life. She was born Agnes Elsie
Diana Thorpe, sometime in the later 1870s. She grew up on the Isle
of Man. Sometime in her youth she married and sometime thereafter she
was widowed. All that is known about her first husband is his surname,
Herbert, which she retained throughout the writing career she commenced after his death. Widowhood apparently suited her; she remarked
at one point that "the widow who marries a second time does not deserve
to be one." Clearly, her widowed status gave her both the freedom and the
funds to indulge her youthful passions—for writing, for travel, and, perhaps most especially, for hunting.

None of these were considered appropriate for young women of her
day. Herbert had been born into a world where the sun never set on the
British empire, where the work and attendant glories of running that
empire fell decidedly to men, and where what one scholar has dubbed the
"Nineteenth-Century hunting cult" played a distinct and vital role in the
construction of imperial masculinity.[1] According to historian John
MacKenzie, "There were some exceptions, but the imperial hunt was a
largely male affair and extolled as such. Its rituals and its alleged charac-
ter-forming qualities were depicted as being 'manly,' a masculine training
for imperial rule and racial domination."[2] The acquisition of trophies
readily symbolized the conquest of peoples and territories, and it was
important in this regard to assert the ideal qualities embodied by the late

Victorian hunt: independence, courage, physical fitness and stamina, moral fiber, and—it almost went without saying—white masculinity. Those women who had the temerity to venture into this landscape of male privilege tended to be sharply criticized; they were as bad as the suffragettes who were making social waves closer to home.[3]

Yet by the turn of the twentieth century, there were a sufficient number of female adventurers—Lord Curzon, Viceroy of India at the time, called them "professional female globetrotters"—that there was a market for the best of their writing about their travels and about the hunting that formed an intrinsic part of many of those travels. Herbert apparently sensed her opportunity. In the opening chapter of her first book, *Two Dianas in Somaliland*, she explained:

> It is not that I imagine the world is panting for another tale about a shoot. I am aware that of the making of sporting books there is no end. Simply—I want to write. And in this unassuming record of a big shoot, engineered and successfully carried through by two women, there may be something of interest; it is surely worth more than a slight endeavour to engage the even passing interest of one person of average intelligence in these days of universal boredom.[4]

Sometime after her husband's death, Agnes and her cousin Cecily (the other "Diana") had embarked on their first international adventure, which initially had nothing to do with hunting. They traveled to North America and hired on in mining camps in the Canadian Rockies to teach cooking to Chinese immigrant workers. "Incidentally," as Herbert would later tell it, "the charm of the chase captured" the two young women, and "we exchanged the gridiron for the gun."[5] They subsequently embarked upon the first of what would turn out to be three major hunting expeditions, a safari in Somaliland. Upon their return to England, Agnes Herbert penned the tale of the two Dianas' exploits, blending keen observation and narrative sense with a wit by turns acerbic and self-effacing.[6]

As the introductory excerpt quoted above makes clear, Herbert was well aware that the key interest of the story she had to tell lay in the fact that these were two women undertaking an expedition so commonly associated with male bravado. This element of the story was intensified early on in the telling, when, as they were assembling their porters and organizing their provisions on arrival in Africa, the women chanced to encounter two countrymen who were similarly bound for the bush. The two—Ralph Windus, a distant relation of Agnes's, and an older comrade of his she refers to only as "the Leader of the Opposition"—were more than a little skeptical about the prospect of two women on safari:

> One evening I heard the two warriors talking and the elder said, not dreaming that his voice would carry so clearly: "Look here, if you are not careful, we shall have those two girls trying to tack on to our show. And I won't have it, for they'll be duffers, of course."
>
> I laughed to myself, even though I was annoyed. Men are conceited ever, but this was too much! To imagine we had gone to all the initial expense and trouble only to join two sportsmen who, true to their masculine nature, would on all occasions take the best of everything and leave us to be contented with any small game we could find!
>
> It is true that being called a girl softened my wrath somewhat. One can't be called a girl at thirty without feeling a glow of pleasure. I am thirty. So is Cecily.[7]

A rivalry was born. Shortly thereafter the two hunting parties went their separate ways, their paths crossing occasionally in the bush until they would reunite at the end of the story . . . at which point it was apparent that while the men had hunted hard and well, the women clearly bested them in the trophy department.

Herbert writes of both men with genial affection, and dedicates *Two Dianas in Somaliland* "To the Leader of the Opposition Shoot: Soldier, Shikari, and Sometime Mysogynist."[8] It is uncertain precisely what sort of relationship may or may not have been developing between Agnes and the Leader, but by story's end Ralph clearly has designs on Cecily—designs which, as we learn early on in this hunt's Alaskan sequel, Cecily has every intention of reciprocating. Hence her demand that she and Agnes travel to Alaska by way of Butte, Montana, where the two women just happen to bump into their erstwhile hunting rivals. The hunt which forms the subject of the present book was undertaken by the foursome. Agnes Herbert shares the task of its retelling with the "Leader"—the "Shikári" of the title page.

The precise identity of this co-author of Herbert's remains unknown. One possibility, based upon a photograph of a moose which appears both in this volume (facing page 290) and in C. R. E. Radclyffe's *Big-Game Shooting in Alaska*, is that Radclyffe was the man. This possibility is born out by the fact the photograph of the Leader (facing page 240) bears a distinct resemblance to Radclyffe.[9] But whoever he may have been, and whatever his reasons for anonymity, it is clear that he and Herbert held each other in very high regard, both as persons and as hunters. And while Herbert could have told the story entirely on her own, the Leader's chapters provide narrative counterpoint which not only amplifies Herbert's own version of various events, but also presents her actions in much more complimentary fashion than she might have allowed herself, given her ironically unpretentious style. The device of co-authorship works brilliantly here to show the book's primary author in her best possible light.[10]

The narrative presence of the Leader also serves at several points to embody the ideal of the imperial white male hunter on the one hand, while at the same time illustrating some significant, and not necessarily subtle, differences between the ways men and women go about hunting. Both of these seem to have been conscious intentions on Herbert's part. With regard to the first, Herbert obviously views the Leader as an Edwardian man's man. For example, as he negotiates a sensitive issue with a group of Inuit guides, she reflects:

> ... the more difficulties the Innuits [sic] set in the way the more resolved seemed the Leader to overcome and overthrow them. As a real leader should do. It always seems to me that a man fitted by nature to lead and govern others never complains of the idiocy of his coadjutors, of their incapability, unsuitability, and other shortcomings. A born leader sees in all these things the proof of his power, his power to meet and beat them. (195–196, below)

For his own part, the Leader unmistakably shares Herbert's view that he is suited to leading others, although less simply "by nature" than by birthright: "England, and Englishmen alone, are those who can still successively rule the native races upon earth. Hence the secret of success in the colonization of the vast Empire which is today ruled by the population of a small island kingdom." (89)

One cannot introduce this volume without acknowledging the sometimes blatant racism of both of its authors. When the Leader observes that "Beneath the skin of a native lies the heart of one born to be ruled by a superior hand" (89), or Herbert herself bemoans "the contamination of race mixings" that give rise to "such low-class half-breeds as we had in camp" (232), it is difficult for a modern reader not to cringe. Yet, to be honest, it was probably just as difficult for a British man or woman of a century ago—particularly a person of some rank and financial means—not to perceive themselves as to the manner of imperial domination born. Indeed, in the passage just cited, the Leader grimly prognosticates the "racial upheavals" that are bound to follow upon the movement toward racial equality in the United States. Herbert most likely shared his view that "Equality between the white and coloured races will eventually end in disaster."

Yet there are some significant differences between the Leader's generally dismissive remarks about natives and Herbert's often more nuanced, and even sympathetic, statements about them. Whereas for the Leader the Alaskan natives are simply "a people without aspirations, or ambitions, with strange fancies and superstitious beliefs, dreamers having the weird imagination of children . . . whose highest intellectual attainments consist in devising means of obtaining food and clothing" (87-88), Herbert sees more complicated characters. She, for example, spends evenings with her Aleut guides around the campfire, learning what she can about native folklore. In the process Herbert discovers not only the richness of Aleutian mythology, but cultural limitations of her own which impede her ability to effectively translate Aleutian stories into an acceptably British idiom:

> And as the native wove his romance into the silence of the night the witchery of the scene and the hour lent a thrill of enchantment and imparted a sentimental feeling of poesy which, perhaps, the story lacks when told again in England, in plain, bald fashion. (269)

Here we have one born storyteller in the spell of another. And Herbert, tentatively to be sure but nonetheless genuinely, expresses their common humanity.

The two Dianas' relationship with the natives is, of course, complicated by virtue of their sex. Here in Alaska, as had been the case in Africa, the Englishwomen have to prove to their native guides that as hunters they can hold their own with men of whatever race:

> Were we not dressed alike, in the quaintest of fur parkas, with a modicum of knickerbockers showing below? and did we shirk damp, danger, or dismay? "I grant that I am a woman; think you I am no stronger than my sex?" Cecily quoted laughingly to Ned [their primary guide].

But in his eyes there was no answering light of recognition. The Immortal One has not as yet been translated
for the benefit of the Aleuts. (67)

Perhaps predictably, the two women are rather less self-assured in
asserting their superiority over their native guides and porters than are
their male counterparts. Herbert clearly finds this fact irksome. She
remarks at several points on the subordinate status of women in the various native cultures they encounter, yet in one way or another she manages
to blame native women for their lower social positioning, rather than
express anything like sisterly feeling for them. Exponent of universal
women's rights she is not; at one point in *Two Dianas in Somaliland* she
chides herself, "Gracious! I am digressing! And talking like a suffra-
gette!"[11] Yet if her relationship with the male of the human species smacks
more of rivalry, and sometime camaraderie, than of anything like equality,
this ultimately says less about Agnes Herbert than about the age in which
she lived and the limits it imposed upon women. As hunters capable of
outdoing the men at their own game, Agnes and Cecily were socially
divergent enough that they probably both felt the pressure to conform, in
other ways, to more conventional cultural expectations.

On one thing regarding their native guides the English women and
men were in total agreement. Alaskan natives, in their view, had no sense
whatsoever for the sport of hunting. This may seem an odd observation
about peoples who have for millennia subsisted by hunting; indeed,
among the surviving hunter/forager groups worldwide, the natives of
northernmost reaches of North America most closely approach a purely
hunting culture in which foraging plays a relatively minor role. Yet herein
lies the difference between Alaskan native subsistence hunting and the
ideal of hunting as sport which developed among Euro-Americans.
Whereas for the latter the thrill of the chase and the procurement of trophies may be equally important as—and sometimes more important
than—the procurement of food, for native hunters the process is all about
meat.[12] Hence Agnes and the Leader fail to comprehend why, after they
both shot badly and lost a Dall ram, their guide Steve (all of the native
guides are given Anglo names) "was heartbroken. Why not kill a ewe, and
have done with it? We could get any quantity, he said, without traveling so
far." To these trophy hunters, that of course would have been to miss the
point of the whole exercise.

Agnes and Cecily were obviously as driven as the men were when it
came to the hunt for trophies. Herbert chalks this up to nature, referring

to "the fierce exultant joy of the chase which can only be understood by those who have experienced it. I should not have been human, and a huntress, if the sight of those two magnificent beasts [two Alaskan brown bears] had not deepened in my heart the lust of sport." (139) Fishing for salmon, she ponders the ethics of a contest so heavily weighted in favor of the anglers. Nonetheless, she admits, "the instinct of pursuit is strong in all of us, and is part of the great scheme of Nature. . . . I was as full of the lust of killing as any of them." (145)

This does not necessarily mean, however, that the two Dianas go about hunting in the same way, or with the same attitudes, as the men. A good example of the differences between them occurs when Agnes is forced, the Leader's rifle having jammed, to shoot and kill a charging she-bear, orphaning its cub. "My heart-strings," she writes, "were tugged with the pity of it! What a brute I felt!" As she takes out her handkerchief, the Leader chides her against weeping. Indignantly she replies that she merely wants to wipe the mother's blood off the cub's paws. "What a woman you are!" the Leader laughs, "Killing one minute, and healing the next. I wonder you have acquired your wonderful collection of trophies at all." To which Herbert replies, level-headedly, "You're jealous." But beneath Herbert's calm demeanor, the Leader senses a tender spirit and endeavors to soothe her feelings about orphaning the cub. (137–138)

On one level, this incident is one of several—including one in which Agnes saves the Leader's life by shooting a wounded bear, and another in which they are trapped and nearly killed by rock-fall—which play up the erotic tension that obviously was at play between them. Yet on another, it illustrates the way Agnes and Cecily challenge and resist those elements of the male-defined model of the chase which dictate leaving one's vulnerabilities back home. At one point when Cecily has lost a wounded bear and night has fallen, she and Agnes spend a sleepless night worrying about the bear's suffering: "It was a great, if impossible-to-be-helped, pity," Herbert writes. She adds, with intentional irony: "We were not sporting enough, I suppose, to be indifferent. Might it be that, being women, we could not learn to take such normal accidents pertaining to the chase with calmness?" (119–120) The women would depart camp before dawn, without breakfast, to track the wounded animal.

When caribou hunting, Herbert finds herself downwind of a female caribou, and when "the scent of a human being . . . reached her nostrils, the sight of the intruder filled her with unnameable horror and dread. . . . The great, soft, round, appealing eyes of the beautiful deer looked full into mine, as though she would read her doom, asking—begging—entreating—

praying." Herbert defers shooting. "Ah, well!" one imagines the sigh in her words. "I like not to war with feminine things. They have enough to contend with as it is. Let her go, and my blessing with her." At which point her native assistant happens upon the scene, casts her a withering look, having "seen his certain chops and steaks vanish on the horizon," and goes off to gather berries on the hillside, "eating them in reproachful mouthfuls." (214–215) Not for the last time will Herbert find herself in a position where her feminine approach to hunting falls short of a male-defined ideal—whether of sport or of subsistence.

Agnes Herbert presents a complex picture when it comes to her depiction of what it means to be a woman hunter. On the one hand, subtle differences like the ones just noted seem to matter deeply to her. So, too, do the logistics of women's hunting, from finding the right gear to the care and discipline of guides and porters. On the other hand, she is explicit in her desire to succeed at a man's activity in roughly the same ways and to the same level of accomplishment (best symbolized by trophies) as a man would. These two sides of her personality are perhaps best summed up in the only two photographs of Herbert that appear in her hunting books. The first is the frontispiece to *Two Dianas in Somaliland*, which shows "The Authoress" rather theatrically posed in a formal studio portrait, hair swept up and wearing a velvet ball gown. The second is the frontispiece to the present volume, "Agnes Herbert in Native Parka Dress," rifle in hand and level gaze fixed on the viewer.

Two Dianas in Alaska was published in 1909 to excellent reviews; indeed several reviewers remarked that the sequel outshone its predecessor. The major British sporting publication *The Field* praised the book's "love of exploration, admiration for the beauty in nature, keenness for sport, and withal a womanly restraint and tender-heartedness." *The Nation* called it "clever to brilliancy." Time and again reviewers on both sides of the Atlantic remarked the book's freshness and wit, Herbert's incisive observations about human as well as animal nature, the freshness of her prose and her literary style. *Vanity Fair*'s reviewer called it "The most fascinating sporting book" of the year "and quite the best written. . . . Miss Herbert's success is as emphatic in book-making as in hunting."[13]

Herbert went on to write one more hunting book, *Casuals in the Causasus: The Diary of a Sporting Holiday* (1912), which chronicled the third of her and Cecily's hunting expeditions. Cecily's marriage to Ralph Windus had formed the conclusion to *Two Dianas in Alaska*. The Leader having dropped out of the narrative picture sometime between the end of this book and the women's adventure in the Russian empire, Agnes Herbert married Commander Archibald Thomas Stewart of the Royal Navy in 1913. She appears to have retired at this point in her life from the sporting life but built upon her reputation as an established travel writer, producing a highly regarded work *The Isle of Man* (1909), and books about her travels in *Northumberland* (1923) and *Korea* (1924). She wrote two books for young readers based in her African experiences, *The Life Story of a Lion* (1911) and *The Elephant* (1917) and one from Alaska, *The Moose* (1913). And she penned a number of short stories and journalistic articles.

Herbert was a member of the Society of Women Journalists, serving as its vice-chair from 1929 to 1933, and as vice-president in 1939. From 1922 to 1929 she edited the *Writer's and Artist's Yearbook*. In 1931, she was named an Officer of the British Empire. While she must undoubtedly have been proud of all of these life-accomplishments, one suspects that for her—as for the historian of women's hunting—her most noteworthy achievement lay in the fact that she and her cousin Cecily hunted three continents in the first decade of the twentieth century under their own steam and on their own terms.

Agnes Herbert died in 1960.

Mary Zeiss Stange
Ekalala, Montana
August 2003

NOTES

1. See John M. MacKenzie, *The Empire of Nature: Hunting, Conservation and British Imperialism* (Manchester and New York: Manchester University Press, 1988), Chapter 2.
2. MacKenzie, 22. The primary "exceptions" he has in mind had to do with fox-hunting, which, from the mid-nineteenth century forward, was in England a relatively equal-opportunity sport.
3. James R. Ryan, *Picturing Empire: Photography and the Visualization of the British Empire* (London: Reaktion Books, 1997), 110.
4. Agnes Herbert, *Two Dianas in Somaliland* (London: John Lane the Bodley Head, 1908), 1.
5. *Two Dianas in Somaliland*, 1–2.
6. The appellation "Diana" is, of course, a reference to the Roman goddess of the hunt (whose Greek name was Artemis). The colloquial use of Diana in reference to female hunters is similar to using the Biblically-derived "Nimrod" for male hunters.

TWO DIANAS IN ALASKA

7. *Two Dianas in Somaliland*, 19.

8. "Shikári," from the Urdu word for hunter, is variously used in writings of the period to refer to expert trackers and hunters of game, more often however with regard to hunting in the Indian subcontinent than in Africa.

9. On this matter, see Kenneth P. Czech, *With Rifle and Petticoat: Women as Big Game Hunters, 1880–1940* (Lanham and New York: The Derrydale Press, 2002), 80–81. Czech raises the issue to refute a charge made by John C. Phillips, in 1930, that Radclyffe was in fact the author of one or more of Herbert's books, including this one. As Czech points out, given Herbert's distinctive writing style, and the fact that her descriptive interests were markedly different from those of Radclyffe, Phillips' accusation appears groundless. Czech does not, however, take the logical next step of entertaining the question whether Radclyffe was Herbert's co-author, as seems likely as far as circumstantial evidence goes.

10. An additional, and more practical, reason for inviting the Leader to provide several chapters may have been that Herbert's publisher John Lane brought this second hunting book of hers out within a year of her first; co-authorship surely meant for less writing time.

11. *Two Dianas in Somaliland*, 205.

12. On this distinction between Alaskan native and Euro-American perspectives on hunting, the tension between these perspectives, and the impact of this tension on the development of game laws in Alaska, see Morgan Sherwood, *Big Game in Alaska: A History of Wildlife and People* (New Haven and London: Yale University Press, 1981).

13. Reviews are culled from the endpapers of *Casuals in the Caucasus* (New York and London: John Lane, 1912).

PREFACE

I DO not know if any words of apology are needed for the mediocrity of the portion of this work which I have contributed. If they are necessary, however, this may be found in the plea that my vocation and lessons in life have been chiefly concerned with the use of the sword before that of the pen. Nothing save the urgent request of my fair co-author would have induced me to undertake such a task. Once, therefore, having committed the awful deed of "putting pen to paper," I can merely crave the indulgence of my readers when they compare my lack of descriptive power with the more accomplished productions emanating from the pen of my colleague. If I have failed in *jus et norma loquendi*, I may claim in extenuation of the offence that my contributions to this book try to represent a true picture of the habits of men and animals as I saw them in the wastes and forests of the dark and silent North.

A SHIKÁRI

CONTENTS

[xix]

ILLUSTRATIONS

TWO DIANAS IN ALASKA

CHAPTER I

WE SET OUT FOR ALASKA

Come, let's go together
Cymbeline

Danger shall seem sport, and I will go
Twelfth Night

MY last book, which was the record of a shooting
trip in Somaliland, has just been returned to me by
a lady to whom I gave a copy, as she said she " didn't
like so much killing." Are we not all killing creatures every day? In savage and animal life it is
done as a matter of course, and if one wants to
describe savage life the killing cannot be left out.
My friend shudders at my slaying a rhinoceros, but
manages to eat part of an unfortunate sheep immediately afterwards. I wonder if the good lady's
words ring true. She may be right, and books on
sport and adventure are only for men and boys, the
sterner sex. If, therefore, you, reader o' mine, should
regard all forms of taking life as unwomanly, read
no more. An you do, it is on your own head. We
went to Alaska to shoot, and—we shot. Perhaps I

B

should like you to persevere, and if for no other reason, because the book is mine.

Our little expedition to Alaska consisted at its onset of the cousin who shot over Somaliland with me, none the less a sportsman for all that she is a woman, and myself. Our preparations consisted in sending on some of the heavy kit to Victoria, British Columbia, which place we meant to use as a base, and where we knew we could garner in all the stores to fit out the small sealing schooner which we meant to hire for the trip. On sport and adventure bent, the ways and means thereof were more or less as yet a matter for conjecture, since nothing could be really definitely decided until our arrival in Victoria.

Leaving England in early December we made New York in record time, and put up for a day or two at one of the largest caravanserais in the town. Our immediate intention was to proceed to Victoria by way of Butte City, Montana, as Cecily, my cousin, wanted to see a young brother of hers who is ranching "Out West." I know now that she had excellent reasons for this strenuous desire to include Butte in our route. It was not her brother who acted as magnet, but some one else's brother.

We were much interested with everything in our short two days in New York, and the hotel was "immense" in every way. So was our bill. When it was presented we thought we really must, inadvertently, have purchased the building. Baths at fifty cents each are not conducive to the state of cleanliness which is next to godliness, for the reason that it is too expensive to indulge in them very often. Our regret was that we hadn't known the charge at the time. We should certainly have run the taps all over again, and had a second dip, in the laudable desire to get our money's worth.

A trip across America is so familiar to most people that there really isn't much that is new to say about it. The gymnastic feat of undressing on one's berth, with the upper one pressing down upon one's head like the lid of a box; the persistency of the ticket collector, who acquires a sort of second wind of most unnecessary activity during the midnight hours; the delight of playing Horatius in the poky little dressing-room, holding it against a crowd of infuriated fellow-passengers, cease to interest at last from constant habit. But the astonishment one feels at the much-vaunted excellence of the sleeping arrangements is ever new. Could publicity farther go? Is a Pullman sleeping-car the place for domesticity run rampant? I only ask mildly. It seems to me that to portion out the car o' nights, half for the men folk, half for the women portion of the travelling community, would improve matters all round. Then, by dropping a curtain in the centre of the passage-way, the joyful consummation of somewhere to undress would be arrived at, and all the embarrassing waving of apparel, muddled up with curtains and cuss-words, would be avoided. But I hate carping, so I'll stop.

It is glorious lying on one's berth, with the blinds of the windows up, as the vast train sweeps up some snow-clad giant slope, and down again to a pathless plain. A panorama which can banish sleep, and give a glimpse into a wonder-scene more perfect than a world of dreams.

I love the friendliness of Americans. Every one on the cars talks to every one else without a suspicion of being taken for a bandit or footpad as is the rule in England. We shared our "section" with a voluble little lady, whose business and hopes and aims were all spread out before us in the first quarter of an hour. Not to be ready to say whither you are bound, and wherefore, is a contemptibly close way of travelling about the States. If you don't want to tell the truth you must tell a fib, but you must tell something, since you will be asked a multitude of questions *instanter* on making a new acquaintance.

Our companion presented us with her visiting-card. It read—

> *Miss Mamie G. Carlson Potts, C.S.,*
> *Great Falls,*
> *Miss.*

I thought C.S. must stand for Civil Servant, but it signifies, Miss Mamie told us, Christian Scientist. She was a "healer," and I suppose that it carries a kind of accolade. It seems odd to have the sect you belong to printed on your visiting-card.

Miss Potts was in a fix. She had so many lovers she did not really know which to select. She told us all about them, and we did our best to help her to choose. Cecily was all for a man "in the dry-goods way," but I strongly advocated the claims of a persistent "drummer." A musical husband is such an acquisition. I did not know until later that "drummer" is merely Americanese for a common or garden commercial traveller. Miss Mamie could not make up her mind. It did seem hard that one woman should have such a glut of would-be husbands, while we two were with not even one husband in sight.

"Husbands ain't come by easy," said Miss Mamie sententiously. "What you two gals need to do is to go out and scratch for 'em."

How energetically she must have scratched! Such a list came up every minute. And Miss Mamie was quite old, older than we were, quite thirty-two, I'm sure. But I notice that the older a woman gets the more proposals she can remember.

Cecily whispered to me what a joke it would be if we could only put all the myriad lovers into the same cage, and let them fight the matter out as bucks and tigers do. I said very likely they wouldn't do it, and it would end like a great scorpion and tarantula battle we once went to see. Instead of fighting they were tremendous pals, and took to one another like anything.

Miss Potts spent her entire day with her front hair wound in and out of a spiky fence of tin arrangements, and this *chevaux-de-frise* was only let out for a brief half-hour before bed-time, when it didn't matter, and in this resplendent condition our friend considered her "bang," as she termed the mass of

short hair tangled to a fuzzy mass of on-endedness,
" real cute."

The most interesting man aboard the cars was a
splendid type of strenuous America, a man with a
mind, a great personality. He had chosen a wife
who made the whole scheme of things inexplicable.
If, as I hope, she touched the spot somewhere, she
could not have touched the machinations of his brain.
They were travelling in great state, with their own
car and servants, and were most hospitably anxious
that we should join them, Miss Potts too, if she
liked, but we thought it would be too much like a
pasha travelling with a harem.

Our friend of the private car had made a vast fortune by coming in at the right moment. Any one
who really studies human nature and discovers what
it is human beings most stand in need of, and then
supplies this want, is bound to lay up treasure on
earth, and, moreover, the cheaper the article the
more universal will be the demand. In Mr. Quilter's
case it was quinine, and through quinine life had
become to him as a gigantic game of draughts,
opposing forces cleared from the board, and all his
men in the king row. One evening we dined with
him in splendour, and Miss Mamie would have gone
to the party with prisoned hair had we not pointed
out to her that no greater occasion was likely to
come her way just then. We had a merry dinner,
only darkened by the upsetting of a cup of scalding
coffee all over Miss Mamie's foot. It was her last
night on the cars, and she retired to her loft early,

telling us that she had "a bad claim," which is, it seems, Christian Science talk for a scalded foot.

We reached Great Falls at breakfast-time, and the cold was so intense the windows of the heated car became steamed beyond a possibility of outlook, and when one wished to view the snow-covered land-scape there was nothing for it but to brave the terrors of the chilly platform of a rear car. Everything in Great Falls was on runners, made into sleighs, and the last we saw of Miss Potts was her departure in a hired hack, its body set right on the snow, and all the portmanteaux and kit bumping along behind, tied on to an improvised platform.

It was a world of dazzling whiteness, the whole of the vast Missouri River, with a water-power second only to Niagara, frozen over.

So at last we came to Butte City, surely the ugliest town in all America. Like some Gargantuan bar-nacle it clings to the hillside, and over it, grey and sombre, looms a pall of smoke, tinged green with the fumes from the famous smelters. No flowers or grass grow in Butte. They cannot. And if some stray enterprising young shoot does peep out it soon alacks the day and withers away in horror at the vista it has been born to. Never was there such a rushing place as Butte. It just seems to take away one's breath. The drum of the energetic Salvationist fights for the mastery over the strident music of the myriad saloons, which, with doors ever a-swing, radiate warmth and Nirvana. All the hurrying men —and no one ever walks slowly—look tense and anxious, everybody is in a furious hurry. They have all the time there is, but not nearly enough. In the hotel each man dips constantly into his pocket for bits of blue ore, and the words "seventy per cent.," "claims," "options," sing in the very air. Does all the ore smelt seventy per cent.? It would seem so. We were invited to take shares in at least six different mining ventures before we had been as many hours in Butte, and all the prospective ore was bound to smelt seventy per cent. For its size no city produces more wealth than Butte, seething whirlpool of plots and plans, and groans and griefs.

Everything was a source of interest. Even to listen to the many mining men who lived at our hotel talking the jargon of the smelters fascinated us. The passing through guest is referred to as "a transient."

"You're a tranjan?" said our chambermaid, dashing in with my *chota hazari*.

"I suppose so," I answered doubtfully, wondering whatever on earth I had claimed to be.

One evening as we sat in the ante-room off the main hall we heard the bustle of a new arrival, and all inquisitive ears caught the sound of an English voice. "All right," it said. "All right," just that. Cecily and I looked at one another, for we should know that voice wherever we heard it in jungle, debate, or Babel of tongues. It could belong to one man only, and that one he whom we had christened the Leader of the opposition party that formerly shot over Somaliland at the same time as we did. My kinsman, Ralph Windus, would of a certainty be here also, for these two never part, if they can help it. They were at Sandhurst together, and afterwards joined the same regiment.

Then, in a flash, I guessed why Cecily had come by way of Butte!

"You are as good at scratching as Miss Mamie Potts," I said sternly.

Cecily looked guilty; and I hope she blushed. We peered round the door, and yes, there was Ralph, running his finger down the back numbers of the hotel register. He turned and spoke to his friend, standing alongside, and in another moment came in like a whirlwind, afire with pleasure at seeing Cecily —us, I mean. Ralph and his *fidus Achates* had been after big-horn and wapiti in Wyoming and Montana, and had come off with some fine heads, which we might see on the morrow. Don't you love to-morrow? To-morrows have but one drawback, they so soon become yesterdays, and I hate yesterday as much as old Omar did.

'Twas such a glorious evening, such a merry dinner, such retrospections, quips, and teasings. If Cecily found a seventh heaven in a corner seat with Ralph, I felt equally contented in my chat with the elder warrior. He caught my meanings so quickly, he loves the same things that I do, the humorous, the playful, the joyous, the pitiful, the pathetic, the imaginative. We discussed the heads they had, and the heads they hadn't, for with the sportsman it is always the heads that are most worth having which are not there. We spoke of our prospective Alaskan trip, and showed them our route so far as we knew it ourselves by the map. And this time our friends threw no cold water on our schemes. They looked at one another. " A splendid trip, isn't it?" said Cecily meditatively.

Then like a bombshell came, " May we go too?" from Ralph.

The silence of intense surprise fell on Cecily and myself.

" May we go too?" repeated Ralph.

" We are going," said his *fidus Achates* firmly, and that seemed to settle it.

Next morning we arranged matters. We four would go together to Alaska, and yet not together. That is to say, in some ways the expeditions would be separate, in others amalgamated. Our camps should at times be one camp, at others, when it suited us, they should be distinct. There should never be any demanding the same hunter at the same time; no seeing too much of each other.

We bestowed the accolade of commander-in-chief of the trip on the one time Leader of the opposition shoot of Somaliland days, but reserved to ourselves the right of vetoing any command he might make. What Mrs. Grundy thought of the whole arrangement I do not venture to say. In the wild such a personage does not exist, and we only thought of the wild. How it called us, how it never ceases to call if once you have answered! Besides, women who have passed the rubicon of thirty—let it be " wropt " in mystery how long since—do not need chaperons anywhere, being by right of age and common-sense each one a full-blown chaperon in herself.

We mapped out the united trip, the route, the ways and means, as well as we could at the time, and collecting our mountains of kit, took train for Seattle, the Sound Port, and from there crossed to Victoria.

The *auberge* we put up at was like all the large Canadian hotels, with the usual quaint notices in the bedrooms.

VISITORS PLACING BOOTS OUTSIDE THE DOOR DO SO
AT THEIR OWN RISK.

Imagine! This was in a really first-class hotel. You must take the risk, or hie you to the basement, where you climb to a majestic lofty perch, reminiscent of a dental chair, and sit enthroned the while your boots are polished!

Cecily took the risk, because she said her boots weren't wearable anyhow, and there was a chance that they might return to her rejuvenated. The door opened suddenly, no tapping, or " By your leave," and a twangy voice said, " Ten cents! Where's the ten cents?"

We were too astonished to do anything but pay up gracefully. Better arrangements for boot-cleaning in Canadian hotels need making.

NO WASHING IN THE BEDROOMS.

This last notice was a considerable puzzle to us at first, for we wondered where else we should be permitted to undertake cleansing operations. We discovered that the curt notice was addressed to remittance men only, and a good many of them board at even somewhat expensive hotels. The hotel proprietors know that in between remittances John Chinaman frequently turns rusty, and says, "Me no washee no more," driving his patrons perforce to the bedroom washing-basin. It is an interesting sight on a moon-lit night to see the upper windows of some of the hotels and boarding-houses.

At nights around us—for we were not in the heart of the town—a few early frogs commenced their evening concert, singing in twisting notes their long drawn-out chirps. So many together made a really big vibrating noise, and the sopranos and contraltos combined to create a most harmonious whole. I liked to hear them, and looked forward to the little choir's entertainment. I tried to get a specimen of the warblers, but they were too wary for me, and as I approached quietly and furtively, I invariably caught nothing but the sound of a gentle splash, as each frog dived for safety. Then—silence awhile. After a few moments, a trying-it-on sort of chirrup, then another in more assertive tones, and soon all the swamp was ringing again with the gay fairy-like music.

Our next procedure was to advertise in a local paper for a sealing schooner. There are many of these strong and powerfully-built ships lying idle at Esquimalt. They are about seventy tons burden, and real stalwarts, able to withstand the terrific seas of the Arctic regions. To have a ship of one's own, even a rough-and-ready affair, on an expedition to Alaska is the next best thing to possessing the magic carpet of the *Arabian Nights*. We should have but to command, and could land on any shore, or inlet, that we chose. We had five replies to our advertisement.

Each owner of a sealer described his property as a veritable *Lusitania*, and, presumably to clinch matters, one of our correspondents enclosed the photograph of his skipper, a piece of quaintness which amused us vastly. The skipper in his pictured presentment was a really personable man, and ought to have pleaded in eloquent silence. Of course a man might be a good sailor with any sort of a face. Besides, photographs fib so. One cannot rely on pictures at all. Even Henry VIII found that out. Do you remember what happened to Henry VIII? The people of England wanted to make the succession doubly sure, and so did old Hal, but he hadn't a wife at the time. Anne of Cleves was thought to be a good political move, and Henry said he would like to see her. The people of England were not to be caught out like that. They knew their Hal. A beautiful portrait was prepared, so flattering that Anne would not have recognized herself. The bluff one was charmed. "Send her along at once," he said. When he saw her—— But history luckily does not cuss in print.

I like a good-looking face, I do confess, but in the case of a skipper good navigation counts more, especially in a trip like ours, covering ground, or rather water, charted indifferently well, rocky, difficult, and fog-bound. We selected the application of a Scandinavian, who sailed his ship for a small company. A good many captains of sealers own their own boats. We went in a body to inspect the chosen. Ugly and massive-looking, she sat the water like a tub of standing. Her deck planks were filthy, every inch of her was smeared with seal-oil, but her name was *Lily*. Her hatches had been white once, but that was æons ago.

Down-stairs—Cecily hints I must say "down the companion," or I shall be taken for a landlubber—there was a large hold for the skins, which we meant to use for stores and kit generally, and, some joyful day, trophies, and a bare compartment we grandiloquently referred to as "the saloon," from which led two insignificant smelling little cabins with two berths apiece. The men all slept in a hideous fo'-castle, where—alas!—our food would have to be cooked.

After coming to an arrangement with the owner by which we were to be allowed to spend a certain sum improving the cabins, etc., we engaged the *Lily*, her skipper, and all hands to take us whithersoever we wished. We carefully inserted a clause to this effect in our agreement, but the skipper pointed out that the *Lily* had her limitations.

The next scheme was for the thorough cleansing of our ship, and the fitting her up so that she might be at least endurable to live in, if not all that one could wish. Clean bedding, knick-knacks for the cabins, a few cushions, and books, made for Sybaritic comfort.

Food of all sorts, tinned and otherwise, we purchased in the Victoria stores, and the majority served us well. One or two of the Chinese seemed inclined to trade on the "take the cash and let the credit go" principle, but a little adroitness put matters to rights. The tents for the trip were made to our order in Chinatown, and when completed weighed a little over seven pounds each. They were ∧-shape, about six feet high at the ridge-pole, and although very thin, withstood any amount of rain.

Camp equipment on an Alaskan trip is a matter for very careful consideration, and luxuries such as beds, chairs, and a plenitude of cooking utensils, which seem so necessary in a country of camel transport, have to be rigidly ignored. There are no pack ponies to be had, and if there were, it would be impossible to take them on occasions aboard *bidarkas*, or get them through the primeval forest after moose. With hunters and packers demanding such exorbitant sums for their services, camp attendants have to be few in number, and the sportsman himself finds it needful very often to shoulder a none too flimsy pack.

Having passed in review the many sleeping-bags now on the market, we decided on the Norwegian variety, made of reindeer skin, and they proved wonderful assets, being so warm, light, and durable. Waterproof bags were provided for carrying our clothes. The general idea which the average person has of Alaska is somewhat hazy, and a traveller bound for the Northern solitudes is regarded very much in the light of a cross between a Nansen and a Peary. The North Pole and Alaska would seem to the man in the street to be synonymous.

As a matter of fact, however, some days of the Alaskan summer are too warm to be pleasant, but in going there a warm outfit is needful, and our *khaki* serge coats were lined through with woollen material of Jaeger make. For hunting moose every hunter has his own idea of the most suitable footgear. Moccasins are very silent, but prone to slip on damp logs and wet ground, and are, of course, useless in the rough country where the white sheep live. Our shooting-boots were made with rubber soles, and for hunting bears in the sleughs we provided American gum-boots, most difficult things to get about in if any speed is required. Since our Somaliland trip my cousin and I had transferred some of our affections—being women, and therefore changeable—from weapons of other days, and now meant to use as our main stand-bys a couple of small-bore magazine rifles, a ˙375 bore, and a ˙256 Mannlicher. We also had in our rifle-cases our old 12-bores, a ˙35 Winchester, a ˙22 Winchester, and a ˙410-bore collector's gun.

We finally made up our minds to send on our schooner to Kodiak *viâ* the west coast of Vancouver Island, we ourselves following some ten days later by steamer from Seattle. The inside passage is very difficult, if not impossible, for a sailing ship, the fiords are so narrow, and the current rushes through the narrows at so great a pace. The west route also is a particularly disagreeable one in spring and autumn, as the wind blows great guns all the time. Everything considered, we felt we should be doing the most sensible thing to join our ship at Kodiak.

During the enforced stay in Victoria we found the time hang rather heavily on our hands. For Ralph and the Leader there was always the open hospitality of that excellent institution the Union Club, but for Cecily and myself there was little to amuse us, save daily visits to the harbour in order to watch what progress was being made in renovating our future quarters on board the *Lily*. I tried to develop an interest in golf, for sheer joy in the wandering over the beautifully-situated links, with the glorious vista across the Sound. There must be some element of sport lacking in my nature, for the mysteries of golf have never seized me in the fierce grip of their charms, as has been the case with so many good sportsmen of my acquaintance.

We took to riding about the neighbourhood on a couple of cayuse ponies hired from a livery stable. Livery stables are very plentiful in Victoria, but the business evidently has its vicissitudes, if we can judge by the following appealing notice which we saw printed on the walls of the establishment patronized by us—

" To trust is to bust, to bust is hell ;
No trust, no bust, no hell."

The cayuse, or Indian-bred pony, breaks into a rocking-horse-like lope the instant it sets out, a most comfortable and easy mode of riding. And they keep up this rolling canter for a very long period. It was rather quaint to notice the manner some butcher-boys and drivers in one or two buggies manœuvred things whenever it was necessary to leave the horse alone for a minute or two. An ordinary two-pound weight was fixed on to a strap which ran to the horse's head, and, at a standstill, the weight was slung out on to the sidewalk, or roadway, and there the horse remained, anchored. Mounting, the butcher-boy would slip the weight into his pocket.

The animal I sampled first had one white eye and one dark brown. I saw him look at me jocosely as I neared him, so I bewared. Sure enough, the instant he felt the weight upon his back he gave two stag-like bounds, and bucked and bucked. Not being a broncho-breaker, I changed my mettlesome steed, willy-nilly.

The second cayuse was an amiable-tempered beast, but rather uncertain in the feet. He never appeared to be able to judge the distance of the next step forward. On the way home from the other side of Goldstream one night I missed the way, and had to cut through seven miles of bush as lonely and dark as night could make them. In a bad place my pony came down, but neither of us was hurt. He was so nice about it, never made a fuss and got frightened, only sort of apologized, and hoped I wasn't injured.

Sometimes we took the road to Esquimalt, and there visited the studio of a sculptor, to whom we had letters of introduction. Isn't there a peculiar fascination about a studio? Sculptured legs, arms, half-finished paintings, studies for heads, horrors of anatomy, all lying helter-skelter in delightful confusion. Light from above. Why are not all rooms lighted from above, open to the sun?

The Chinese theatre in the large Chinese quarter in Victoria attracted us, but when we got there we wished ourselves anywhere else. The Chinese have passed us. Our problem plays are food for babes compared with Chinese drama. They have left the Problems behind, and overtaken the Purpose. If you must go to a Chinese theatre, go alone. It is very embarrassing to go in company.

In between the appalling situations we four rushed into conversation, nervously, to cover up our tracks, as civilized people do, seizing on immaterial details and discussing them with the fierce grip of drowning men clutching at straws.

" In this indistinct light," the Leader said, " your hair looks quite red."

" Very likely it is so," I responded, having to laugh at last, " I'm a magenta-coloured blush from head to heel."

The heat and the smell of a Chinese theatre make a visit very short. The silence is so dispiriting also. There is no applause. How, I wonder, does an actor in China know when he reaches the constellation stage?

The ordinary theatre in Victoria was not open regularly, week by week, when we were there, but the companies coming in from the States and Canada were often very good. The boards were sacred too, for they had been trodden by " the Bernhardt," as the divine Sarah is always referred to " out there," and other famous touring stars.

One evening we went to hear a very much advertised American band. I mustn't particularize. It was a very excellent band indeed. Before almost everything they played they produced a board with " By desire " printed upon it in very large type. Some one had expressed a desire apparently for almost every item. I was so amused to hear a languid-looking, rather unintelligent lady, who was seated just in front of me, remark *sotto voce* to her cavalier—

" What a large number of pieces this man ' Desire ' has written, hasn't he? Have you ever heard of him ?"

The amusing part of it all was that the man she questioned was equally at sea, and they both agreed that they must lose no time in acquiring some of " Desire's " taking efforts from a Government Street music store!

In between the buying of stores and the getting the *Lily* started off, Ralph managed to find time in which to make a complete stupid of himself. It was all brought about, he afterwards confided to me, by Cecily's apparent indifference, and came of a desire to make her jealous. A foolish idea at any time—

to stir up jealousy. It is ever unwise to take jealousy lightly, as if it were an insignificant thing that may be disregarded. With people that feel deeply it is a very serious thing, and it is a very curious thing, for it is often strongest where there is least cause. How came the Bard to paint Othello as he did? Can he have tasted jealousy himself to portray it so?

Ralph's ladye—for of course a woman was the cause of all the trouble—was staying at our hotel, in between moments of globe-trotting. We had not talked to her for half-an-hour before she told us how completely misunderstood she was by her lord and master, an elderly, well-meaning person, far too good for the draw he'd made from the matrimonial lucky-bag. Yes, she was hopelessly misunderstood, her "soul was starved," whatever that might mean. Her husband, she said pitifully, was a "mere money-making machine, an insensate log, who could never do aught but drag her down from the heights of poetic fancy." She had soaked herself in such a lot of psychological nonsense it was really difficult at times to follow her meanderings.

First she slid out her minnow to the Leader, but he would not bite, being by way of practising misogyny; next she tried Ralph with a fine cast, and he swallowed her bait greedily. Every one of us had to listen to the mournful recital of imaginary woes all brought about by the unsympathetic conduct of the husband. Madam was looking, she said, for a real love, which should be "an ethereal fantasy, sweetly idealistic—in short, a poem."

"My husband says a woman should be content to remain within what he calls her limitations," she sighed.

"Sounds fairly sensible," I said.

"But what if she has none?" the absurd creature said grandiloquently. "I am not a woman with limitations. I can soar and soar."

"Where to?" I asked vaguely.

"With one beloved, be he prince or pauper, anywhere. On and on, into infinite space."

"You couldn't soar far with a pauper," I quibbled; "ballooning is exceedingly expensive, and even in space you will find some one who needs tipping."

"If only my husband understood me! What a lot of poor suffering women are misunderstood by their husbands."

"And understood by other people's," I added. "One cannot help noticing it."

Evidently in Ralph Madam thought she saw the embodiment of all her idealistic dreams. She was of a very coming-on disposition, and did not let the grass grow beneath her feet. The climax was reached one night at a little dance, and Master Ralph was very nearly caught out.

The Leader and myself were sitting on the verandah, when we heard voices below us in the garden, and without any previous intention of eavesdropping heard enough to make us long to hear every word. Yes, wasn't it mean of us? But—there it is.

"'Tis on such nights," Madam Misunderstood murmured in soft caressing tones, "that our hearts are filled to overflowing, and we respond with all the vigour of our pent-up longing. We grope with our puny words to comment upon situations which cannot even be comprehended. I throw out my arms—so —and gasp, as for air."

"Bad business," said Ralph, in an alarmed voice. "Do you feel faint?"

"I merely spoke figuratively," very reproachfully. "*You* might have known that. I gasp for the air that is outside us, beyond, above, not the commonplace every-day air we breathe into our lungs. Give me true ventilation, the ventilation of our psychic natures. You follow me?"

"It's a bit clever for me, don't you know," Ralph replied, in a trying-to-appear-enlightened tone, "but I thoroughly enter into the thing. It is on the lines of the Johnnies who go in for star-gazing, dissecting beetles, and other occult sciences, isn't it?"

"You dear boy! The very thing, but crudely expressed. Can it be that you are a kindred spirit?"

"Of yours? Yes, always."

"Can I trust you?" asked Madam pensively.

"Entirely. I am wholly at your service. You must have guessed that."

"Yes, I guessed by the wonderful power which is given to so few of us. We are so material. But by the means of thought transference, by the very sensitiveness of my mind, by the aid of its acute mental photographing process I can follow and grasp all the thoughts that come to an affinity."

"Good business!" said Ralph admiringly. "Can you see what is working in my mind now?"

"In your mind—now. I see—it is coming, taking shape."

"A face," broke in the shameless Ralph. "Some one's face. Whose?"

"You must not speak, you blur the colours."

"The colours!"

"Yes," the ridiculous woman went on, "it is I, myself, in a rainbow of cloud, purple—orange—mauve."

"I say! Can you really see all that?"

"And does your imagination dress me in those sweetly Oriental shades, this lovely colour scheme reminiscent of the Old Masters in all the profusion of the National Gallery?"

"No pigments ever mixed," affirmed the excited Ralph, "could equal the—er—the er—whatever it is you are so sweet as to have divined in my feeling for your charming self."

"Ralph," persevered the outrageous creature, "I love you. With a love that had seemed impossible in aught but theory. My affections have wandered before, but now It has come! I have found my ideal."

"I only meet ideals in dreams," said Ralph nervously, trying to hedge a little.

"We have met in dreams. I know it now. It is you I have been seeking, even whilst I have been following will-o'-the-wisps, mere purple illusionary myths. And now, what is to be done, now that the long dark age of groping is over. And you *have* groped, dear?''

"I suppose so," replied Ralph, completely be-fogged, but, masculine-like, desirous of pleasing to the last.

"We will live up to our ethics," said the com-ing-on lady. "We will go to the ends of the earth."

"But, I say, don't you know, I—er—I'm bound for Alaska, and—and——"

Here the Leader, who could not keep quiet any longer, laughed like anything, and we both had to run away, and hide our eavesdropping heads.

Tap-tap at my door that night. It was Ralph, duly penitent and ashamed.

"I've a good mind *not* to help you, Ralph," I said in my wrath. "I've a good mind to let her elope with you to the ends of the earth."

"But I don't want to go there," he maintained, "I don't want her to elope with me. I want to go to Alaska with you and Cecily."

"Cecily! If she only knew!" I said viciously.

Well! of course I agreed to save him, but only on condition that he went to Seattle next day, whither we all speedily betook ourselves, having seen the *Lily* started off on her voyage to Kodiak.

CHAPTER II

THE VOYAGE NORTH

Hence, and bestow your luggage
The Tempest
Here in this island we arriv'd
The Tempest

ON arriving at the Rainier Grand Hotel in Seattle we
found that the *Nome City* was timed to sail from the
Schwabacher Dock on April the 3rd, two days earlier
than we had thought. It was a very good thing we
turned up when we did. To have missed the boat
would have meant a serious alteration in our well-laid
plans.

At Seattle the taking of the census was in progress,
or rather the arriving at a conclusion as to the growth
of the city since the previous year. We helped to
swell the population, and filled in the forms we found
placed in our bedrooms. The questions were alarm-
ingly of the order known as " leading," the one anent
age being most difficult to get over, in spite of a carefully worded reassuring sentence explaining that the
number of the years should remain a mystery for ever
save to the powers that be. Another interrogation
seemed a trifle intimate, I thought. " How many im-
beciles are there in your family ?" As though families
ever gave away things like that! The invariable

26

scheme is to make out the weak-minded members to be profoundly learned people with one or two fads.

Cecily set herself down as twenty-eight, and was immensely glad of the opportunity, and I wrote " full age " on my paper, forgetting that I was not at last filling in a matrimonial certificate. We gave Ralph as the only imbecile of the quartet, agreeing that if he wasn't one he ought to be, after that near thing in elopements with the coming-on lady on the look-out for an affinity.

April the 3rd saw us taking up our quarters in the state-rooms secured, and with winds in varying moods the *Nome City* steamed off on her northward voyage, a voyage that has no parallel in any clime.

Except that the sea was not always peaceful the trip was like an excursion up some great river, for always the beautiful peaks of distant ranges were in sight to charm us with their myriad-tinted glories, and the dark green of the firs and cedars fringed the country to the very edge of the sea. For a thousand miles there is but a half-day of open water. In and out among the islands dotting her path, down straits so narrow that at times a well-thrown stone would strike either shore, the *Nome City* threaded her way. One fears illimitable tragedy as, in the hours of darkness, our ship steams nonchalantly along, no lighthouses to guide her, come what, come may, through rock-strewn channels, hardly slowing up for fogs. Indeed, the only difference these maritime horrors made to our complete contentment was the constant shrieking of the horn.

This was not intended as a warning to other ships that pass in the fog, for the waters hereabouts are not busy, and the times and likely positions of the few ships that ply over them can be arrived at more or less by a little calculation beforehand. The fog-horn wakens the echoes, and the echoes call back the degree of danger the ship is running into. If it is desperate the news is given from such close quarters that the helmsman guesses immediately whether port or starboard means the road to safety. The whole journey is crammed with amazing sensations, and one cannot help speculating very often on the slightness of the barrier that at times appears to be the only block to a swift eternity.

One day we had to anchor for a whole twelve hours, owing to some defect in the steering gear, and we four annexed a boat and hied us ashore forthwith, penetrating the woods of Vancouver Island. Landing was easy, for the prettiest of little shingly beaches, covered with baulks of timber, washed white by the waves, were inset into the frowning rock and moss-grown ramparts of the isle.

The silence of the bush was very impressive. Birds there were, but they had no singing voices, the tap-tap-tapping of the woodpecker alone breaking the stillness. I penetrated far into the thick cover, the forest was a dream of beauty in its new spring green. Many black-tailed deer took the fallen boulders in lithe, swinging bounds, in small bunches of twos and threes they crossed the path frequently. The large bird that does duty in Canada for the robin, brown-

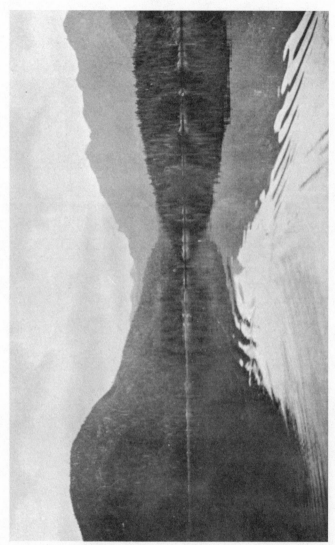

FIRS AND CEDARS FRINGED THE COUNTRY TO THE VERY EDGE OF THE SEA

coated, red-breasted, and as big as a thrush, crept in and out the fallen pine stems—in the Canadian forests there are as many trees lying down as standing, growing again and overgrown—brilliant blue-jays, with crests erect, flew round in chattering dismay.

In the midst of the thick tangle of green, ever and again one comes on a blackened oasis with bare standing tree-stems holding up their maimed limbs skywards in piteous appeal. Desolate bits of country licked up by the forest fires, but with a kindly carpet of the ready growing deer's-foot to make the poor nakedness seem less acute.

Afar in the bush I heard the booming of the blue grouse. They make the most remarkable love-notes, exactly like the deep tones of a drum, and appear to evolve them from the depths of their inner consciousness. It is remarkable how hard it is for untrained eyes to detect these birds when they remain motionless. I crept along on the line of sound, and the drum-like noise guided me to a beautiful forest glade. So silent was I that the beautiful bird pirouetting for the delight of his ladye was in no way disturbed, and from my fastness of wreathed syringa I could watch the little drama quite unnoticed.

On a great fallen cedar the grouse " cake-walked " from end to end, his thick black ruff of neck feathers erect, his tail an extended fan. Every few seconds he boomed forth his love-song, so loud a noise for so small a bird. Sometimes he jumped into the air, alighting most gracefully. On a tree near-by Miss Grouse sat criticizing. She was bored almost to death, 'twas plain to see from her demeanour, but she bravely tried to hide it from her suitor. When he turned to trip along his log, she preened her feathers, and took no count of him; but as he finished his length, she affected alertness, interest, and delight. A true feminine, little Miss Grouse, who would screen from her admirer any failing of hers. Very human too, for it is human for all feminine things to shun showing their faults to the masculine creatures who admire them. It is the law of nature. In wild life the male puts on his gaudiest colours, and the female chooses. In the long run she selects what is best for her species, and we get the survival of the fittest. In civilization the woman decks herself. It all comes to the same thing.

A rustle of my making, my shooting boot, not suited to this silent tracking, crunched a protesting twig. The blue grouse paused, his head alert, listening, and his little ladye flew off, glad of the excuse, and vanished among the feathery fir tops. My friend sat on defiant. Perhaps he guessed that I would not take his life even though the pot cried out in emptiness, for it is not thus that we reward such well-graced players.

"Begone!" I called. "Go after her. You've done very well. I admire you exceedingly."

He deserved the compliment, and that made it worth having. Flattery is not often sincere, rarely, indeed; it usually has an end, "that thrift may follow fawning."

In one clear rocky inlet Ralph and the Leader

longed to bathe, but it was far too cold as yet in these waters to think of swimming. I should never want to try it at any time, for that lurking terror, the octopus, is not uncommon in the deep recesses of the Vancouver rocks. That very morning as Cecily and I paddled our boat round a jutting headland, where the water was as clear as crystal right down to the rocks below, we saw a small octopus swimming for home, long arms and suckers extended, travelling tail first, an odd method of locomotion. We hung over the side, interested spectators, and as we did so the long-armed horror seemed to turn the water around it to an inky shade, hiding its whereabouts, making it impossible for us to trace its course to its rocky lair.

The evenings were rather long on board the *Nome City*. Had Cecily and I been enthusiastic card-players the hours, I suppose, would have seemed too few. Ralph and the Leader said it wasn't whist we played, but some fearsome hybrid that made time impossible to bear. So we took to reading aloud. It is always rather interesting, I think, to see the sort of literature individuals rush to if given free choice. Ralph was very trivial, and mostly went in for French novels, and when he read these got so tied up in making expurgated editions we really were often fogged as to what the tale was all about. He only gave us what he liked, and " bowdlerized " the story out of all sense.

The Leader on the other hand never wearied of Max Nordau, and read *Degeneration* aloud with gusto.

Well, I like Max Nordau when he writes of Paul
Verlaine, the French Mystics, and the Pre-Raphael-
ites. How he puts his knife into that variety of poet
who delights in fogging everybody, including himself. Max Nordau is quite right. Healthy-minded
poets like Shakespeare and Dante never mystified, and
yet how deep and magnificent they are. How he
tears our faults to tatters, and unpicks humbugs un-
erringly and relentlessly, yet he realizes all the forces
of nature, and even admits love and tenderness. He
is right also when he says that if we behave less
punctiliously than civilization decrees we are degener-
ate. And Nature says degeneration is bad, though
she does not allow it to breed more than a generation
or so. In her scheme all works for good. But what
I want to know—I asked the Leader, and he only
cried "Help!"—is, did God make the ethics of
Nature for civilization, as civilization is the outcome
of Nature?

The passenger list of the *Nome City* was a curious
one, and I think it would be perhaps the most descriptive thing to say of our fellow-voyagers that one
and all had their hearts in the right place. I do not
know where else a heart could be kept, but the phrase
aptly describes the entire worthiness of human beings
without dwelling too unnecessarily upon the polish
and veneer which is, after all, but the result of an
effete civilization. Miners mostly, trappers, traders,
remittance men, prospectors, an *olla podrida* of
classes, and only three ladies to grace the show.

The third lady was an acidulate who cared very

little what she said or how she said it, and with her husband was travelling to some hot springs at Hoonia, the other side of Sitka. Ruskin said that wherever men are noble they love bright colour. This lady was the acme of nobility, and dazzled every one with the radiance of her peacock plumes. She was an amateur dressmaker, of the variety who do not consider it worth while to trouble to supply hooks and eyes, and the entire structure was always apparently dependent on the staying powers of one pin. I used to meditate on the awful happenings if it should fall out. She came on board attired in her latest triumph, a velveteen dress in shades of violet, with a yellow lace collar. Her hair was brushed back with precise neatness, and arranged into an infinitesimal knot held together with one solitary hair-pin. All her pinning arrangements seemed to go in ones. The husband was a pastor of a Seattle church, to which they always referred as " The Episcopalian." He began life as a veterinary surgeon, but, realizing his error in time, fled to the nearest back door and entered the Church. A very kindly, well-intentioned man, harassed and jaded looking. You could tell that he was married on sight. He had long ago discovered that matrimony is very much like a dinner at a big restaurant—you get everything but what you want.

The poor man used to try and join us at the make-believe whist occasionally, but Madam always dragged him back. One night he did manage a rubber, thinking that his lady had retired, but she rattled her cabin door so vigorously, as a signal for the game to cease, that some disturbed person sent a message to ask why the donkey-engine had started.

" Did you not hear me pounding on my door last night, young man ?" she asked Ralph.   " Gee ! I did pound it !"

She always called Ralph " young man."   Once she asked him if he belonged to the Episcopalians, and not understanding what she meant in the least, or pretending not to, he claimed to be a Plymouth Rock ! Mixing up the hens with the Brethren.

For two days rain fell in waterspouts, which was curious considering that the coast we were hugging was sunny and dry.   In between times, on sloppy decks, we tried to play cricket, on a tiny cricket field about the size of a handkerchief.   The enjoyment I personally derived was a half-broken head received through running into what Ralph called " a bob-stay."   The game was no sort of a success, because the Leader in his delight at the chance of making half a run rammed the skipper, who was nothing like the same weight, and sent him flying.

Filthy dug-out canoes came to greet us from every Indian settlement.   The Siwash—Siwash is the name of the fish-eating Indians of the Pacific coast—women do a great part of the work of paddling, and are very difficult indeed to tell from their lords and masters. The men clothe themselves in antiquated raiment bearing a far-off resemblance to the sartorial—I hope I am using the right word—developments of the white man, and the blanket of the North American Indian is unknown.   A klootchman—which means woman in the Chinook lingo—is an absolutely shapeless creature, in short, nondescript skirts, with usually a gay plaid shawl folded about her, tied in with string at the place where her waist would be if she had one. Sometimes a belle Indian adds a check apron. Very different all this to the royal braves of Fenimore Cooper, with their leather leggings, shoulder skins and feathers. There is nothing magnificent or romantic about the Siwash. He is a very low-grade person indeed, is always a Siwash, and perpetually smells of fish. Of no stature to speak of, bullet-headed, non-intelligent, he is everything the Indian of the prairie is not. It almost seems to argue that a fish diet for generations does not make for the betterment of the race.

The Chinook language, which is mostly used by the coast Indians, was manufactured years and years ago by a fur trader who found the necessity for some more direct means of communication in his bartering deals than arm wavings and signs. Now his invention has spread far and wide, and even the Chinese use it. With no grammar to bother one, the few words of its composition may be picked up very quickly. They are very few, and only need to be juggled with this way and that. Always put the cart before the horse, so to speak, and you've got it.

The Indian reservations are a collection of ill-built, rough-timbered barn-like houses of large size, and lofty, roofed with shingles split from cedar-trees. So far as we could make out, from observations at Sitka, and other places, the men and women all camped together in the same big earth-floored domiciles.

Miserable bunk beds, aheap with piles of dirty clothes, and blankets, were all round the walls, and in the middle of the apartment a wood fire smouldered, with fish grilling in the cinders, a hole in the roof letting out some of the smoke.

Many of the Indian dug-outs are enormous, hewn from forest giants, and—relic of the more warlike times of the grim Haida, and his Northerners—they call each extra-sized vessel a " war-canoe."

In these primitive ships a whole Indian family annually sets out from Vancouver Island to cross the Gulf to the Fraser River to take part in the salmon harvest. From the aged grandfather, his cheeks in the deepest furrows Time can plough, to the latest addition in the way of the quaintest of babies. Youth at the prow, old age at the helm, the father of the family asleep, and the mother, the grandmother, and the daughters doing all the paddling amidships.

Almost all the journeys taken by the coast Indians are by water, and even babies of four and five have the ubiquitous paddle thrust into their tiny hands, and speedily learn to use it with agility. Paddles vary slightly according to the tribes, but nearly all the blades are roughly carved, and decorated with blue and red stain. They taper to a point, and the whole thing is about four feet in length, slightly longer for use in canoes of great size. The wonderfully adroit use of the single paddle interested me extremely. By a firm touch at the psychological moment the frail craft is held at " safety," and answers the command immediately. The paddler seems one with the craft, the rhythm, the balance, and the easy grace is so perfect.

Some of their great war canoes scale seventy feet or more in length, and are so deep that a man standing in the centre cannot see over the gunwale. All hewn from a single tree, a cedar if possible, and to their aid the Indians summon the Spirit of fire, controlling the havoc he would make in his fierce excavations by water. After a big deep hole is formed in the rough trunk native chisels are called into requisition, and slice off the wood outside and inside. They have no measurements to guide them, no set dimensions, and yet these rough builders invariably turn out a graceful craft of correct lines, seaworthy, and lasting. The vessels are nearly always carved, and ornamented with the inevitable bear, beaver, and eagle. Weird contortions of all three, picked out in indelible blue and red stain.

On the morning of the sixth day out from Seattle we made Juneau, which nestles at the foot of a Gibraltar-like rock, and snow covered as the summit was, with the dark green relief of the spruce-trees on its hoary cliffs it would be hard to find a more exquisite scene. The whole beauteous panorama lay reflected in the still waters around our ship. We did not go ashore, and left almost at once for Sitka, the one-time capital of Russian Alaska, now the seat of satrapy of the United States.

Here, at Sitka, we said farewell to the Episcopalians, who were going to remain awhile in the capital, as it was rather early as yet to go into camp at Hoonia. I did not envy the padre his summer holiday; even as they got on to the wharf they were verging on what Hardy calls " the antipathetic, recriminatory mood of the average husband and wife in Christendom."

Leaving Sitka we stood out for the open sea, crossing the Gulf, making for Yakutat, over three hundred miles distant, and for the next few hours such glories were laid before our astonished eyes as my poor pen can in no way adequately describe. The mighty Mount Fairweather compelled admiration first, but appeared almost insignificant as Mount St. Elias burst upon our vision. Perhaps it is no exaggeration to say that this mountain is the most awe-inspiring in all the world, outdoing Cotopaxi and its 19,600 feet, for it must be remembered that Mount St. Elias rears its 18,200 feet from the very edge of the sea, and most mountains can only be viewed from an already high level.

A wealth of beautiful scenes held us spellbound. Mountains rising to great heights with bold and lofty peaks covered with an everlasting snow mantle, supported on their giant sides the wondrous glaciers. Contrasted with the even-coloured snow above, these frozen sunlit ways seemed to glitter in all imaginable tints, blue and green, green and deeper blue. Range upon range of peaks, and each valley filled with the wonderfully iridescent glaciers. Great blocks of ice are perpetually tearing off with a splitting reverberation, and sometimes the effect on the water was terrific, as the disturbed waves lashed around the berg, and then passed on to spend themselves in battle with each opposing crest.

Before we reached Yakutat we touched the fringe of a majestic storm. It began in sudden squalls from the mountains, termed in Alaska " woollies," though there is nothing soft or wool-like about them, and before long we had to lie to in a heavy sea. The tempest raged for three hours, and often we could see nothing for the spray driven before the wind. Banks of foamy clouds were piled up on a lurid sky, and at intervals lightning played about the horizon. It was a dark, impressive scene, and had a very sobering effect on all our spirits. The men were drenched to the skin in the war with the elements.

An albatross, with great stretch of wings, hung over us, in the teeth of the gale, his head slowly turning from side to side. The vast wings never flapped, the bird seemed to cleave the air in graceful lengthy curves and slants. Now and again it disappeared into the mists, to return like some strange solitary spirit of the storm, whose air of complete disregard for weather and wind was magnificent in its spontaneity.

To the north-west of Yakutat lies the great glacier which is christened after Malespina, the Spanish navigator who explored for the North-west Passage more than a century ago. Monarch of all the glaciers it has a frontage of fifty miles, and goes back thirty more to the ranges of Mount St. Elias. The sea for miles around is tinged with the " glacier milk."

As the sun set, the snow fields took on the rosy light called by the Swiss "Alpine Gluehn." The exquisite blazing shades, luminous, prismatic, changed constantly from tones of pale pink to crimson, and lasted some evenings for an hour or more, until the twilight shadows quenched the glowing glories.

The next place of any account after Yakutat, for we stopped occasionally to put down prospectors at God-forsaken inlets once or twice, was Valdez, and nearly all our passengers quitted the ship here. The glaciers surrounded the spot on every side, and we felt the cold considerably. Valdez is at the head of Prince William Sound, with its islands and fiords running up into the land.

After leaving Valdez we got into an amazing tide rip, which carried the *Nome City* a great deal nearer shore than was exactly pleasant. We hugged the coast as we crawled along.

Here the canoes which shot out to meet and greet us were manned by Aleuts, and the Siwash type appeared to have been left behind. The boats, too, were not of heavy dug-out variety, but light and portable. These *bidarkas*, as the natives call them, are constructed of a skeleton framework, covered with seals' skin, sewn together, and no nails are used. There is a little hole for each person to sit in, one, two or three, or more, as the *bidarka* builder most requires. They are propelled by paddles, Indian fashion, from one side, and the man in the stern does all the steering. Very, very easily upset, they yet can travel over and through tremendous seas, but the balance must be perfect. Up rivers the *bidarka* is ideal, because so little depth is required to float them, and they are so easily carried over portages. In rough weather the *bidarka* mariner dons a quaint variety of shirt called a *cameleeka*, and made of bear or seal gut, fastened round the neck and then over the hatchway wherein he squats to paddle. This protective arrangement prevents the boat from shipping water and being swamped. So, equipped with a spare paddle in case of accidents, and a row of spears, the Aleut will go to sea in any weather. We learnt to manœuvre these frail craft quite creditably, having had considerable experience in managing tiny Berthon boats in the roughish waters of the Irish Sea.

Near Cape Elizabeth the *Nome City* skirted past some rocks alive with sea-lions. A shriek from our fog-horn sent hundreds of the creatures scuttling to the sea. Some swam out towards us, with childish faces upraised in interested wonderment. Gloomily coated cormorants shared the rocks, beautifully tinted in iridescent greens, and the harlequin duck breasted the waves, tossing lightly over the crests; puffins, too, scurried over the face of the waters. Flocks of scoters fished assiduously, and the graceful Arctic tern, looking like a first cousin to the swallows, gyrated round about us.

Two days out from Valdez we made Saldovia, and reached the latter place early in the morning. It is situated at the entrance of Cook's Inlet, the largest bay in Alaska, for it runs one hundred and fifty miles inland, and is over fifty across at the mouth. Mountain monarchs frowned down upon us, and across the Inlet, wrapped in a spotless white mantle, Iliamna and Redoubt reared their volcanic peaks, and from the former a jet of steam issued, and hung low about the summit.

Towards Kodiak, which lies south of Cook's Inlet, the climate grew a little milder with the balmier airs blowing from Southern seas. The village of Kodiak lies on the east end of the island, and as we skirted the shores, still under snow, the slopes reminded us of the lawns at Richmond. The wilderness of forest was absent, and here and there we caught glimpses of park-like expanses, home-reminding pasture country.

Through tortuous channels winding in and out of tiny islands we ventured, feeling our way, up the strait whereon lies Kodiak, the St. Paul of Russian days. From the rear of the town a mountain covered with snow added picturesqueness to the beautiful scene.

The enchantment of the northern solitudes had laid its spell on us. Winter and spring commingled. The island was a paradise, and all for us.

THE TOWN OF KODIAK

CHAPTER III

ON KODIAK ISLAND

(By the Leader of the Expedition)

Such a worthy leader, wanting aid
King Henry VI

Thou hast astonished me with thy high terms
King Henry VI

As we imagined, our arrival in Kodiak caused no small stir in that peaceful settlement, and on the news spreading that the whole party, including the ladies, were "mighty hunters before the Lord" we were soon inspected by most of the residents. Having regard to the fact that the weather was comparatively mild for the time of year, and everything pointed to an early spring, we were anxious to make a move as soon as possible in quest of bears, and although confident that they were more numerous on the mainland of the Alaska Peninsula than on Kodiak Island, we felt that our trip would not be complete unless at least one specimen of the Kodiak bear (*Ursus middendorffi*) figured in the bag, since these beasts are the largest specimens of the bear tribe now living on the earth.

The chief thing which we required to procure from Kodiak was the services of some good native hunters, with a knowledge of the surrounding country and the habits of the various animals found there. Thanks to the assistance of a local storekeeper four natives were found who undertook to accompany our expedition at a price which seemed to us somewhat exorbitant, namely one and a half dollars pay per diem. Compared with our former experience of the amounts demanded by natives in India and Africa, where a few annas will engage good men, these Alaskan terms seemed excessively high. But we had yet to learn that the Alaskan natives are probably the most independent and highly paid members of the race of hunters on earth, and this may chiefly be ascribed to the fact of the ease with which they can obtain a living from the unlimited supply of fish, flesh, and fowl that still abounds in the waters and untrodden lands of the Alaskan shores. Moreover, the scarcity of white men along these coasts enables the native to demand, and obtain, extraordinarily high wages if he is inclined to work in such places as the mines, or any of the numerous commercial enterprises which are being rapidly opened up in Alaska.

The four men who had volunteered to accompany us rejoiced in the names of Ivan, Pete, Steve, and Ned, but their weird-sounding family names were utterly unpronounceable by our foreign tongues, and hence they were always hereafter referred to by their Christian names. As regards their racial type they were half-breeds between Russians and Aleut natives, and spoke Russian and Aleut far better than English, although their conversation and vocabulary comprised a certain amount of quaint American sayings.

The men were informed that they would be required to accompany us on a trip extending far beyond the confines of their native island, but this appeared to have no terrors for them since they had all made expeditions in former days along the shores of the Alaska Peninsula, when engaged on board sailing vessels in quest of the valuable sea-otter and fur seals, which then were plentiful along those coasts.

We were advised to take on board the schooner two or three of the native *bidarkas*, and our men assured us that these little craft would be found most useful when making expeditions up any of the numerous rivers of the country, and this indeed subsequently proved to be a fact. We also purchased two flat-bottomed boats known as "dories," which we were told would be invaluable for landing in shallow places.

One more day was given up to making final arrangements for our departure from Kodiak, and a few more necessaries and supplies which had been omitted in Victoria, were laid in from the local stores in order to make the commissariat department as complete as possible.

It had been decided to make a trip to the westward along the southern shores of Kodiak, and to look for bears in some of the bays which indent the island's coast. The men assured us that in a certain bay, well known to them, we should find a good anchorage for the schooner, near a place where bears had once been very numerous. But they added that persistent killing of them for years by the natives had greatly diminished the number of bears on the island.

As the month of April was now well advanced, and the snow was fast disappearing from the low grounds, we were anxious to get on the hunting ground as soon as possible. Therefore, early next morning, as Captain Clemsen pronounced the wind favourable, we bid farewell to the kindly residents in Kodiak, who had displayed to us every hospitality within their power during our short stay in the settlement. The morning was bright and clear, with that peculiar crispness, and bracing feeling, in the air which in arctic regions impart to men a wondrous sensation of rejuvenescent energy. A fair breeze was blowing when once we were free from the harbour's shelter, and as the white wings—on reading this part Agnes ejaculated, " You know they were as black as ink, really !"—of the *Lily* were unfurled, and as we went gliding out between the picturesque islands of Kodiak and its neighbour, Wood Island, on to the broad bosom of the Pacific, the gods and the face of nature alike seemed propitious for the commencement of our trip.

During our stay in Kodiak we had wisely procured complete outfits of fur costumes similar to those worn by the native Aleuts and Eskimos. The most useful of these garments is one known locally by the name of a *parka*, and consists of a whole skin coat with a hood to it and no opening down the front, the coats being pulled over the head like a jersey. The skins used in the making of them are usually those of the caribou, or marmot, and the fur is worn on the out-side. Some of them are highly decorated ingeniously by the natives, and are marvellously constructed when it is considered that they are often made with crude ivory needles, and sewn with the sinews of animals in place of thread.

Robed in these new furs our whole party spent most of the day on deck watching the picturesque scenery as we glided by the innumerable bays and inlets which thickly stud the shores of Kodiak Island. Captain Clemsen told us that if the wind held as favourable as it then was, we should reach our destination ere next morning. Towards evening it got bitterly cold, and we were glad to seek the welcome warmth below decks around the cabin stove. After dinner a rubber of whist whiled away the time until we turned in, and then, having taken a parting glimpse at the stars from the deck, we retired shivering, none of us envying the man at the wheel, nor his attendant look-out watchman in the schooner's bows, nor the untiring captain who seemed to spend most of the hours of the day or night on deck so long as we were in proximity of land.

Being a remarkably sound sleeper I have only a dim recollection of hearing some unusual noise during the night, which can have been nothing but the running out of the chain as the anchor was dropped, for on being roused next morning by Tom the cabin boy he informed me that we were at anchor in the bay. Hastily dressing, I went on deck. Here the view was magnificent, as the schooner lay calmly in a land-locked bay some five miles long and over a mile in width. Four big valleys debouched into the bay, through each of which a river ran, and between the valleys rose lofty mountains of which the tops and higher slopes were thickly clothed in snow. The open channel leading outwards to the sea, through which we had entered this snug bay, was screened from view by mountain spurs, and high rocky bluffs, which gave this fine natural harbour the appearance of an inland loch.

Shortly after my arrival on deck the ladies appeared with Ralph, and universal delight was expressed by every one at the magnificent scenery with which we were surrounded on every side. Although we lay anchored fully a mile from the nearest point of land, the hills in this rarefied northern atmosphere looked almost near enough to be within a stone's throw of the schooner.

Since we were all eager to make our first landing, and inspect the happy hunting grounds, a hasty breakfast was the next move. Immediately afterwards the largest dory was launched and manned by two of the crew, rifles and telescopes were quickly produced, and all four of our party proceeded to pack ourselves rapidly into the boat. The natives preferred to launch their *bidarkas,* and led the way, paddling far quicker than our men could row the heavy dory. These *bidarkas* are wonderful little craft, and the natives kneel in them in a crouching position, sitting on their heels, but to any person unaccustomed to it, this is a most uncomfortable position and generally produces violent cramp if it is adopted for any length of time. My advice, there-

THE SITE OF OUR FIRST LANDING

fore, to any stranger who occupies a *bidarka* for the first time is to adopt a sitting position, and to remain very still at that, for these little canoes are as easily capsized as a child's toy boat if one is unused to their peculiarities.

We steered for the nearest river's mouth, and on arrival there the ladies expressed a desire to explore the river for some distance up stream, and Ralph and I set out again in the dory to inspect the neighbouring valley which lay some two miles distant and further up the bay. Promising to return late in the afternoon we said *au revoir* to the huntresses, and being favoured with a slight breeze hoisted the sail of the dory, thus making good time by travelling close along shore. On arrival at the next river we hauled the dory ashore, and leaving the men in charge to amuse themselves as best they could, Ralph and I taking our rifles walked up the river bank. If ever the river had been frozen in winter it was now entirely free from ice, and although about fifty or sixty yards wide was very shallow at the mouth, particularly at low tide. On its lower reaches it ran through a wide open valley, which was mostly bare of timber, and intersected with numerous back lakes, or small lagoons, which were the haunt of numerous mallards, harlequin ducks, teal, and other wild fowl that rose in great numbers as we advanced up the valley. In summer the grass and vegetation must attain a considerable height, but it was then all lying flat and dead from the effects of its heavy winter covering of snow.

As we proceeded further up the valley, clumps of

E

fir and cottonwood came into view, and soon we found ourselves amidst a thick growth of trees interspersed by dense alders and willow bushes. Here in the sheltered valleys timber grew abundantly, although the trees did not reach any considerable size in height or girth. Here also the river ran more swiftly as it wound a serpentine course, now rushing over rocky shallows, here and there hollowing out deep pools beneath the overhanging banks, whilst in other spots the foaming waters came tumbling down a seething, boisterous mass, where the river had for centuries past cut deep gorges through the solid rocks which rose dark and frowning sheer on either side above the raging waters.

Along the river banks great sunken bear trails ran, showing where for ages past these huge beasts had wandered up and down the stream in quest of salmon, which teem at spawning time in most Alaskan rivers. Even now, dead bodies and decaying skeletons of fish were thickly strewn along the banks or lying in the eddies of deep pools, grim relics of a strange fate which befalls Alaskan salmon after they have spawned.

Bears were not in evidence, but their tracks of recent date showed up plainly on the snow, where they had been wandering on the hillsides seeking patches of grass which forms their earliest food on issuing from winter quarters.

Having pushed on some four or five miles up the valley without seeing a living thing, save a few willow grouse, and after searching the hillsides in vain with glasses for sight of a moving bear, we decided to retrace our steps. By the time we reached the boat the sky had become overcast, and lowering banks of clouds looming on the horizon to windward betokened bad weather. No time was lost, therefore, in making for the small cove where we had parted from the ladies, the men having a hard pull to get the dory against a rising wind and tide.

I was fully prepared for an indefinite period of waiting, and was agreeably surprised to see the whole party coming along the river bank soon after our arrival. The natives, it appeared, had wisely advised a hasty retreat in view of the threatening weather, knowing that, although in the sheltered bay, an Alaskan wind can make even inland waters dangerous. We noticed that Pete was carrying something on his back, which on closer inspection proved to be a fine specimen of a red fox. This had been seen creeping along the river bank in quest of any form of food, which was as yet scarce enough in these parts. The ladies had tossed up in true sportsmanlike fashion for who should take the chance of bagging reynard. Agnes, who persistently declares that she cannot win at any game of chance, maintained her reputation by losing the toss, and thus a short stalk, and a good long shot had rewarded Cecily with the first blood of our expedition. But she, with true feminine caprice, was less elated by the excellency of her shooting performance, which had much impressed the natives, than by the prospect of what a splendid muff that skin would make on our return to civilization.

Our return to the *Lily* was not unalloyed joy, for

a heavy, choppy sea was running in the bay, and the dory kept shipping small seas as she went smashing into the crest of each big wave, so that every one was drenched to the skin ere we reached the vessel. It was little short of marvellous to watch the way the natives handled the small *bidarkas*, as they rode like ducks over the seething mass of waters. And ever afterwards the scene remained vividly impressed on my mind, since it was a revelation to see in what waters these cockleshell craft could live when properly handled.

All that evening the wind rose and came howling down from unknown space beyond the mountain heights. By way of extra precaution the captain ordered a second anchor to be dropped lest we should find a premature ending to our trip by drifting ashore. All night the *Lily* tugged and strained at her anchors, rolling and tossing as huge waves came thundering neath her bows, whilst overhead a biting icy wind went whistling and shrieking through the rigging. And then we had a foretaste of Alaskan hail and sleet, which cut the hands and face like whip lashes, in fact it seemed as if all elements combined to make night hideous with a satanic pandemonium.

CHAPTER IV

BROWN BEARS

Thou'dst shun a bear
King Lear

Will not the ladies be afeard?
Midsummer Night's Dream

AFTER leaving Kodiak in the *Lily* and reaching the Mecca of our hopes, a land-locked bay, on the south side of the island, we had a preliminary canter from ship to shore, and finding it such a nuisance to have to return to sleep aboard, we decided that, cold as it might be, we would camp for a time, a course which would enable us to cover more ground than if we had to return to our ship every night.

We landed with a considerable quantity of kit, the four hunters and the *bidarkas*. Ralph and I actually made shore in the two-hatch *bidarka*, chiefly because he bet me I dared not trust myself in it with him for pilot. He paddled in such a wavering fashion that I breathed a prayer, and thought my last hour had come. He said that the *bidarka* had a permanent list to starboard, and we flew along well on the side of our fragile vessel full steam ahead. If I hadn't understood the laws of equilibrium, which prompted me to shift ballast at the right moment, I should have been hurtled into the sea. Fate is kind

53

to amateur sailors, as we know from watching them at seaside resorts, and the game was exciting.

We portioned out the loads, and some of the stores were placed in the *bidarkas* to be paddled up stream, and the rest every one took a share of. We were not going to make the mistake of trekking too far away from the coast, for, in the spring, when the new grass is shooting up, the bears come to the slopes of the coast line to feed.

The great brown bear, *Ursus middendorffi*, of Kodiak, Uganuk, and Afognak, is the largest of the tribe to be found in the world, and there is not much difference between it and the brown *Ursus dalli gyas* of the Alaskan Peninsula, at least to the average person who cannot detect the difference in the conformation of skull when the great heads are covered. The variations from the grizzly type may be plainly seen by the veriest tyro, for the Alaskan bear has not the long, straight, white claws which are so characteristic of his cousin, neither has he the furtive snake-like head. The brown bear grows to a much greater size than the grizzly, and his claws, though immensely powerful and long, are curved and dark in colour. The head also is extraordinarily large, and seems unduly big even on so vast a body.

We followed the river closely as well as we could, but here and there on its sloping banks alder clumps dodged our every step, holding us back in dogged persuasion. Save for the waterfowl the island was as yet untenanted by birds, and the solitudes were still in thrall to the grip of winter. We came on

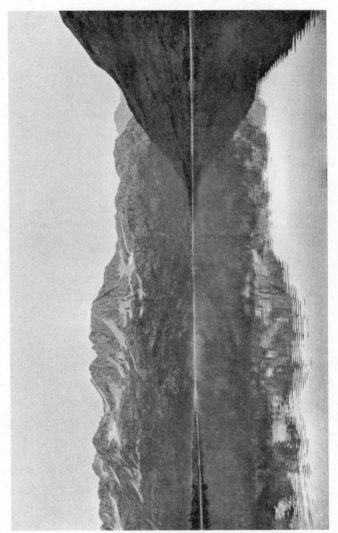

OUR FIRST ANCHORAGE AT KODIAK ISLAND

belts of cottonwood trees, but none of any girth, rested about noon, and after a further trek in the afternoon hours lighted on a place which seemed an ideal camping ground. With ready hospitality the trees gave us of their best, and the ridge poles for our tents were fitted with agility. That night, in spite of the reindeer sleeping-bags, we felt the cold intensely, and next morning, like Balbus, we built a wall around us, on the zareba principle, and it was not long before we felt the difference of temperature in the tents.

The Leader came into camp with news of the most wonderful fall of water, a small Niagara, he said, and dwelt so long on its myriad charms that I was up and off with him the instant we finished breakfast. The booming of the water came to our ears before we breasted the intervening hill, and as we got nearer and nearer the wild music seemed to vibrate in all the air. Then, suddenly, without any warning, the glory of the falls burst on my delighted vision. A great torrent rolled down the precipitous sides of a gigantic granite kloof in exceeding volume, and then broke up, descending quite slowly, like snow.

How I should love to see the chaos that the rains would bring. The early sun gave a glint to the whiteness which was indescribably beautiful, the etchings were limned so clearly, the colours painted so definitely. At the bottom where the fall met the river was an indistinguishable boiling, seething pot; and the tossed spray arose, enshrouding the falls, and as it lighted on the Titanic masses of granite, meeting a different temperature, it condensed, and formed thousands of tiny cascades in the rocks.

After a very disappointing day as regards sport, without the encouragement of coming on the smallest traces of bears, save evidences of year-old perambulations, the Leader and Ralph decided to trek on the morrow to some distant bays and try their luck there. We chose the two best-tempered hunters to remain with us, and settled down to stalk the country for miles round.

For three whole days Cecily and I roamed those hillsides, wandered by the river, swept the country with anxious glasses, and did all we knew to find the smallest evidence that Kodiak was then inhabited by bears at all. With no result, and we could not help being a trifle cast down. Our luck seemed wonderfully on the up-grade when, within three miles of camp, we struck the trail of a large-footed bear, hitherto overlooked. It was quite recent, damp and oozy, and the ground yielded up the secret of the passing of a monster creature. Our hands trembled with excitement as we got out the tape. The impress of the hind feet measured fourteen and a quarter inches in length, so we judged we were really on the way at last to bagging a worth-having specimen of the bear tribe. From the crisscross of fainter tracks we judged that Bruin had come this way to the river very often.

We followed along the trail for some way, sinking up to our knees in swampy ground in places, in others held back by a veritable fastness of alders and inter-

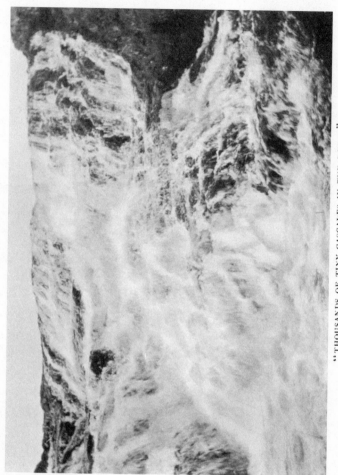

"THOUSANDS OF TINY CASCADES IN THE ROCKS"

laced willows. Tracking back to the river we discovered that on the banks the most succulent grass grew, one side being tinted emerald by the slender spears. It was quite late afternoon when we came on our great find, and although we lay in ambush until the twilight fell nothing happened, and the real campaign had to be put off until the morrow.

We rose with the day, for bears come out early and late as a rule, and we breakfasted in excited haste, saw to our rifles, and warned both our men not to go near the bit of river we meant to watch all day if needful. They looked at us in ill-disguised amusement, and crouched over the embers of the fire again.

Cecily and I hurried to the bear track, and entrenched ourselves on the other side of the river, in a vantage ground of alders, directly opposite the beginning of the path, thereby enfilading the whole position. We were some eighty yards from the place where our quarry should, if he had any consideration at all, emerge. For the time being the wind was propitious, but there is absolutely no reliance to be placed on Alaskan winds. It is never in the same mood for two hours together.

Cecily lay flat, in excellent position, and I sat, Joss-like, in cramped uncomfortable attitude, for the cover was so sparse there was not sufficient of it to go round, and there was no room to spare. The forest growth was much denser opposite us, up above the grass-covered slopes. We should not be likely to get a good glimpse of Bruin until he was right on us, even if he came. Oh, but he must come! He surely must!

Our fervent faith got a trifle dashed as half-hours crept by with no sort of result. Save for the rippling of the river the silence was unbroken. My foot went to sleep, and pins and needles racked it. I felt that I must move, though I ruined every chance I had. Then, even as I essayed a changed position, with an electric-like shock I realized that the opposite alder tops moved gently, sinuously, one after the other a-quiver, all down the pathway which we watched, lynx-fashion, with keen, alert eyes. A great beast was travelling, the thrill in the very air held us as in a vice.

Out he came, right into the open, as magnificent a picture of wild life as it has ever been my lot to see. His vast bulk outlined against the green of the undergrowth behind him, his head carried so low that the great arches of his shoulders appeared to equalize the width of the wide skull, and the depth from nose to ear.

Pausing for an instant the bear came to the very edge of the water, and presently actually drank from it. With his mouth dripping, the ponderous animal mounted the bank again, and fell to, like some great ox, on the grass round about him. We could have shot him easiest as he slaked his thirst, but held our fire in the desire to watch this drama of the wild. Even as we watched, the bear seemed meditating a move to a more distant patch of country. Cecily looked at me. I nodded. I raised my rifle with a momentary fear in my heart that the cramped attitude of my position might render it next door to impossible to rely on a steady aim. I drew a bead on the swelling shoulder, just behind the blade, and—phut! The bullet found its billet right enough. The great creature gave a deep-toned " woof " and looked about him in astonished amaze, which was an opportunity not to be missed. Cecily hit him fair and square in the region of the heart.

Like a clockwork toy the bear automatically raised himself on his hind feet, snorting or rather gasping in little spurts of sound, and faced us gallantly, looking for all the world like a very annoyed and irritated chauffeur; with a pair of goggles the disguise would have been complete. He looked so human that I felt like a murderess. Standing for a second thus, the massive legs gave way suddenly, and the bear dropped in his tracks. Over and over the body rolled, down the slope to the edge of the river; a little farther and he had been in the water. On the verge he rested, one forearm extended, more like a chauffeur than ever. I hoped all the bears wouldn't look quite so human, or I should have to leave them for more game-like game.

We got across the intervening river lower down, through it somehow, afire to investigate our prize. What a colossal beast, immovable in majesty! The pelt was in excellent condition, thick and even, and the face bore signs of vigorous contests, one great gash extending from eye to jaw.

Cecily went back to camp, and I kept guard until the men came to take over. The glamour of the scene crept over me, the witching stillness lured every sense to pleasurable emotion. What wonder of civilization can compare with the mysterious fascination of the wild? The weird enchantment, the silence, the space, the intangible something of everything. Ah, it is living indeed.

Steve and Ned commenced with delighted ejaculations to skin our treasure, answering our myriad questions the while. For we would know how old he was, and hear how great a weight it was surmised our bear would be. It was an astonishing sight as the skin was stripped to see the great layers of fat covering the carcase. One would imagine that after the long hibernation the bears would emerge thin and poor. This one was none the worse for his long fast. Just before " holing up " for the winter they are rolling in fat, and put it on all through the summer at a great pace. The splendid pelt was a biggish load to pack back to camp, and when we weighed it the scale turned at sixty-eight pounds. From the nose to the end of the tail Bruin measured ten feet two inches, and this result was arrived at very fairly, with the skin laid casually upon the ground before pegging out.

We spent the rest of the afternoon watching Steve clean the green skin. This he was most careful and particular over. All Aleuts are past masters at preparing furs.

The cooking in our small camp was absolutely haphazard, any one who was idle cooked. Ptarmigan stew occurred with clockwork regularity and our men drank quarts of tea.

The management of native guides and hunters in Alaska is quite different from anything one is used to in Africa. The numbers are so many less, wages being so high, and what one loses in quantity is not gained in quality either. The all-round capability of the average African head-man is non-existent in any follower one may acquire in Alaska. To hand over the whole domestic mechanism of camp affairs to an Alaskan servant would just mean utter chaos. They have not attained the smallest notion of the duties of a head-man. They can guide, know the whereabouts of game, and some of them are excellent still-hunters—though none of them, in my opinion, come up to the black shikári—and all of them are splendid at carrying terrific loads. I am hard to please now, as regards hunters, and am for ever trying to find in each new man I go out with some of the attributes my old Somali shikári possessed. And it is absurd, since I shall never look upon his like again.

All of the Alaskan tribes, Aleut, Innuit, and rag-tag-and-bobtail of indiscriminate race mixings, can remember happenings of a week back, and not a day beyond.

The ordinary humdrum man of all work round camp asks a dollar and a half a day, but the real finished article, especially if he is a white, or half-breed, demands his five, and can get it too. The mines claim so much labour, and raise the scale of wages.

Steve, our first hand—first by right of the amount

of his pay—was a stolid individual of no brains or acumen whatever. We called him the hunted instead of the hunter because he always contrived to be somewhere else when wanted. The son of an Aleut mother and a Russian father, the blend did not seem altogether successful. When we first met he was practically a man of two words, and those two most aggressive, if expressive. " Oh, hell!" he said when anything good or bad happened. There is nothing in a swear-word really, if you come to analyze, but this particular word was not " ben trovato." It grated, and worried us. One day I heard Cecily who sat beside Steve on a fallen log ask our henchman if he would like to learn a better safety-valve.

" 'O-badiah' is a much more expressive thing to say than ' Oh, hell,' Steve," she said persuasively. " And quite as easy. Try it. Say it after me. O-badiah."

" O-badiah " practised Steve diligently, and ever afterwards he used the joyful find, and we had much ado not to laugh at it. Purists will say that O-badiah said viciously enough is just as shocking as any cuss-word. Perhaps it is. But it didn't grate on our sensibilities so much, and that was the main point.

Ned, a more general factotum, was a pure Aleut, and all the knowledge of fish-craft, sea-craft, and forest-craft was his by right of birth. His stature was infinitesimal but his strength amazing. His voice came from the depths somewhere, and clanked with the sepulchral ring of footsteps going down a stone entry. His lightest whisper conjured up church-

yards. Neither of the men washed, or ever thought
of washing.

For ten days more we spoored in every direction
with the most disappointing results, and but for year-
old trails we found no signs of bears at all. We
appeared to have bagged the one and only specimen
of the Kodiak bear in the vicinity. Talking it over
together, Cecily and I decided to get back to the coast,
and try our luck there. Steve said he thought the
journey might be made in the *bidarkas*, as it was a
down-stream trip, and a lot of the stores could be
placed in the spare hatch-way, the rest must be piled
in with each individual. We struck camp on a pour-
ing wet day, and commenced the voyage, a gloriously
exciting affair, the men piloting the fragile craft over
swirling rapids, shallows, and currents with the most
surprising agility. We made the coast by late
afternoon, and bivouacked near the alders which
fringed the land-locked beach. Fortunately driftwood was plentiful, and we soon had a roaring fire
going, a fire large enough to defy the wetting mist
which continued to envelop the whole scene for some
twelve hours longer.

On the pools of sea-water which intersected the
country for some way into the island hereabouts we
saw many kinds of wildfowl. One variety of wader
looked as though he walked on stilts, so tall were his
stick-like legs. Yet he was not inelegant, and strode
about in the shallow water with proud and lofty mien.

Early next morning we put on gum-boots and wandered in and out of the backwaters until we had

covered a mile or more of coast line. In Alaska a backwater is a " sleugh," unless you happen to meet a French Canadian, who terms it " *n'cha*."

Leaving the water-line we struck up into the alder belt, and as fair Fate would have it, suddenly came on a bear track, and amid the countless indents of Bruin's fairy footsteps discoved some that were obviously very new indeed, going towards the sleugh. The sodden ground held the impress like a mould, there was the long flat expanse of the foot, there, well defined and clear, the imprints of the great claws, and at the ends of them the earth furred up slightly.

There was a low exclamation from Cecily, and right out on the sand-spit, grovelling in the sand for clams, we saw a cumbersome bulk, very much the colour of the scene around him. A bear at last! Stolidly he hunted, nor guessed the presence of enemies in his vicinity. The wind, what little there was, blew over the sea, landwards. We practically held all the trump cards, for the bear was in the open, we were concealed, and the odds seemed unfairly against our quarry. He scraped awhile, and then commenced to walk with rolling gait and slow, obviously his purpose was to enter the alder scrub much lower down than his usual path.

" Cut him off !" I whispered, and as lightly as we could encumbered with our difficult-to-manœuvre foot-gear, in silent rushes we ran up the bear-path, and onwards at right angles to the point where we ought to intercept our quarry. Intercept him we did, but I mustn't lay too much stress on our condition of readiness. Bruin arrived some seconds before we expected him, and we dashed practically into his way. We were considerably taken aback at the finesse of the creature. More I must not say, or I shall remind you of that American fugitive who called out to the officer who attempted to rally the regiment, "For heaven's sake, don't try to stop me; I am so fearfully demoralized."

The bear must have galloped the instant we lost sight of him, perhaps even, he had some premonition of the threatening danger. On seeing us scattering to right and left the bear, who seemed absolutely enormous to my untrained gaze, stiffened all over, and his little eyes grew oblique with rage. He appeared to pull up almost on to his haunches. Cecily and I fired simultaneously, and at such close quarters that both shots were bound to be effective. With an extraordinary noise, half groan, half rage, the beast rose on hind feet, appearing to tower high above us, his wide head and massive neck turning from side to side. Like all the fiends he laid about him with great quivering arms, striking the air with weighty blows, helpless, a Samson shorn of his wondrous strength; and even as he strove to avenge the manner of his death the bullets did their work. With a lurch forward the vast creature tottered, righted himself erect once more, and then fell on his face with a dull, resounding crash. An awe-inspiring and impressive sight.

We did not approach the prostrate heap for some time. Many a man has met his end by investigating a supposed dead Alaskan bear.

F

Feeling desperately hungry, we began to feast off biscuits and tinned beef, and presently Ned appeared up the trail, telling us that the shots had called him out. We knew he could not possibly have heard them in our distant camp, and I suspect that he was tracking us in the furtive, secretive way these people have. Very often a lurking form glided phantom-wise between the tree-stems, causing me to pause a moment, only to find that it was no forest-dweller, but one of our own hunters hunting us. A strange trait of inquisitiveness; dangerous too.

Ned had a string of ptarmigan over his arm, and our '22 Winchester on his shoulder, but the whole lot gave way at the sight of the bear, and he dropped on his knees beside the carcase.

" You shoot all right, you bet," he said in sepulchral tones of amazement. We had known from the very first that our men regarded the feminine part of our expedition very much in the light of an American dime show—a great deal of fuss and palaver, and very little when you really get to it. We did not mind. It was a matter of indifference to us what they thought. Why talk to them of other experiences—days with rhino, lion, leopard, as though one could not do them again? It always seems to me that when anything you have done in the past looms very large and splendid in your eyes, it argues that you have not accomplished much to-day. Deeds, not words, count with natives.

By this time Ned had seen enough to convince him that we were fairly safe to go out with, and knew the use of firearms. He handled my Mannlicher next, as though he would wrest from it the secret of our astonishing success. Then thoughtfully he laid the weapon down. I think this last hunt completely converted Ned, who ever afterwards treated us with the same consideration and respect which he accorded the masculine element of the expedition. And wherefore not?

Were we not dressed alike, in the quaintest of fur *parkas*, with a modicum of knickerbocker showing below? and did we shirk damp, danger, or dismay? " I grant I am a woman; think you I am no stronger than my sex?" Cecily quoted laughingly to Ned. But in his eyes there was no answering light of recognition. The Immortal One has not as yet been translated for the benefit of the Aleuts.

Next—to the skinning, and though we did not take any part in it, we helped at intervals to shift the massive bear to a more get-at-able position. The " he," I regret to say, was a " she " of " uncertain age," with much-worn teeth and claws.

All Ned had with him was an insignificant bit of string, so, producing all we could offer, he tied the pelt together, and with the skull hanging over his shoulder we set out campwards. We also took a little of the meat, because of course we wanted to be able to say that bear steak had at least been sampled.

The ground was very bad going, and at intervals we sank in marshy hollows above our knees. We wondered how on earth our man could struggle on impeded as he was, forgetting the immense strength of these Aleuts. Very likely he did not feel the pack he was carrying half so much as we did the two rifles. Nature suits her strength to the burdens, as the burdens to the strength.

" You do not mind my weight ?" said the apologetic fly in the elephant's ear.

" Not at all," replied the elephant; " I really did not know that you were there."

We passed by a tract of country very much like an Indian snipe *jheel*, and sure enough we saw a few snipe rise from the marshy ground.

The bear steak we took back to camp with us was very dark in colour, the darkest flesh I have ever seen, most unappetizing to look at, and the fibre was coarse and tough. It was not really downright disagreeable when cooked, but nothing very special. When the bears get on to a fish diet the meat becomes very strong and unpalatable.

As our stores were ominously low we set about repairing to the *Lily,* which lay at anchor not more than five miles away, and she seemed a very pleasant home, sweet home, to us as we climbed on to her deck from out the dory.

CHAPTER V

COASTING ALONG THE ALASKA PENINSULA

She sings like one immortal
Pericles

'Tis gold which makes Diana's rangers false themselves
Cymbeline

By this time we had discovered that we had great cause to complain of the ship's *chef*. He could cook all right when he was able, but, then, he was so often *hors de combat*. He told me that he was " saved," but from what did not transpire. Certainly not from whisky, of which he appeared to own an illicit still. Fortunately our cabin boy, Tom, a first-class youth, was able to cope with the duties so often thrust upon him, the while our cook lay huddled in his berth crooning, " Yes, there'll be glory for me, for me. Oh yes, there'll be glory for me."

Tom, in a burst of confidence, told me that an end to the carousals must come, because the whisky supply would not continue to meet the demands made upon it. So there was nothing to do but wait the coming of that day of days.

Routine on board our ship as regards the saloon department was only noticeable in the mornings. As a rule breakfast was forthcoming in good time, but the day following the bear hunt appeared to be a *dies non* so far as getting anything to eat was concerned. At last—Tom being nowhere to be seen—I ventured into the fo'castle to investigate. The cabin boy was busily cutting bacon, running the risk of losing his head, for he was attacking half the side of an out-sized pig, and he cut towards himself, the knife being just level with his neck. The cook was helpless in a bunk, assuring any one who cared to listen of his complete confidence in the fact that there would be glory for him, for him.

There was nothing like enough coal in the stove to cook anything upon, and so I went to find some. The "open sesame" to the most used coal-locker was set in the flooring of the passage leading to the saloon. Most unfortunately I forgot, in my hurry, to replace the lid. The next instant such a crash and such language! I rushed to see whatever had happened, and there, half in and half out of the coal-hole, was the Leader of the expedition. He had not noticed the absence of the top board, and I do think it was silly of him. Somehow or other I got him back into the saloon, and he was very hurt and very huffy. I should have offered to get him some brandy if I hadn't known that the cook had made away with all there was available. It was no use precipitating a rumpus.

The Leader sat ruefully rubbing his knee, and I explained about the breakfast and everything, and tried not to laugh, and just then remembered to replace the board over the coal-locker before any one else fell down it. Then such a groan from the fo'castle! I felt absolutely certain that the knife had slipped after a further parley with the bacon, and Tom was decapitated. As I know nothing whatever of ambulance work, and had had quite enough worry for one morning, before breakfast too, I went on deck.

Presently the Leader came to me. The cook, he said, was in a species of fit, and would I help? I was so relieved to hear that it was not the bacon knife I went willingly, though I am completely ignorant of any workable method for the suppression of fits. I once helped to suppress a swarm of bees, and danced about crashing two pan lids together; but fits are another story. If it had not been for a wonderful little paper, a domestic encyclopædia, called *Home Snips*, engineered by the clever man who runs the *Daily Wail*, we should have been in parlous case indeed.

Luckily the cabin boy had a copy in his kit, and presented it to us. Fortunately there was an article on "Fits: and how to cure them," and we did all it said. *Home Snips* is such a remarkable little paper, quite indispensable to housewives it claimed to be, and I should think with reason. I found a recipe for making a good imitation of tomatoes, should tomatoes happen to be expensive, by parboiling some strips of red flannel, and another invaluable hint for converting turnips into a creditable representation of mushrooms by carving them into shape, and then serving up the deceptions with a covering of mushroom ketchup.

We finally breakfasted at 11 A.M., and by that time the *Lily* was under weigh, heading for the Trinity Isles.

The entire route of the expedition had now to be definitely mapped out, for it was hardly fair to our captain that our plans should be so very much *en l'air*.

The season for sheep and moose commencing on September the 1st, we had to arrange matters so that we should be in the best possible part of the country at that time. The Sheep Creek district having been the Mecca of so many sportsmen for so long, we decided that our chances of procuring a few really fine specimens of *Ovis dalli* thereabouts were small. All the plans were very chaotic, owing to the fact that Cecily and I had already formulated a scheme which we fully intended to carry into effect, and Ralph had another, and the Leader yet another, but every one wanted to hunt in the other's vicinity.

"*Will* you listen to reason, Ralph?" said the Leader, testily, as Ralph suggested the Mount St. Elias ranges, and pushed his views strenuously. It is nice when a person will listen to reason. It gives the reasoner such a chance to talk.

The route planned by Cecily and myself, to take effect after the summer hunts along the coast of the Bering Sea, was to the mouth of the Kuskokwim River, where we would quit the *Lily*, leaving instructions with her skipper to sail his boat back to Cook's Inlet, there to await our arrival, whenever that might be. He was to engage suitable men at the Sushitna settlement and send them, with *bidarkas,* up the Sushitna to meet us. We, landed at the mouth of the Kuskokwim, would hire Innuits on the spot and have them guide us up that river to the headwaters, and on meeting the contingent from the Cook's Inlet side our hunters from the Bering Sea could return to their homes. Our present men from Kodiak could return with the *Lily* as she sailed back to Cook's Inlet.

With every one wanting to set sail for a different locality matters got a trifle difficult. On talking it over with Cecily we decided that the plan of plans was to get the Leader of the expedition into a belief that the proposed trip up the Kuskokwim was his idea solely, when, man-like, he would hang on to it, and run it for all he was worth. If a man is judiciously allowed to think he is having his own way completely a woman can do anything with him, and, by the law of contraries, let a woman get but a glimmering notion that she is having her own way and a man can do nothing with her.

The thing worked like a charm. By adroit manœuvres, hints, and fragile suggestions we initiated the Leader into the first steps of the already arranged trip, and by lunch-time he was confident that he had thought out the details of it, and by tea-time he would have sworn by all his gods that he alone had evolved the scheme. The Sushitna-Kuskokwim route was carried. When I was asked had I ever considered that it would be a good line of country for the expedition to travel over, I didn't remember. Cecily, too, had a most astonishing lapse of memory. It is well for a woman to have a faulty memory on occasion, in fact, it is rather stupid for a woman over thirty to have a memory at all. Her object is, or should be, to keep young, and memories are fatal, mere aiders and abettors of Anno Domini.

We sailed by the Trinity Islands to the Semidi Islands. On the North Semidi the first fox ranche was established with the idea of making a great industry of raising blue foxes to supply the fur markets of the world. Nobody has made a fortune out of it, but the foxes can be reared to great perfection, the animals being killed between November and January. The blue fox living wild is now exceedingly rare in Alaska, but the islands set apart for the raising of them in domesticity are numerous, the *sine qûa non* being that it must be two miles away from any other land. This to prevent the foxes swimming away. Some of the islands have as many as a thousand head. The food provided is meal and fish, mixed together, given once a day. The beautiful creatures get to know the hand that feeds them, not dreaming that some day it will turn and rend them. It takes about nine months for the cubs to grow to maturity, and the litters usually number six to eight.

One or two islands go in for propagating the silver-grey fox, whose pelt is worth so much more than the blue. The silver-grey, however, is less profitable in the long run, because it is so difficult to take them without harming the fur. A blue fox will readily enter his death chamber, the box trap, without inquiry. Not so his cousin, the silver-grey. No scheming will induce him to enter anything of the trap variety, and poison does not answer because males and females alike swallow it.

The blue fox pelts vary, naturally, in quality, and as much as fifty dollars is paid for a really excellent skin.

Anchoring at last in a land-locked cove we found ourselves on the shores of a fox ranche, set on an infinitesimal island, and proceeded to go ashore to say " Salaam."

We made our way between scanty bushes to a little shack, with a stove pipe through the roof for chimney, and a heterogeneous collection of empty coal-oil cans doing duty for buckets beside the door. On a clothes line slung from the house to a pole a pair of dainty clocked stockings waved in the breeze.

Clocked stockings on a fox ranche !

Instantly we longed to quest for the Golden Girl who sometimes wore them. What would she be like ? It was a burning question of unbridled curiosity. In the distance, coming from a group of ill-built sheds, we heard some one singing. 'Twas like the trills of a nightingale. The singer came nearer, the owner, it must be, of the clocked stockings. Well, she was like her foot-gear, dainty, charming, quite young. A French Canadian, as pretty as they make them. Here she had lived for two years, winter and summer, caring for the foxes, helping her partner to bear the lonely lot of a fox rancher in the Northern wilds. There was some deep-set mystery about this couple, which we, of course, did not seek to probe. They were not the type of people to be where they were, to work as they were working, and thereon, I suspect, hangs a tale. The owner of the fox ranche was a well set up Englishman, whose mellifluous tones proclaimed him thoroughbred. He spoke of knowledge, so it was not difficult to guess where he had graduated.

Our new friends came to dinner on board the *Lily* after much persuasion. The dainty little lady was so retiring, but we could see the pleasure it gave her to meet white women again. The acoustic properties of the cabin on a sealing schooner are not of the best, so we took to the deck, and our nightingale consented to sing after we had convinced her that we all wanted to hear more of her voice.

Ralph accompanied her on his violin. First it was Auber's laughing song, then a gay little French ditty, next Saint Saëns.

The more I heard of her voice the more marvellous it seemed to be. So full of infinite variety that she never appeared to produce the same effect twice, so wonderfully tender that she must love royally, so delicate, so grand, so sonorous, so full of pathos, fire, feeling, art, laughter, tears, so thrilling, so moving, I have never heard a voice like it. I would rather hear it than any other living. It started so sweet, and sank, and rose, and swelled, and trembled, and dwelt, and enraptured, and died away, like some beautiful dream. It was a wondrous thing. It was divine. My very heartstrings were vibrating.

"If you would but go to Europe, you would have no need to raise foxes any more," said Ralph, as soon as he could speak for the witchery of the singer and the song. "The world would be at your feet."

" My world is here," said she, and her eyes smiled at her man.

" My world is here." That was her reason for remaining on that hideously bare island, whatever her partner's might be. Though possessing a gift of song unparalleled this Northern nightingale loved her grim cage too well to fly away from it, to flash, meteor-like, into a firmament of stars, outclassing all.

She is quite unforgetable, this dainty songstress, for her presence on the earth is so hard to explain. Nature has made types, but she was not a type. Darwin says that all types have their exceptions, but Tennyson has it that Nature is most careful of the type.

We anchored for a whole twenty-four hours at Sand Point, a bay inset on Popof Island, driven thither by the wrath of the elements. The *Lily* had groaned and creaked in the battering onslaughts of the sea. A large length of the gunwale resigned office suddenly, and we had to run for shelter without delay.

The storm was heralded by an ominously fine mirage, an enchanting illusion of unsurpassed clearness. Every shore, and point, and peak, and island were piled one above the other, fancifully painted in shadowy tones, as if reflected in a mirror suspended over the ship.

We had sailed by Aniakchak Bay, Afognak, and other bear-hunting grounds, wanting to get ashore, yet refraining, and bottling up our ardour for the chase. We knew that the farther afield we got, the more out of the beaten track, the better our chances of procuring some good specimens of brown bears on the mainland.

The mighty forests were a thing of the past, and from now onwards we saw nothing but beautifully green slopes, dotted with infinitesimal patches of alder or stunted willows in the valleys, and sheltered grounds, varied by the rolling tundras of the barren lands.

Here at Sand Point the familiar magpie was very much *en evidence*. The old Nursery rhymes about him were useless—the " One for sorrow, two for mirth "—because the magpies were so numerous there were not enough verses to meet the case. Bald-headed eagles sat on the rocks, silently meditating with that air of profound reflection which dominates the genus.

As soon as the storm abated we set sail for Unalaska, and though the sea was still troubled the atmospheric conditions were ideal, a delightful piece of luck, for we were thereby enabled to obtain a much more comprehensive view of the Pavlof volcanic peaks than is often the case. Indeed, our skipper told us that he had never before seen the peaks so clearly. Weird and majestic cones, about eight thousand feet high, with snow-clad sides blackened with the smoke, which belched forth, from one of the peaks, as though from a mill chimney in Lancashire. All the Alaska Peninsula and its islands are of volcanic origin, and everywhere one notes the typical " transition periods " of volcanic architecture.

Beating against a head wind we remained in sight of the Aghileen Pinnacles for hours. So needle-pointed are they that not even the snow clings to their spires. Thence past emerald tinted expanses, grey pyramidal cliffs, valleys, and strangely shaped rocks alive with sea-birds. Murres, the commonest of all the Alaskan diving birds, in myriads, and hundreds of tufted puffins with the wondrously tinted extra-sized bill adopted for the breeding season, to aid and abet the charms of the wooer, which is cast away, just as it is with us human things, and our adopted attractions, when he is married and a'.

Following steadily in our wake sailed a slender fulmar, a very distant relative of the albatross, whom in many ways it imitates. The fulmar is a very rigid flier, but it cannot glide indefinitely with never flapping pinions, neither has it that air of absolute mastery of all the laws of graceful flight which the albatross exhibits.

At the tip of the Peninsula, on Unimak Island, the volcanic peaks of Shishaldin and Isanotski reared their nine thousand feet of altitude. One of them looked impressively sombre, with a great white ruffle of pure coloured snow around the base. The snow line extended from the sea level to half way up the mighty cone, where it ceased suddenly, straight edged, to give place to blackness. Its mountain twin appeared to be leaking vapour at every pore, and from each rent and fissure jets of steam issued.

Now between Akun Island and Unimak we turn at last into the Bering Sea. It looks like any other sea. What had I expected, I wonder? Seals and sealers, whales and icebergs, Eskimos and walruses. Of these expected treats the whales alone turned up to give us greeting. They were belugas, or white whales, and of various sizes, the largest probably about twenty-five feet long. The big ones were very white in colour, and the small ones slate-grey. They appeared and disappeared with clockwork regularity, until we ran into a belt of fog, and so lost sight of them.

From out the enveloping mist a wonderful bird gyrated, curving in and out of our rigging with unswerving rigid wings. Again and again it uttered a mournful cry, low and penetrating, the voice of the Arctic. " The wilderness has a mysterious tongue," and it seemed to call to us insidiously through the medium of this seafaring bird. I knew it must be a shearwater, because I saw the similarity to the shearwater (*Puffinus anglorum*) which at one time frequented the more remote parts of the Isle of Man. Since that once delightful spot has become tripper-ridden, and every cave and cranny of its most distant rocks given over to the rampant love-making of the lower orders, the shearwater has sought islands new. It chooses the lonely, storm-swept countries, unfrequented by man. This agile bird would never seek *terra firma* at all save for the need of somewhere to lay its solitary egg upon. The nest is built in a hole, in some half-inaccessible part of the chosen island, and only the one egg is laid. The shell is remarkable for a strong scent of musk, and exceedingly fine texture. Most aptly named, this shearwater, for often it sails right through the crested breakers.

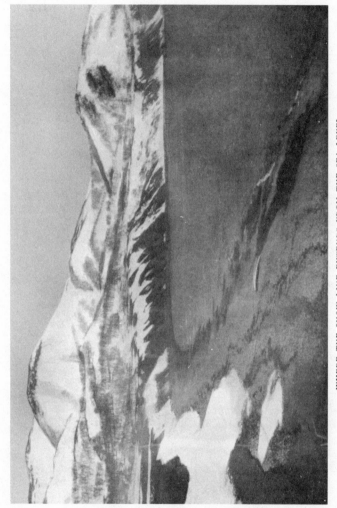

WHERE THE SNOW LINE EXTENDS FROM THE SEA LEVEL.

We went on to Dutch Harbour, on Unalaska, most beautiful of islands, where we found to our surprise another hunting camp located, preparatory to moving on. It was that of a solitary Englishman, out after brown bears, and he had made Unalaska from Kodiak on a chance trading vessel. He now intended creeping back to the mainland of the Peninsula in a dory, a very sporting thing to dare to do.

Such a dare-devil trip would, I imagine, have resulted in the complete exodus of the venturesome sportsman from Alaskan waters, and for his sake we were very relieved to hear of the purchase of an ancient brig, much the worse for time and inaction, which might, with a little fettling up, be persuaded to make a sort of swan-song trip of a voyage back along the Pacific Coast.

Our wayfaring countryman was an Imperial Yeoman. He did not look imperial, but he was, oh very. HE HAD BEEN TO SOUTH AFRICA. And could not forget the fact. He demonstrated with the few forks our limited supply ran to, how he turned the Wakkerstrom turning movement, built a Vaal Krantz with the salt-cellars, and rode into Ladysmith on the mustard-pot.

" He sailed away at break of day," before we were up; and not until we needed them did we discover that two of Diana's rangers had falsed themselves, and enlisted under the banner of the Imperial Yeoman. He would not know, of course, that the avaricious renegades were under contract of sorts to hunt with us, and probably agreed to pay the two dollars

G

a day or so which would be demanded of him to what he assumed were a couple of unattached hunters on the lookout for a likely billet. Steve and Ned remained true, and this, I suspect, because they had not had a chance of bettering themselves.

We were very cynical these days on the native hunter question.

We remained in Dutch Harbour almost five days, and it was the 2nd of June ere we quitted the beautiful place. The day previous to sailing Cecily and I had an ideal ramble on the hillsides, and up the slopes of a silvery river. Spring was in all the air, and countless birds sang to us of summer days to come. Deep moss upholstered every solitude, and in the green gardens the golden crown, a sparrow of exalted plumage, crept in and out the grass spears, he was just everywhere, this plaintive minstrel.

The various thrushes were in full spring song, the tender cadence of the exquisite love-notes cleaving the air in liquid trilling tones. Here, too, we noticed that most beautiful of all small birds, that little ball of fluff one longs to hold awhile in sheer delight in its wondrous charms, the chestnut-backed chickadee. Anything more perfectly sweet does not live in the world of birds.

On the river we saw the belted kingfisher, his crest in spring splendour, and all else of him iridescent. His flight was not the accurate darting motion of our home birds, but wavering and hesitating.

I often wondered, during my sojourn in Alaska, whether any one understands the laws of the country as now evolved, even the administrators. For every law that stands there appears to be another to nullify. All over the territory liquor is a prohibited import, the Act says so, and it ought to know, and if, when smuggling, you are careless enough to be caught red-handed fines and confiscation will result. But get the stuff into the country, by fair means or foul, and every one is delighted to welcome it, and the said prohibited drink is sold quite openly and above-board. Another Act sets forth, with due decorum, that no white man shall live with an Indian woman unless he is married to her, but as very few of the Alaskan padres are minded to "put a blessing" on such unions, the Act is of very little moral use.

CHAPTER VI

DUTCH HARBOUR AND ITS ENVIRONS

(By the Leader of the Expedition)

> This little world,
> This precious stone set in the silver sea
> *King Richard II*

ON an island, where the turbulent sea washes its shores, there stands to-day a town nestling cosily at the head of the picturesque land-locked harbour. The town itself is of mushroom growth, having its origin in one of the great gold rushes so common in Alaska. The buildings are of wood, and replete with such comforts as men can construct under prevailing conditions in the far North-West of America. Among the dwellings may be seen a fine hotel, and numerous comfortable houses, all now entirely deserted, save for the presence of a few residents who still cling to the abandoned town, either in hopes of better times reviving or lacking other places in which to cast their lot. On rare occasions a ship calls here to replenish her coal supply, since the town lays proud claim to being a coaling station. What matters it if the coal store is seldom replenished or depleted? So sudden has been the exodus, and houses now standing in empty silence bear such recent traces of habitation, that the spectator is reminded of a city of the dead, as it were forsaken owing to some terrible visitation of pestilence.

The island's beauty is entrancing, and a dreamer is bewitched in its solitudes by the glamour of Nature's graces. To appreciate the surroundings in all their glory one needs to climb one of the many small hills, whence the eye may revel in the charm and wonder of the scenery.

It is evening, and all the air is redolent with mingled perfumes of sweet flowers and soft deciduous grasses. The panorama is bewildering in its diversity. The island lies in a sheltered bay, surrounded by hills, lofty and majestic, of the mainland, through which a narrow entrance leads out to meet the ocean.

Clothed with a verdant carpet of innumerable flowers and grasses, the isle resembles a bright emerald surrounded with transparent blue setting formed by the bay's calm waters. The varieties of flowers are multitudinous, and their beauty and colouring are exquisite. Let the eye roam far out across the bay, and there we have on every side glimpses of lofty hills which assume all forms of shapes found in mountain scenery. Conical, serrated, concave, or convex, the sharp curves of hills and valleys stand out in bold relief, each line accentuated by the clearness of this Northern atmosphere. The setting sun is sinking behind the distant peaks in an effulgent glory peculiar to the Arctic regions. Dying rays shining on motionless clouds are reflected in wondrous colour tints, and softly clothe the highest snow-clad peaks with a golden mantle.

The scene is of surpassing loveliness, whilst over all there hangs a death-like stillness lending weird charms to this island of solitude, once so full of human life, but to-day wrapped in silence. Even the birds flit noiselessly amongst the luxuriant grasses, seeming as if smitten with sad forebodings of winter, For are not they, even as us, wanderers, in this land of short, fickle summers, and the days are not far distant when perforce they needs must undertake once more those long, weary flights, battling their way over countless miles of watery wastes, or crossing dark forests, in quest of warmer climes.

If the wanderer who visits these shores explores the neighbourhood his reward will be strange and novel sights. If his course lies to the westward there are islands innumerable, barren, desolate, inhospitable spots. The home of gigantic volcanoes, and even to-day a new island has recently been bodily erupted from the ocean's depths, so that where less than two years since vessels sailed in deep waters, now there stands a forbidding emblem of Nature's handiwork, with a rocky mountain top rising sheer from the sea. Volumes of steam and smoke issue from its summit.

If destiny turns the wanderer eastward his ship may take him to a land of low-lying shores which during winter months lie fast locked in the chill grip of ice and snow. Here, on isolated sandbanks, are the haunts of countless sea-birds, whose weird

ABANDONED AND SILENT LIES A NOBLE THREE-MASTED VESSEL

cries by day and night find responsive echoes in the
hoarse bellowing of walruses, or shriller barking of
the roving seals, all seeking here a harbour of refuge
in sanctums where the murderous hand of man
seldom leaves its mark. Weird, desolate, wind-
swept coasts, on which neither trees nor bushes
flourish, where life seems to be a continuous struggle
against Nature's fiercest elements, and where the call
of the wild speaks loudest in hearts of man and
beasts alike. Here we see the ravages of a higher
power, which defies man's labour, and bids defiance
to his skill. Abandoned and silent, lies a noble
three-masted vessel, high and dry on the sands, grim
relic of an ocean's wrath. Her sole occupant a bold
fox, which has somehow found its way in quest of
food on to this desert island, and made its home on
board the ship. What more touching sight is there
than this gallant craft, perfect in all respects, save
that her sails will never carry her again proudly over
those waves which she, in her pristine beauty and
strength, defied. Fast embedded in the sand, long
will she remain an object of superstitious dread to
the natives who know that on her brave men met
their death.

Strange indeed, to the minds of civilized beings in
the twentieth century, is the anomaly of life amongst
the denizens of this chill and lonesome North. Here
may still be seen a race little affected by the march
of civilization, as regards the customs and habits
ruling their daily life. A people without aspirations,
or ambitions, with strange fancies and superstitious

beliefs, dreamers having the weird imagination of
children, but happy, content to live and die as their
ancestors have done before, representing a fast disappearing form of primeval man, whose highest
intellectual attainments consist in devising means of
obtaining food and clothing. Suffering much, in
various periods of their history, at the hands of more
powerfully armed marauders from far-distant climes.
Gaining little in return for the importation of vile
spirits, or unknown diseases, which have wrought
havoc amongst their numbers. A race of fishermen
and hunters, but under the improved conditions of
the American rule, they have developed the industry
of fur trading. Formerly the valuable furs collected
for their own use too often fell a prey to the hands
of their marauding enemies, or Russian taskmasters.

With the purchase of Alaska by the Americans
from Russia in 1867, a new era dawned for the
natives. A rule of bloodshed, murder, and plunder
was succeeded by what is to-day an equally lenient
and in some cases too considerate form of government. Some laws have been enacted giving them
certain privileges denied to many white men. This
applies more particularly to the framing of the
Alaskan Game Laws, whereby the natives are practically unrestricted as to time, numbers, or anything
else in their wanton destruction of game, both great
and small, throughout the country. Many wise rules
have been made to protect the game from too indiscriminate slaughter by sportsmen and others. No
doubt can be entertained that such policy is an error

of judgment, since it leads the natives in certain districts to consider themselves the equals, or superiors, of the white men visiting the country.

Time and experience have taught Englishmen throughout the world that the only successful way to rule natives is by firmness tempered with justice, compelling them to feel a certain dependency upon their white associates. Beneath the skin of a native lies the heart of one born to be ruled by a superior hand, whether it be that of his own kind or that of an alien race. Kindness is too often interpreted by them as a form of weakness, familiarity breeds contempt, and equality between the white and coloured races will eventually end in disaster.

It is with the latter terrible problem, a demon yearly increasing in size and significance, that the whole American nation is faced to-day, nor can any man say what will be the final outcome of the great racial upheavals which are bound to arise at some future date. Slow, methodical, behind the times, in the onward rush of civilization as we are to-day, England, and Englishmen alone, are those who can still successively rule the native races upon earth. Hence the secret of success in the colonization of the vast Empire which is to-day ruled by the population of a small island kingdom.

Perhaps the one point on which the Americans display more judgment in the treatment of natives than is the case with many Governments of the old world, is in the matter of so-called religious teaching. As a rule, little is done to try and convert the natives from the religion and beliefs of their ancestors. Consequently we see little of what has caused so many of our own petty wars, where the missionaries are followed by fire and sword, to quell the disturbances which their well-meant, but ill-advised teachings have aroused, in their devoted attempts to overthrow the traditions and customs of centuries.

The writer is full well aware of the storm which may be aroused in certain quarters by these remarks, but, nevertheless, speaking from experience of natives in various countries, he has no hesitation in saying that for corruptness in all its branches there is nothing which equals the semi-Christianized native, in comparison with whom, their savage brethren, acting according to the traditions and teachings of their community, are often paragons of perfection.

The number of different tribes (if they may be thus designated) inhabiting the coast line of Alaska is almost bewildering to an amateur in the study of anthropology, ranging as they do from races of the low-class Siwash Indians in the South, to Aleuts on the Alaska Peninsula and Aleutian Islands, and again to wandering bands of Eskimo found on the shores of the Arctic and Bering Sea. The Babel of languages is even more confusing, since inhabitants of one settlement have often considerable difficulty to make themselves understood in their native tongue, when speaking to dwellers in other settlements situated at no great distance apart. In such cases they often have to resort to the Russian language, which is still in vogue among them, and even now is taught by priests of the Russian Church in certain districts.

It is a noticeable fact that except amongst the Northern tribes of Eskimo, the majority of native settlements past and present are situated on or very near the coast. This may probably be attributed to the fact that the one staple food amongst the inhabitants has for centuries been fish. In spring, or early summer, the ocean supplied their needs, and later the countless salmon running up the various rivers were easily captured and dried for winter use. In recent times the purchase of firearms by natives has become a real menace to all forms of game in the country. Bears, moose, caribou, seals, and other forms of fur-bearing animals supplied them with their clothing, and formerly, when armed with primitive weapons of their own construction, these animals were in no danger of extermination. But, alas, to-day the use of firearms, traps, and the more villainous poison, have wrought havoc and destruction in the numbers of both the great and small mammals throughout the country. No longer are even the hardy, keen-eyed mountain sheep immune from ruthless slaughter by those men armed with modern weapons of destruction, and many boatloads of these fine animals' carcasses are annually brought down from the mountains by the rivers.

At present the American Government is wisely making strenuous efforts to put down the sale of hides, or heads, of the big game, in which considerable traffic has recently been done by natives, and a few professional hunters of white persuasion. As a sample of what is still done in this way by certain men of the country, I may mention that I saw the return of a well-known professional hunter with three boats containing the horns and skins of moose, sheep, caribou, all killed in a celebrated game district. And this, moreover, a part in which now all the species of game mentioned are strictly protected from the few wandering sportsmen who occasionally find their way to far distant Alaska.

The greatest annual function amongst the dwellers on the coast, is the capture and drying of salmon for winter use. For this purpose whole settlements of men, women, and children adjourn to the banks of some river where the salmon ascend during the summer months in countless millions, the men using nets, spears, and every kind of appliance to capture the fish, the women and children remaining in their temporary camp to clean and dry the catch. The latter process is simple, as the fish are merely cleaned, split open, and the heads removed. They are then hung in rows on rails, ropes, or trees to dry in the sun and wind.

The terrible smell arising from the offal, carelessly thrown in heaps near the dwellings, is so overpowering that the average white man is glad to escape as soon as possible from a visit to one of these camps.

When found in immediate proximity to American trading posts, salmon canneries, or mining camps, the inhabitants of native settlements show a tendency

NATIVES OUTSIDE A BORABARA

to adopt the habitations and dress of civilization. Here, in consequence, the natives are indolent, impudent, and, if possible, more avaricious than their less cultured brethren.

Amongst the Aleuts, where timber is scarce, the ordinary dwellings, locally called *baraboras,* are small dug-out huts, half below the ground level, having the sides and roofs composed of logs covered with earth. Poor, miserable hovels, scarcely suited for dog-kennels in a civilized land. The hardy Eskimo are nomads, dwellers in tents during the summer, or houses made from the skins of walrus, called *topeks,* but with the commencement of winter, and the first heavy snow-falls, they construct snow houses, which are known as *iglus,* and in these they dwell until the approach of spring.

The true Eskimo, or Husky, of the barren lands, still remain unsullied by the tarnish of civilization. Their character has been well described by Mr. David Hanbury in his book, *Travel in the Northland of Canada.* Few men are better qualified to speak of the Eskimo as they are to-day, he having " lived their life, shared their habitations, clad in deerskins, and subsisted on caribou and musk-ox meat in winter, and on fish in summer."

He says : " The Husky character is naturally easy-going, happy and contented. To counterbalance an occasional display of sulks he has many good, even noble, qualities. The good Husky knows no fear, and never gets excited either on land or water.

Among them there is no knowledge and no idea of a Supreme Being, nor of a future state. One whom I questioned said, 'Husky die, no more Husky.' They have no account of the creation of the world, and their story of the origin of the human race is incoherent."

Is it then a matter for wonderment that these wild children of illimited barren wastes, dwellers in a land of mournful solitudes, should cherish in their hearts strange illusions, or weird phantasies of the dread unknown? In a land where the fickle and short-lived summer gives place for long weary months to the chill, fierce grip of ice and snow, when nature is clothed in garbs of cruelty, and seldom smiles in gentle moods; where in southern regions the sighing of the wind moans through dense, silent forests, or across northern wastes, icy blasts rush down from snow-clad mountain tops to mingle in wild cadence with tempestuous waves on a storm-swept, desolate coast.

During our brief stay in Dutch Harbour we paid several visits to the adjacent picturesque little settlement of Unalaska, and upon one of these occasions we were fortunate enough to encounter a man named Macdonald. He had spent many years on these coasts, having been skipper of a sealing schooner in the palmy days when the valuable sea-otter and fur seals were still numerous along the Bering Sea shores. In course of conversation with Captain Clemsen, this man displayed such an intimate know-

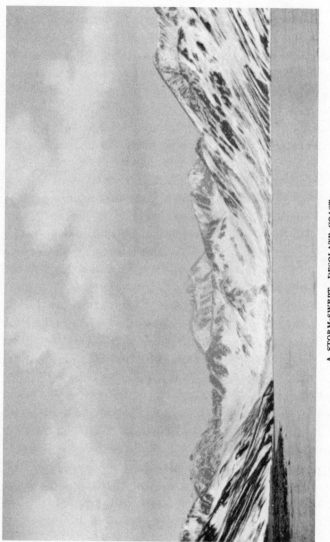

A STORM-SWEPT, DESOLATE COAST

ledge of the various bays, islands, and rivers along
the coast that the former felt Macdonald's services
would be a welcome addition to our party. So,
finally, on fairly reasonable terms for a white man
in Alaska, we induced him to accompany us as far as
the Kuskokwim River, whence we promised to send
him back to Unalaska in the *Lily*, as she returned
to await our arrival in Cook's Inlet.

Macdonald's local knowledge proved of the greatest
benefit to us, and also to our skipper, for probably
without his assistance we should never have successfully sailed along those treacherous coasts, nor found
the haunts of several species of big game which we
sought.

As the season was now so far advanced, and the
weather getting decidedly warm, we were anxious
to push on in order to obtain a few specimens of the
great bears which inhabit the Bering Sea coasts of
Alaska. As soon, then, as a favourable breeze set
in we bade "adieu" to Dutch Harbour, and shaped
our course N.E., standing in along the shore as near
as we dared to sail.

Making good progress under a full spread of
canvas the *Lily* glided past Akutan Island, affording
us magnificent views of its lofty snow-clad mountain
peak, and then past Akun Island, across the entrance
to Unimak Pass. Here countless thousands of sea
birds congregated, the most numerous species seeming to be a large dark-coloured petrel, which wheeled
and flew about the vessel in huge flocks. Far as the

eye could reach the air was black with pinions. Here were wheeling flights of eider ducks, guillemots, puffins, scoters, and various kinds of gulls, all passing to and fro in bewildering profusion, winging their way by day and night either from or to their breeding grounds which are situated far from the haunts of men.

Never throughout my travels in many lands have I seen such countless numbers of birds assembled in one place, and probably the reason of it was that Unimak Pass is the main highroad through which these birds passage from North to South, and *vice versâ*. In fact it may be called the parting of the ways between Arctic regions and more temperate climes, for here is the spot where first the mighty Pacific Ocean meets in endless strife with those turbulent waters of the Bering Sea. Few men who have sailed along these coasts can relate that they have ever seen the waters here peaceful and calm.

As night came on the wind veered round and almost died away, leaving us floundering and wallowing in that most unpleasant thing of all, a heavy tide rip. For sheer discomfort commend me to a sailing vessel becalmed in such a place. The utter feeling of helplessness, added to the qualms of *mal-de-mer*, with a glorious uncertainty as to when the next breeze may come, whilst with idly flapping sails a ship wallows in the trough of choppy waves, this indeed is the acme of misery.

Next morning those of us who could sleep under

these trying conditions awoke to find the *Lily* engaged in tacking against a head wind. This again in rough waters is neither pleasant nor a speedy means of progress, and as Agnes graphically described it, the whole business reminded her of a mouse which runs around a washing tub, taking endless trouble in travelling a long way to reach the point from which it first started.

It is a long lane, however, which has no turning, and rarer still is a wind in the Bering Sea which does not quickly shift. Thus, as once more the wind veered round and blew steadily off shore, we soon found our good ship tearing along through the waters helped by a spanking breeze. Close hauled, under every stitch of canvas which the skipper dared set up, the *Lily* displayed her finest sailing powers. Heeling over with our starboard gunwale half under water she went ploughing through the waves, sending showers of spray from beneath her bows as we leapt buoyantly over the deep, smashing and driving her sharp prow into those foaming crests as if rejoicing in taking revenge upon the wicked waters which had buffeted her for long weary hours whilst she lay helpless on their bosom.

Swiftly we sped along the shores of Unimak Island, a barren, desolate coast, but the island is interesting to sportsmen, for it is the most western point of Alaska upon which both bears and caribou are found. According to the natives these latter animals repeatedly swim from the mainland to the island, a distance of some two or three miles across Falk's Pass or

H

Isanotski Straits. Here we would fain have landed, but Macdonald said no safe anchorage could be found along the Bering Sea coasts of the island, and if we persisted and insisted on doing so the *Lily* must perforce abandon us, and sail on many miles ere she could find a sheltered harbour.

CHAPTER VII

A BEAR HUNT AND AN EPISODE

(*By the Leader of the Expedition*)

Thus will I save my credit in the shoot
Love's Labour's Lost
Was ever man had such luck
Cymbeline
You seem to me as Dian
Much Ado About Nothing

At last we came to a place called Izenbeck Bay, and
here Macdonald said we should find a harbour of
refuge, and moreover declared that bears were plentiful upon the mainland near this spot. The entrance
to this bay was sheltered by a chain of low sandy
islands, which occur at intervals with great regularity
along the Bering Sea coast, and are perhaps the
most uninviting, dreary-looking spots on earth.
Nevertheless, after many hours of enforced idleness
and certain discomforts since our departure from
Dutch Harbour, we all yearned to go ashore and
stretch our legs once more. So our skipper steered
a course between the islands and dropped anchor in
the sheltered bay.

It was too late in the day to attempt a landing on
our arrival, but early next morning we decided on
making two expeditions from the ship, Agnes to

99

accompany me, Ralph taking Cecily to another point upon the mainland; each party taking one native, and two men rowing the flat-bottomed dories. The latter boats we found most useful for drawing close in to shore, since here the gently sloping, sandy bottom was often only covered with a few inches of water fully a mile from shore. It usually ended in what the Americans call "a gum-boot proposition," since every one had to don rubber boots and wade ashore for considerable distances; men being always left in charge of the boat to pull her farther in, or push her farther out, as the tide came in or receded.

After going through the customary performance of wading ashore, Agnes and I landed on a small sand-spit, near which a little river flowed into the lagoon. In the river countless humpbacks and dog salmon were running up to spawn, and far as the eye could reach up the stream was seen an endless piscine procession. In many places the stream was only a few inches deep, but, nothing daunted, here the fish were seen struggling upwards in thousands with their fins and backs clear out of the water, all going to their spawning beds.

Here they mate, and soon afterwards perish miserably, since none of these fish ever live to return to the sea when once they have spawned. Whether it is the action of fresh water upon them after sojourning in the sea, or whether it is the actual process of spawning which exhausts these fish, it is hard to say, but the fact remains that of the countless millions of

these salmon which ascend the rivers of the Bering
Sea and Pacific Ocean none ever live to return again
into the sea. Their anadromous habits appear to
be the cause of a cruel waste of life amongst these
fish. If they would only take any form of lure in
fresh water an angler might break all world's records
with a rod and line upon some of these far Northern
rivers.

Although we repeatedly tried with flies and spoons,
we never moved a salmon of any kind when once
they had entered and commenced to run in any of
the rivers which we visited. This remark does not,
however, apply to certain of the salmon on these
shores when they are in tidal waters, and in fact we
took a number of the fine king salmon, and also
many of the silver salmon by trolling and casting
a spoon at the mouths of the rivers where these fish
were running. During summer, and in the fall,
salmon form the staple food of the Alaskan bears,
and it was easy to see from recent tracks along the
banks and sandy beach that this river was the haunt
of more than one of these four-footed fishermen.
But as the afternoon sun was still high in the heavens,
and as by now we had learned the habits of these
bears sufficiently to know that their feeding times are
late in the evenings or early mornings, we rightly
surmised that it was wasting time to go in quest of
game just then.

Since Agnes had come out with murderous intent,
she needs must slay something to while away an
hour. And thus she set off to the boat, again return-

ing triumphant with a boat-hook which she said was to be improvised as a new form of fishing-rod. In vain I pleaded that we had been told that these two kinds of salmon were not really nice to eat. She merely retorted—

" How do you know until you have tried them yourself? I do not believe all I hear in Alaska, and not always what I see, so therefore you can watch me catch a salmon, and help me eat it afterwards."

True to her word she very soon hooked out several fine fish, weighing about eight or ten pounds each; in fact the whole procedure was ridiculously easy, since the fish kept jostling each other up over the shallows in such crowds that many of them were almost driven ashore by sheer weight of numbers. Agnes, who does not profess to be a fisherman, had no compunction in slaying about half-a-dozen in this unsportsmanlike fashion. I am bound to confess that when subsequently cooked on our return to the ship these fish were by no means bad eating, although the colour of their flesh was almost white, and they could not compare, in my opinion, with the magnificent king salmon, which when fresh killed is almost as good as the true *Salmo salar* of European waters.

As it drew towards evening we decided to follow up the river bank and take up some position whence we could obtain a view towards the distant foothills from which we knew bears must come, since it was here that they laid up by day, hidden in dense alders which heavily fringe the hillsides. In its lower reaches the river flowed through a low, sandy plain on which in places long patches of coarse grass were growing, whilst here and there we crossed soft boggy spots covered with dwarf moss and rushes, typical tundra of barren Arctic lands.

A mile or more ahead of us there rose a sandy hill which domineered the whole country. So bidding the men remain with the boat until we should return, Agnes and I set out to reconnoitre from the distant hillock. On arrival there we found that all the ground between us and the foothills for at least a mile was clearly visible from the summit.

Outlined on the plain lay the snake-like windings of the river, till it disappeared from view behind a distant spur of the foothills. Dotted at intervals over the open tundra were a few roving caribou, which in this district are classified by American mammalogists under the scientific name of *Rangifer granti*. Knowing that the bulls' horns were still in velvet we left them unmolested, contenting ourselves with a careful scrutiny of the river banks on which we hoped ere long to see our friends the ursine fishermen.

All along the river banks well-worn bear trails ran, signs that for generations these huge beasts had wandered up and down the stream. Beside the shallow places numerous fresh tracks, some of them gigantic in size, showed that bears came daily down to fish. In many spots we found partly-eaten bodies of dead salmon, where the bears had hauled the fish out into the high patches of grass, and there devoured their bodies, leaving usually the head and tail parts only.

Whilst walking up the stream, and even on the

hilltop, countless hordes of mosquitoes viciously attacked us, and as this was our first experience of these pests, we had come out unprovided with mosquito nets. No one, until they have seen mosquitoes in these northern latitudes, can imagine what their numbers are, nor the misery which they inflict on men and beasts alike, and although I have battled with these pests in torrid zones and tropical climes, yet never have their numbers and ferocity equalled anything which I have encountered amongst these voracious blood-suckers in the Arctic regions of Alaska and Siberia, where during the summer months men and beasts are seldom free from their attacks by day or night. Since the breeze was blowing downwards from the hills I ventured then to light a pipe, and by this means repelled a number of the venomous insects, but for Agnes, who does not smoke "penny poisons," otherwise cigarettes, there was little peace, until at last a gentle rain commenced to fall and drove away our unwelcome visitors to shelter beneath the clustering grasses.

We scarcely hoped to see a bear before the dim and mystic hours of twilight, but a fact that never entered into our calculations was that here, remote from even the haunts of native men, these beasts had roamed for ages immune from all attacks of their dread enemies the human race.

And so perchance they had grown callous or far bolder than their species is in the hunted districts of Alaska. Thus it was with no small joy, whilst the light was good, we simultaneously espied a huge skulking form slowly emerge from a distant patch of alders, and there in the full light of a setting sun stood the most gigantic specimen of a bear which either of us had ever seen.

Although fully half-a-mile from us it needed not the assistance of our glasses to tell us that here indeed was a king amongst bears, for standing on a patch of the bare hillside the brute looked, as Agnes said, as big as an elephant.

He seemed in no hurry to descend the hillside, but remained a while as if listening, lifting his great head as though sniffing the air in quest of scenting any hidden danger. We knew that as far as we were concerned everything was safe, since the wind was blowing straight towards us.

Presently the bear began to move, and slowly, with a rolling gait, he descended to the river bank. On arriving there a curious metamorphosis took place in the antics of the bear, for suddenly the ungainly brute appeared as active as a kitten. After standing motionless on the bank for a moment he sprang into the water, and a second afterwards appeared galloping up the bank with a salmon in his mouth. The whole performance was so quick, and the distance was so great, that we were unable to see how the actual capture of this fish had been effected. But upon subsequent occasions when closely watching these great bears fishing, I observed that they always pounce upon a fish, transfixing it in shallow water with their claws, and then carry it to the bank in their mouth. Once on land they retire to some thick patch of grass, or friendly screen of bushes, where they eat their prey, and soon return in quest of others. One salmon of ten pounds by no means suffices these monsters for a single meal.

Then the question arose as to how best we should make an approach and get within shooting distance of the bear. The whole ground lying between us was destitute of cover, save for the high grass growing on the river banks, and the only thing to do appeared to be to follow the water course. Quickly then we clambered down, and hastened at our best pace up along the river side. Fortunately the stream was very low, and had receded from the banks, leaving on either side a miniature beach of sand and pebbles, over which the travelling was easy. Thanks to the winding course, the river bed was securely screened from the spot where Bruin fished. And fish he did, for not even Agnes with her boat-hook was as certain as this beast whenever he essayed a strike. During our stalk, which lasted barely twenty minutes, we observed the bear make a raid three successive times, and each time he returned triumphant with a salmon to his feeding spot upon the bank. So intent was he on his fishing operations that I think we might have crawled to within a few yards of his lair if an unforeseen *contretemps* had not arisen.

Agnes and I had called a temporary halt behind some tall overhanging grasses, to regain breath ere making the final advance nearer to the spot at which the bear came down each time to a shallow place, and close by which we knew he was still devouring his last caught fish. We had been so intent on watching the particular patch of grass in which we knew our quarry lay that neither of us looked to right or left. Suddenly, as though it were from out of space above us, on the bank there loomed the head and shoulders of another bear. So close indeed it stood that we could well have hit it with a twelve-foot fishing-rod. Just for a moment I cannot say who looked the most surprised, but of the three of us the bear was the quickest to recover, and then, with a snort and kind of frightened squeal, it dashed off up the bank towards where the other beast was feeding.

Standing erect I quickly saw the newcomer was a small beast compared with our former friend. But one thing now was certain, namely, that the smaller beast would pass and warn the other of approaching danger by its mad stampede. Seeing this I said to Agnes, "Come quickly, and follow me."

We started running along the bank towards the high grass where we last had seen the big bear disappear. As we reached a point about a hundred yards away from this spot the huge beast stood erect, and for an instant gazed towards us as we ran. Realizing that this was our last chance for a steady shot, I stopped and bade Agnes take the first shot at the beast. As she hurriedly took aim the great bear swung round and started off at a lumbering gallop for the nearest cover, which was a large patch of alders growing on the hillside. Agnes was using a double-barrelled ·375 rifle, and at her first shot I saw the sand fly up just beneath the bear, and he passed on untouched. At her second shot the beast lurched forward and almost fell, but in a moment had recovered and started off again as if not badly wounded. Seeing that we were likely to lose the animal unless I could contribute to his discomfort, I drew a bead upon him, and just as Agnes had done I pulled off and shot low at my first attempt, but the second bullet from my heavy 450 cordite rifle fairly bowled the bear upon its side.

By this time he had almost gained the shelter of the bushes, and ere either of us could reload the beast once more recovered, and though apparently very sick, disappeared into the high alders.

My disgust at seeing the huge beast disappear can be better imagined than described, and although I knew that he was mortally wounded there was little hope of finding him if left till the morrow, because a soaking rain had then set in which would probably obliterate all tracks and blood trail within a few hours' time.

Turning to Agnes I said, " If you will stay here a little while, I am going to try and find that bear."

I was fully prepared for her laconic reply, " And me too."

It is characteristic of Agnes Herbert that she does not waste words on such occasions as these, and realizing that to argue with her under the circumstances was but a useless waste of time and breath, I was at some trouble to make up my mind as to what was the right course to follow, knowing full well that to pursue a wounded bear into such dense brush was, to put it mildly, looking for trouble.

Therefore I reluctantly said, "Very well, then we will leave him till to-morrow, and send the men to look for the brute."

Assuming great indignation, Agnes said, "I believe you are afraid to follow a wounded bear into the bush."

It has always been a mystery to me why Eve had not sufficient cunning to outwit a snake, because her descendants have more than enough sagacity to outwit the average man. Agnes is no exception to this rule, since full well she knew that nothing could have stung me to action quicker than this taunt.

"Very well," I said, falling into her trap, "if you think so come and see, but you are to keep behind me all the way."

Now Bruin had entered the brush by a well-worn trail, and soon we found ourselves threading a way between the dense alders and thick grasses which grew beneath them, the latter often reaching to our shoulders. The huge tracks were plainly visible every yard along the trail, whilst here and there great blood tracks, deep splashes on the grass and twigs, showed that our quarry was badly wounded. Our rate of progress was not rapid, since in many places it was necessary to crawl between big alder stems which these huge bears, owing to their weight, can force aside as easily as we could do with grass or rushes.

How far we had gone I reckoned not, as with my

eyes intently fixed upon the tracks I slowly plodded on.

Suddenly, without any perceptible sound, a huge body rose beside me, scarcely two yards away, and so quiet and silent was the movement that Agnes had uttered a warning cry of, "Look to your left!" ere I realized that the wounded animal was standing almost within arm's-reach of me.

Just for a moment I stood irresolute, since I have proved to my own personal satisfaction that the old adage, "quick as thought," is a misnomer when applied to minute seconds in which we face a mortal peril. And although both sight and sound warned me now of this threatening danger, it took the torpid mind a second before it bade my limbs bestir themselves to fend off a disaster. In one brief instant a thousand schemes were crowded into one, the net result of which was that I needs must shoot or run. By many writers we have seen these moments spoken of as if they lasted ages, yet for me the fleeting second seemed too short a space in which to come to a decision.

And, *horresco referens,* just for a moment also I forgot the imminent danger in which my companion stood.

But with her it was otherwise, for even now the scene comes vividly back to me of seeing Agnes raise her rifle, and ere yet my inert muscles could obey the brain's command, a shot rang out, and reeling like a drunken man the vast brute crashed forward with a bullet through his skull; so close indeed it was that only by jumping nimbly aside was I enabled to avoid the impact of the fall.

Then to me there came that moment of reaction in which, reflecting on a recent peril, we think what might have happened had things turned out otherwise. Such moments do not come often in a lifetime, and still rarer are the occasions on which men owe their lives to the cool courage of a woman. As a full significance of the facts broke upon my clouded senses, I found Agnes smiling, and furtively regarding both me and the fallen beast. Suddenly the magnitude of my debt to her arose clear in my mind, high above all other thoughts, and thereby possibly awakening sentiments which hitherto I had done my best to despise.

Here, reader of mine, lest you should expect a dissertation or a treatise on the gentle arts of Cupid, let me preface the following remarks with a statement that, according to strict compact with my collaborator in this " work," I am excused from the recording of all sentimental episodes.

Suffice it therefore if I say that I walked to where Agnes stood, and as she held her smoking rifle in one hand, I took possession of the other, and looking squarely into her brave eyes I said, " Little woman, you have saved my life, and for that I pay thee toll."

What the nature of the toll was is left for you to conjecture.

CHAPTER VIII

FURTHER TRIPS ON THE PENINSULA

Fortune brings in some ships that are not steer'd
Cymbeline

AFTER the Izenbeck Bay hunting, during which we bagged two fine specimens of *Ursus dalli gyas*, our pilot, whose knowledge of the Bering Sea was said to be like Sam Weller's acquaintance with London, "extensive and peculiar," advised making for a bay in the vicinity of Cape Rodgnof, and the *Lily* set her nose into a bank of fog which rose, white and insidious, before us. But if one waits for the fog to clear in these parts one may wait for ever. Fog is the normal condition of the Bering Sea.

Captain Clemsen did not profess to have any great knowledge of the coves and inlets where we would fain hunt; his acquaintance with the regions northward was confined to the ordinary route taken by sailing vessels. He struck me as being most cordially thankful to have some one aboard who would undertake to manœuvre our craft through the rocky, treacherous sea which lay ahead of us.

The following morning, very early, our new man, a canny Scotchman too, surpassed himself and inaugurated his reign with *éclat*, and no mistake about it.

The day broke very cold, so cold that I had gone back to my *parka*, a costume we had discarded since June came in with smiling days. We were feeling our way—for the breeze was light, and the sea for a wonder calm—through a dense fog, doing our best to creep into a safe anchorage in a near-by creek thoroughly well known to our pilot, when suddenly, apropos of nothing, with a horrible grating sound we struck a submerged rock, and swung there on its table top like a see-saw. The serious side of the affair was quite swamped for me by the ludicrous conduct of the Leader, who rushed to me in the greatest excitement, and made the most embarrassingly strenuous efforts to tear my *parka* from my back. " Get the thing off at once," he said; " if the ship goes down you'll be drowned like a rat in a trap," which was quite a mistake, I imagine, for my *parka* was of caribou-skin, and a caribou is an animated lifebuoy, every hair being hollow, and consequently buoyant. That is the reason, I think, why caribou swim so exceptionally high out of the water.

But I am digressing, and I left the *Lily* in a terrible quandary upon a rocky pinnacle.

We all calmed down in a moment or two, as nothing more untoward appeared likely to happen, and as the tide rose—fortunately for us the tide was coming in at the time of the disaster—the ship rose also, and presently got some way on, and we knew that we were clear. None of the planks seemed to have started or suffered from the impact so far as we could judge, but the steering gear was totally disabled, and

I

the schooner did not answer to her helm at all. As it was not the moment to try conclusions, we got out a dory and towed. Hard work and slow, but effective enough, and by nightfall we had run the gauntlet of the fog, and made the looked-for creek set in a waste of tundra.

On the greater part of the Bering Sea the low-lying tundra rises from the beaches or coast line like vast, rolling prairie meadows. So smooth and inviting it looks, and yet appearances are deceptive in tundras as in so many other things, and the whole place is more often than not a quagmire and morass. In places the marshes are really deep, in others just wet and spongy. Beneath the tundra the ground is for ever frozen, and only the surface thaws out each year. The grassy plains in summer are gardens full of blazing flowers—lupines, yellow anemones, calypso orchids—a scheme of tints impossible to any master mind save that of nature. With the dull brown for background, the wonderful colours spread with lavish hand in labyrinthine splendour look like a matchless carpet of fairy weaving.

Here on the tundras countless birds build their nests—black and red throated divers, geese, terns, scoters—and all the air vibrates with the numerous calls. Again and again ring out the newly-acquired love-notes of the golden plover, his shrill whistle changed to a tender cry, alluring and joyous. In solitary pairs, with chequered wings, the golden plovers lighted on the grassy expanse and sang " their wild notes to the listening waste." As our home birds do, the plovers of the tundras play-acted little comedies of death in life to detract our attention from the nesting-place. One bird flew on before me one afternoon feigning to be wounded, dropping with ruffled feathers, helpless, into a crumpled mass, and even as I stopped to raise the piteous little heap was up and off again, fluttering on stronger wing away and away from the zone of her nest.

The *Lily* being on the sick-list, we decided to take our chance of getting a bear or so in the country round about us. The creek in which we lay up was on the Unimak side of Cape Rodgnof, and a serviceable little river flowed down the valley to the sea.

Prospecting round, we came on undoubted traces of the former presence of caribou, numberless shed antlers denoting the fact that, as our men told us, the caribou in their hundreds seek this part of the peninsula in the fall of the year. Careful scrutiny of all the hills around with powerful glasses failed to reveal to us a caribou in the flesh, but Ned, backed up by the beautiful and beneficent arrangement which permits natives to kill game in and out of season, went off on a shoot of his own, and spoored to some purpose, for he returned with a caribou bull with the tiniest of horns, protruding about four inches from the head, and as soft as putty. Our hunter said he required the animal for food, when I remarked that it seemed a pity to kill so wantonly. Which was pretty cool of him, considering that both our men had been, up to then, gorging like boa-constrictors daily at our expense.

Our idea was to camp up river some way, and

reaching the foot-hills we might calculate on wood for fires. Here, on the desolate coast, timber was at a premium, and the great white, wave-washed baulks, which are so large a feature of the beaches fringing the Pacific, were few and far between.

A native settlement of three huts lay a mile to our westward, and one of the inhabitants promptly arrived to offer his services. Being rather short handed for a tow up-stream we engaged our find after some difficulty. He could not speak a word of English, and everything we said had to be arranged and translated by Ned.

We loaded up a dory, and with our new man in his *bidarka* towing another, conveying more stores, we set out up the banks of the river. This towing business was very heavy work, as the water rushed very heavily down stream, and frequently our men could make no headway at all, and the only means of forward progression was to give the tow-rope a turn round a rock some way ahead, and then pull up to it. On the second day we reached quite dense alder scrub. Here on the river sides, and in the marshy hollows where an evil-smelling yellow plant grew, we discovered fairly recent tracks of bears, and deciding that this particular spot would do us very nicely, Cecily and I suggested to the Leader and Ralph that they should seek pastures new up the stream, and shoot over the neighbourhood some miles farther on. This plan was carried *nem. con.;* and Steve and Ned, being allotted to us, set about halving the stores, and setting up the tents.

A LANDING ON THE BERING SEA COAST

Hanging on to the end of a bough of a dwarf alder
I found the nest of the golden-crown kinglet, an
exquisite in tiny birds, so aptly named too. The
majestic title of king would o'erweight so small a
monarch, and a monarch he is, for he is crowned with
gold. The nest was a very dainty residence. Moss
comprised the outer covering and feathers lined the
inside, and to compact and cement the whole structure
the spiders had contributed of their webs. The
golden-crowned kinglet fluttered round me in
anguished dismay as I neared his domicile, for his
queen was at home, and her smaller tiara flashed in
the sun as she slid out and made a bid for safety.
There were seven eggs in the nest, white, with yellow-
brown speckles, and I withdrew to a little distance,
and lay concealed until I saw the little queen return
in complete contentment.

That very same evening our luck was astonishing,
for, prowling along the river slopes, over ground
which must have been covered by Ralph and the
Leader, we saw a large bear standing meditating on
a little knoll. We were all on the same side of the
river, and probably not more than two hundred yards
separated us.

The bear instantaneously scented danger and whipped
off, with surprising agility for so large a bulk, towards
the alder scrub. I threw up my rifle, and at that
same instant Steve, who was immediately behind me,
took it on himself to order the proceedings, and in
quite loud tones said, "Shoot, shoot now!" To
emphasize his remark he gave me a decidedly vigor-

ous push as though to indicate the precise moment for me to pull the trigger. My shot, naturally, fell very wide indeed, and went ricochetting into space. Cecily got in two, which she declared were effective, because she saw the disappearing animal half stop and raise himself as the bullets told. As the bear must by then have been quite two hundred yards away from us I confess I had my doubts. Cecily had none, and we followed our bear up immediately. It was as though the earth had swallowed him.

We spoored in every direction, trying to pick up the trail, but there was nothing to guide us. The grass-covered ground gave no sign of the bear's passing, and every clump of alders looked like another. At last Cecily, stooping, discovered the faintest spot of blood, and taking lines to various points we came on another and another. A dense fastness of alders lay ahead, and as we cautiously neared the place a low continuous growling met our ears, changing to ugly snarls and short, savage throaty mutterings. We prepared for action, confidently expecting to be charged. We could see nothing but the alders stirring in the light breeze, and though they were so stunted they were thick enough to be a bit of a poser. To go in recklessly meant a certain mauling, to remain outside and await developments required time, and this last was just what we had not got.

Night, like "the big black crow" of Alice's adventures, darkened all the sky. The only common-sense solution of the difficulty was to wait for the morning hours. The bear could not travel far, he was evidently seriously disabled, and as Steve said, "Him very sick." Reluctantly and regretfully we abandoned the chase for the day, and it was well we did so, for the sky grew black and overcast ere we made camp, and our bearings were not of the clearest. This because Steve took us what he called "a short cut," and like many other short routes it proved in the end to be the longest way round.

As to Steve—well, I expressed to him, in no mild terms, what George Moore calls "the thought at the back of one's mind." Cecily backed me up, and said that speaking from the point of view of an unbiassed observer she considered Steve to be a real rotter as far as bear hunting is concerned. That made me laugh, and I forgot to be cross any more. For there are so few fair and unbiassed observers in the world. The majority of us can only count one, and natural modesty won't allow us to give him a name.

All that night Cecily worried on about the wounded bear left out in the bush. It was a great, if impossible-to-be-helped, pity. It is a hateful thought that you didn't kill your animal straight out, and that, in consequence of some negligence on your part, the creature is at large, suffering. "A small thing, but it troubled me," said Mr. Pepys, as he tore his new cloak on the door, and this small trouble weighed on us all night and drove sleep away. We were not sporting enough, I suppose, to be indifferent.

Might it be that, being women, we could not learn to take such normal accidents pertaining to the chase with calmness? After all, are not pin-pricks notoriously harder to bear than a good rapier-thrust, which needs must be attended to? Balzac, most wonderful of observers, held that more men commit suicide because a few pin-pricks follow one on the other than from some terrific trouble. Of course we didn't feel like committing suicide, but we got up in an agreeable blend between night and morning, and went out after the wounded bear before we had our breakfast. Which is suicidal in tendency. Breakfast is the main stand-by of the Briton, and by their breakfasts ye shall know them.

We decided to have nothing to do with either of our hunters, whose methods of stalking were much too slap-dash for us, and sallied forth alone. We took the exact route of the previous night, and gained the alder fastness in no time. Everything was very silent. Save for the liquid notes of a hermit thrush carolling his song to the dawn, the wilderness was not awake. Cautiously we investigated, keeping together. It was no use entering the place from opposite sides, for, in the event of a scrimmage, we might shoot one another.

Making a wide detour, circling the spot, we came up in the rear of the place where last night our enemy had entrenched himself. The citadel was much easier carried thus. With great care and discretion we penetrated the clump of alders, and each step we took was on the impress of myriad bear tracks. This way and that the trails ran, evidently the fastness was a favourite haunt of Bruin's. As we progressed we

FINDING THE BULLET

passed bed after bed, and then—through a maze of intervening boughs—we caught sight of something bulky, something brown, lying on the pressed down branches of a fragile tree. It was our bear! Cecily touched my arm, and signed to me to ask whether or no she should make certain sure by putting a bullet into the prone form. It was, of course, the most sensible thing to do, but I did not like the idea at all. Talk about hitting a man when he's down!

We shouted instead and beat the bushes, but the great brown bear never stirred. He was dead indeed, and had lain so for some hours. As he lay huddled up we recognized that he was a fine beast, of huge size and girth, and belonged to the variety known as *Ursus dalli gyas*.

Getting back to camp for breakfast we sent out the men to commence skinning operations, and made them take an axe along in order that the ground might be cleared around the carcase and permit of the business being thoroughly done. After a little time we returned to the scene of action, because we were rather curious to discover how and why Cecily's bullets had taken effect so expeditiously, when, as it appeared to us, she was badly placed for a shot, and the possibilities were against her. The first bullet had entered behind the shoulder joint, and raking through had passed the heart by a quarter of an inch only, and expanding had caused considerable internal havoc. The second shot had splintered a rib and finally lodged in the off-shoulder muscles.

On the way back to camp we found the first ptarmigan's nest, and the hen was sitting. It was placed on a hillside exposed to the sun, and farther on we came on quite a small colony of nests. Most of them had five eggs and some three.

We spent the rest of the day cleaning our bear's skull and watching the men prepare the skin for drying. They sat down on the ground, tailor-fashion, with the pelt across their knees, holding a bit of it between the teeth, and then, with a sharp knife, every piece of fat and meat adhering to the hide was rapidly picked off. The dexterity displayed was amazing, and must have come of years of practice.

Cecily compounded some bear soup that evening, and rendered camp hideous with its smell. It was a very poor imitation of soup, for though we stewed it and stewed it the strength of the flesh did not seem to go into the liquid at all, which remained much as it came from the river, save for masses of floating fat and nauseating taste.

The day had been so perfect, the great day of the finding of our bear, dead in his sanctuary. We had even seen the frail wraith of a butterfly, fluttering weakly over the river into which it fell, and ended its brief career. The air blew warm until late evening, and the mosquitoes advanced on us in force, with reserve battalions and flanking parties. We had to light smudge fires all about us, cost what labour they might in gathering wood. We turned in at last to get away from the pests, and left the river bank reluctantly, for Mr. and Mrs. Otter, who lived next door to us, had not been out to say " Salaam." We had watched their holt for an hour or more with no sort of success.

We slept cosily until the dawn, to waken to hear the wild god Boreas rushing down from the mountain tops to beat with tempestuous purple wings against the walls of spring.

"Tarry yet awhile!" whistled the keen breath of the snow-sheeted mountains. "Tarry yet awhile!"

And as if in mockery the proud and laughing chuckle of the cock ptarmigan echoed across the river.

Then followed a couple of days of icy blasts, driving rains and hail. Our tents could scarce stand up against the war of Nature's forces. Fireless we lived in philosophical discomfort. I think we made more of our uncomfortable situation than needs be, because, all the time, the proximity of the *Lily*, and the recollection of her comforts, made odious comparisons to our minds.

Another day of villainous weather finished us off, but as the Leader and Ralph had taken the flotilla along with them, we could do nothing but wait until they called for us on the way coastwards. We began to formulate impossible schemes for a trek, and just then, fortunately, the dory came swirling by and drove right into a bank below us, she had so much way on. We soon got our trophy and the tents aboard, and with the Leader for pilot I set out in a *bidarka*, Cecily, Ralph and Ned annexing the other.

We had a lively time on our lightning voyage, for

the water ran strong, and the eddies and rapids were numerous. There was little for the paddler to do but keep the canoe head on. We flashed down to the coast in the shortest of short times, mud banks, gravel reaches, stunted alders, rocky ramparts, and grass-grown slopes passing in kaleidoscopic swift array. A red fox stood by the river side as the first *bidarka* raced by, and I saw him loping off, with bushy brush held straight out, in flurried surprise.

At the cove where the *Lily* lay we were quite aston-ished to notice the numbers of hair seals, which had arrived in their myriads since our departure. The lure of the salmon so soon about to run up the river had caused the influx. We did not try to shoot a specimen, because when the seals are thin and in spare condition it is impossible to recover the carcases, which sink to the bottom like stones. The natives kill these seals for *bidarka* coverings, shoes, etc., etc., in the late season, August and September, when the creatures are fat and rolling in blubber. Buoyed up with good living the dead bodies float to the surface.

" Once aboard the lugger " things were not exactly halcyon. The cook, who was now a teetotaler from force of circumstances, refused to make porridge, or " mush," as they always called it, for the pilot, who, being Scotch, required porridge to sustain his strength. When asked why he did not make porridge without so much fuss, the cook replied that the pilot could not really need such a dish, and if he did he ought not to. They were both at loggerheads of the most cross-grained variety.

Tom, our cabin boy, confided to me that the porridge question was merely a side issue, and the cause of the rumpus lay in the fact that the pilot had, inadvertently, it is to be hoped, drunk the last remaining bottle of the cook's whisky, his one ewe lamb of a bottle. Tom told each of us in turn, and always as a great secret. He knew, I suppose, that a secret is not thoroughly established as a secret until it has been confided to several people. A one-man secret is a make-believe affair.

The cook was bribed with a bottle of whisky from our stores, a casual, no-reason-at-all sort of present; so the porridge was forthcoming and the pilot's strength supported, though whether the piloting was any better—— but the Leader wants to talk about that before very long.

Many varieties of ducks paddled about the cove, and helped us in the commissariat department. Pintail were the best eating, and very easy to shoot. The male pintail has two great feathers which give the bird much the appearance of a pheasant, and the alert head and jerky movements foster the likeness. Scoters were difficult to bag, as they swim, almost invariably, in " open order." We sampled one of this species— Cecily shot it from the dory—and it tasted just like flying-fish. Indeed, our mate, who was a tepid Roman Catholic, told us that his church allows scoters to be eaten in Lent because the flesh is fish-like enough for anything. I should think it is a fairly safe permission to give to a fasting person. First catch your scoter.

Of all the beautifully coated ducks the most exquisite is the golden-eye. His beauty is but skin deep, for he is a most unpleasant bird at table. As these birds fly the beating of their wings is a musical rustle, a whistling patter of sound almost impossible to describe, but something akin to the shivering rattle with which a peacock animates his feathers as he sets his tail into a fan. Most alert of birds, golden-eyes, never still, for ever diving, flying hither and thither, restless as a petrel. I think they have solved the mystery of perpetual motion. Here, in Alaska, they frequented the coast and rivers.

The natives told us that these birds nest in holes of trees. In Lapland, I know, the golden-eye chooses a hole in a tree to build in, but on the Bering Sea coast I do not know how the habit can be fostered. A very far journey would have to be taken before a tree calculated to support even the most emaciated golden-eye could be discovered. The parent birds, Steve told us, carry the little ducks to the water when the right moment comes. A tremendous business. Like an excursion to Margate of *Punch* variety. For the golden-eyes have enormous families, eight or ten as a rule.

The phalaropes were the most taking little birds, so solemn in face and mien, so sombre in plumage. Picture a sandpiper riding on the breast of the waves, buoyant as a cork, lightsome as a bit of thistledown, and you have the phalarope. Like a sandpiper he is ashore, for this bird of many parts is as agile on land as on sea, flitting gaily here and there, and running with tricky darts along the sand-spits. Such quick dexterous paddling is amazing in so small a bird, but the feet are exceedingly broad-lobed, like those of a coot, and perhaps in this lies the secret of such speed and safety.

CHAPTER IX

A VARIETY OF SHOOTING AND FISHING INCIDENTS

Weaving spiders, come not here ;
Hence, you long-legg'd spinners, hence
Midsummer Night's Dream

Come on, poor babe,
Poor thing, condemn'd to loss
Winter's Tale

IN the days of my youth I was expected to make myself familiar with the philosophies of a wise old gentleman, one Thales of Miletus, and among the aphorisms which he scattered about his writings like the pebbles of Little Poucet, I remember this, "Water is the beginning of all things." I wonder if Thales had been exploring in Alaska, and penetrated the sleughs and barren lands fringing the coast line in some parts. Water is certainly the beginning of all things there, the end too, very often. The sea and rivers meet, intersecting the land, and one may try sleugh after sleugh and not find fresh water for the kettle.

The Leader and I had four days' hunting amid a scene of desolation which would have been hard to beat anywhere, and the *Lily*, meanwhile, took Cecily and Ralph onwards to a bay famous for its bears. We decided to try our luck on this bit of Never-

Never country, because our pilot spun us such in-spiriting yarns about the numbers of bears bagged in the region last season.

We landed with tents, a *bidarka*, and Steve in attendance, on a waste of sand, water, and tundra. There were no sticks big enough to support our canvas residences, and it looked like camping out in the open until, fortunately, after wandering along the coast line for a mile or more, we came on a native burial ground, and borrowed some of the poles we found set up over the graves. The natives arrange that the poles shall be tall enough to show above the snow in winter, for they will not walk over the dead. On one or two graves a row of spears and a paddle were placed, on others nothing. We thought it must be that the men only are given the advantage of implements to be of use to them in the Happy Hunting Grounds.

Here gum-boots were stern necessities. I found them most uncomfortable of foot-gear, but we should certainly have got very wet without their protection. Salmon, flocking to the rivers, lay dead in dozens all along the reaches, and we wandered in and out among the decaying bodies searching for bear tracks. Anxiety over the commissariat was quite set at rest, for we had salmon, salmon, and again salmon for the taking. The Leader annexed a monster fish, wresting it from a bald-headed eagle, to whom by all the laws of first blood the trophy belonged. I watched the struggle from camp. The eagle was endeavouring to dig his talons deeply into the silver

K

fish, which lay on the edge of a sleugh. Sometimes the great bird got a fair start, and rose into the air for a few feet, to drop the heavy salmon to earth again. The Leader dashed up just as the salmon had descended for the second time, and said in effect " Shoo !" to the king of birds. A most familiar way to treat majesty. The eagle resented it, and seemed to me to strike out fiercely, wheeling low about the Leader's shoulders. Then realizing defeat, disappointed, it soared away foodless, to hunt again under more propitious circumstances.

What a cook Steve was ! Or rather what a cook he was not ! If he had to boil the kettle he must upset it, and extinguish the valuable tiny fire, whose wood was so precious and so scarce ; if he fried he set the fat on fire, and if he stewed he forgot to add water, and set a solid in the pan, alone, until it burnt away.

In the late evening a red fox came down to the sleughs to drink. I thought a bear had arrived at last from Steve's excitement, for he windmilled impossible-to-understand messages of joy and excitement, and rolled his eyes in startling manner. I was cooking supper at the time, and the Leader was prowling somewhere after the bears that were not. My patch of ground had been part of Alaska when we struck it first, now it was busily trying to make a separate island of itself. Like Canute, I had been stemming the tide for an hour or more, in futile endeavours to keep back the embracing sea. My rifle was " over the water," on the farther shore, and to possess myself of my weapon I needs must show myself very much in full view.

By the time I had crossed the sleugh, and grasped my rifle Reynard had a good start, running low. Ten to one I miss him! I fired, but the bullet went wide, and I saw the sand spurt up in a little jet. Raising the three hundred yards' sight, and taking in plenty of foresight, I had another try. The fox sat down as suddenly as though he were a mechanical toy worked by a string. Running nearer, I got in a shot which somewhat damaged the beautiful coat, but put the beast out of pain. Steve soon had the pelt drying before the atom of fire, and the ravens and kites made short work of the remains.

We had Steve carry the *bidarka* to a river which ran between ugly mud banks down into a wide estuary. From early dawn the Leader and I paddled energetically up stream, hoping that the lure of the salmon would call out the bears to the banks. We took it in turns to paddle, and when one of us got cramped up with the awkward attitude necessitated, we landed, and gingerly changing places set off again. We worked so hard that although a strong current ran against us, we covered some miles of river, and actually discovered a belt of dwarf alders, which were almost as scarce hereabouts as the bears. Getting ashore we spoored this way and that, with poor results. A bear trail was discernible, but it was very ancient, and not, I think, of our season.

Ptarmigan were very plentiful and very tame. Throwing stones would not dislodge a bird which meant to remain. Rambling on down a path through the alder scrub, a lonely track of dwellers in the wild, I strode right into the midst of a fluffy band of cheeping yellow chickens. To the right and left they scattered, and at my boot in a flash came the gallant little mother, making a reconnaissance in force until the helpless chickens found safety, her tiny eyes aflame with anger, feathers ruffled up, hissing defiance at me. Brave little hen! Again and again my small foe returned to the attack, pecking my boots, screaming in furious chuckles her commands to me to begone. I could not help smiling at her tactics, they were so obvious, even whilst I loved the small thing's courage and forgetfulness of self. I ran backwards, and with a whirr of wings the ptarmigan flew off into a patch of salmon berry bushes.

Cheep! Cheep! I crept warily along, and there, ever and again, in and out the sanctuary of cover, I caught glimpses of my tiny enemy collecting her babies beneath shelterings wings.

Down-stream again, and all suddenly the atmosphere changed to a muggy dampness which clung to our coats in dew-like moisture. And as the light *bidarka* sped over the shallows of the gently-rushing river, the whole air in the vicinity of the banks became like passing through the finest of fine gauze. Hair, eyes, all of us was enveloped in the silken mesh. Our protesting fingers broke through a maze of interlacing webs.

Myriads of tiny red spiders were entangled in the gossamer, and all the atmosphere was thick with the

venturesome little aeronauts, hanging apparently
from fragile single threads beginning and ending
Heaven knows where, all tangled with each other's
films of silk. On every side the fairy gossamer enfiladed our position.

Some of the little spiders sailed away on their
silken wires like pantomime fairies, other enterprising
spirits investigated the *bidarka* thoroughly, running
over her skin decks on to the paddle blade, and then
on the endless threads over the side into the water.
Even then they did not drown, but seemed to skim
over the surface lightly, deftly, with the grace of a
coryphée. About twenty yards or so of river was
enchained by this gossamer web, a sort of spider
"Cook's Excursion" somewhere. I am afraid we
must have upset the calculations of the little travellers
very much.

The next day we crossed the river, skirted the
estuary, and covered the coast-line for some distance,
until the face of the country changed and low alders
grew to the edge of a little creek, whose reaches were
covered with decaying salmon. On our horizon some
moving forms loomed, and in great excitement we
made out, through the glasses, that the perambulat-
ing bears were four in number, two fully grown, and
two cubs.

This was a most unusual thing. Sometimes a she-
bear wanders in company with a previous youngster
of two seasons back and this year's baby—the natives
have it that bears seldom breed two years in succession—but it is certainly unusual for the little band

to be escorted by paterfamilias. It seemed to me
that in between courting times the males of the bear
tribe roam alone, seeking "the great waste places,"
like the very much married gentleman in Ibsen.
Lo! here, evidently, was a big bear doing the heavy
father to the top of his bent, for, looking closely,
I saw him cuff the larger cub as though to teach it
better manners.

The old bears were turning over the salmon, and
our difficulty was to get within range unobserved,
since there was no cover, only the patch of alders
which grew in some profusion on the far side of the
bears.

Here I suggested an entirely novel way of stalking, namely, that we should get back a little and
work round until we were dead level with the patch
of alder cover the bears would have to make for, and
then, at the right moment, with nothing but the open
ground between us, it would simply be who could
run the fastest. It would be three points of a
triangle, the bears in the open, ourselves preparing
to run into the open ground, and all making straight
for the scrubby bushes. The Leader formally
adopted this plan because he could not think up a
better; besides, it was such a chance anyway that
we could detach Mr. Bruin, if Mr. Bruin he proved
to be, from the bosom of his family, and of course
we had no intention of trying to bag Madam or the
little ones.

The whole thing worked like a charm at first. Our
hunter remained at the spot from which we first

sighted the bears, very glad of the chance to rest and doze. Two were quite sufficient to run the blockade, and our man had been very bored all the morning. It makes a wonderful difference to a native whether he is hunting because he is hungry, or just for sport. Which is, after all, natural enough. But one would like to see the sporting instinct have some place.

We trailed across the open space carefully, warily, dropping flat whenever it seemed likely that we must be noticed, and took an apparently unconscionable time getting to our vantage ground. A few moments to get breath, and—now must we run like Atalanta, and see what we should see. The Leader outstripped me and gained a few paces. It was a race of races. Our feet crushed the summer flowers, and took the little grassy hummocks in bounds.

The bears in wonder pulled together for the fraction of a moment, as though thinking out the manner of defence, then the larger cub, with the greatest of acumen, broke back, and went for all he was worth, until, in the excitement of the moment, I lost sight of him.

The larger bear, which we knew to be undoubtedly a fine male, cantered towards the cover without a thought for the safety of his companions, followed by the she-bear and the tiny cub, going very slowly and painstakingly. The Leader dropped on one knee, and at some two hundred yards planted a well-placed bullet into the neck of the foremost animal. It seemed to check the onrush, for the wounded creature pulled up in a great hunched slide, half rose, then dropped to four feet again. Another shot, and another, and the great brown bear tottered and fell over prone, motionless, on to his side. That was undoubtedly the moment when we should have remembered that discretion is the better part of valour, and called to mind the useful little axiom, slightly paraphrased, "He who shoots and runs away, lives to shoot another day." For we were now exceedingly close to the alder patch, and fairly in the way of the oncoming she-bear. With a sort of beautiful and refreshing trust in Providence, we both imagined that her ursine highness would turn aside and avoid us. A she-bear with a cub to protect is a big thing to tackle in any country, in Alaska she is a fiend let loose.

With a short sharp yell of rage, voicing the fury of her rage and offended majesty, she came straight for us. How she travelled! And the very small cub ambled behind as though nothing untoward was afoot. The front claws of the bear appeared to take a real grip of the ground as she propelled herself in great gallops over the coarse, knotted grass, through the maze of blazing buttercups.

"I leave it to you," I said, hardly knowing the tone of my own voice, it was so huskily excited.

The Leader threw up his rifle, fired, and for a moment the oncoming bear certainly checked her speed. I saw, in a kind of dazed wonder, my companion wrestling with his rifle, hurriedly, anxiously, feverishly—something was wrong—the cartridge would not rise into the magazine.

" Kill her !" said the Leader laconically, with the greatest *sang-froid*.

Of course it had to be. I was using my old 12-bore —best of friends—a terrifically hard-hitting, heavy weapon, and had just time to get in a shot at a near thing of thirty yards, but it was well in the forehead. Still the game and courageous animal came on, her head dipping low to earth, and as I danced backwards she crashed over, so close to me that I could have touched her as she fell. A brave and gallant beast !

" Thus she passed over, and all the trumpets sounded for her on the other side " the Happy Hunting Grounds.

To have had to kill a she-bear ! 'Twas the way luck went. Would that it had gone some other way.

The poor little cub stood bewildered a little way off, and presently he advanced to the great prone form and stood beside it, with his quaint little feet, and tiny growing claws, set in a faint trickle of blood. My heart-strings were tugged with the pity of it ! What a brute I felt ! I took out my very grimy handkerchief.

" You aren't going to cry about it, Agnes, are you ?" the Leader asked apprehensively.

" You know I'm not," I answered indignantly; " I'm going to wipe the cub's feet, if I can catch it. I do think it is dreadful for it to be standing in the blood of its own mother."

" What a woman you are !" laughed the Leader. " Killing one minute, and healing the next. I wonder you have acquired your wonderful collection of trophies at all."

" You're jealous," I said calmly.

We played "You're another " until we managed to catch the little cub, a most beautiful little thing, very young and furry. As soon as the Leader saw that I did indeed mind very much having helped to make an orphan of the cub, he gave over chaffing, and did all he knew to comfort me. It was the truest fellowship. In countless tender ways he made the deed of blood seem less gory and revengeful.

Tendernesses are so dainty, so delicate, they are the work of Nature's genius. So long as a man can bring himself to give a woman tenderness—and I use the word in its highest sense—then she may know she has his love safe.

" I wonder who the little beggar takes after," said the Leader meditatively, as he held the little animal, struggling fiercely, in his arms; "its father or its mother ?"

" Neither. It is just like Lord Kitchener."

And so it was. An amazing likeness. I often notice the extraordinary resemblance of expression which some animals have to some people. This cub was an excellent photograph of K. of K. We christened him Kitchener in consequence. And the small animal who had crept so unexpectedly into our lives crept into our hearts as well during the short three weeks he lived aboard the *Lily* with us. We so hoped to be able, somehow, to get him home, for he was evidently on the way to being a fine speci-

men of *Ursus dalli gyas;* but, alas! it was not thus
to be. Kindness killed him. Or indigestion. The
crew, though forbidden to do so, would feed the
cub, and one morning we were greeted with the
sad intelligence that our Kitchener lay dead. But
I anticipate, as the novelists say.

Our man had by this time joined us, and we were
faced with the stupendous task of skinning the two
great bears. First we had lunch, which we badly
needed, and sitting beside the brown carcases, I am
bound to say that one by one my qualms vanished,
and in their place raged the fierce exultant joy of the
chase which can only be understood by those who
have experienced it. I should not have been human,
and a huntress, if the sight of those magnificent
beasts had not deepened in my heart the lust of sport.

> " Fill the cup, and in the fire of Spring
> The winter garment of repentance fling."

The Leader owned a ridiculous pocket compactum
knife and fork, which, when opened and unfolded,
worked all right, and made lunch away from camp
quite civilized. Of course he always had to offer
it to me, and use his fingers himself. The thing
was no use unless its proprietor was at hand to undo
it, its mechanism defied the ordinary brain, which
curtailed its usefulness somewhat.

" Well, I will always touch the spring for you,"
the Leader said, when I complained of the limitations
of the combination cutlery. It was rather like the reply
of the young man to some one who inquired whether

he still kept a samovar. "I did," he answered, "until the engineer struck."

Far as the eye could reach, the surrounding tundra was wreathed in flowers. In grim Alaska summer is like a magician who changes as with a wand of gold the harsh face of the earth to a verdant paradise. Every yard brimmed over with blossoms, a blaze of narcissus buttercups made a glowing carpet of gorgeous yellow, the blue of the polemonium and the bluer forget-me-not commingled, a riot of colour tints; every gentle wind wafted the fragrance of this wealth of scented flora, and rustled the nodding plumed heads of the myriad grasses.

In and out of the flowers white and purple butterflies flickered on trembling wings, slender, gossamer-pinioned, Ariel-like.

We carefully examined the Leader's rifle, which was his favourite Mannlicher, and found that a small bit of grit had got into the breech, and thus jammed the bolt action. The trouble was merely a small affair, and was soon rectified by removing the bolt. Fortunately this disaster, which is so common with all magazine rifles, did not entail any loss of life, as has happened before when men will use these rifles for dangerous game. The careful skinning of the bears occupied some hours; the Leader set to work upon the larger bear, and Steve commenced operations on the other. The animals were much the lightest-coloured bears I had seen in Alaska, being of a very pale fawn tint. The baby was much darker, and his fur very frizzy. I had to hold him

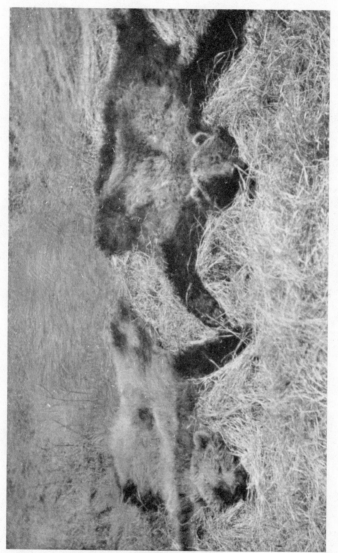

THE SKINS OF OUR TWO BEARS

during the *modus operandi* of the dismemberment of his parents. His little eyes were dimmed with a great wonder, but he fell to licking my fingers with a rough tongue, and soon the little creature curled itself up to sleep, trustfully and peacefully, just as a St. Bernard puppy might do.

Steve, being a practised hand, finished his bear first, and then helped the Leader, who was nearly eaten alive by mosquitoes. At last the messy business was over, and laying the skins casually upon the ground we put the tape over them, and quite unstretched, the pelt of the she-bear, from head to tail, came out at six feet five inches, and that of the male just seven feet.

Bald-headed eagles gathered in the blue ether, sailing round and round, swooping low to earth, then rising high to the heavens again, scenting from afar the mighty banquet.

The carrying of the rolled skins, with skulls and feet, was a heavy and daunting affair. I took no hand in it; but I consider that I did not shirk hard work also, considering that it fell to my lot to convey Kitchener in my arms to the river, and he must have scaled twenty pounds or more. We had to make two or three journeys over, having but the one *bidarka*, and I did pray, as I stepped into the hatchway of the frail craft, that the small bear had his fur parted directly in the middle, and that he would refrain from struggling and kicking out. He was very good, and every one, and everything, got over serenely.

Arriving at our forsaken-looking camp, we tied our little visitor to a pole of the Leader's tent, and mixed up some Nestle's milk, which the cub would not touch. We administered some of the liquid in medicinal-like doses, a spoonful at a time. Kitchener could eat, he wished us to know, and had a decided preference for licking very high salmon which Steve procured from the coast-line.

The next day the *Lily* returned for us, but in the early morning we sought the estuary and the river, to discover the reason for the presence of so many bobbing seals and wheeling birds of prey. The salmon were running up the river, seeking the lake away up in the distant foothills. As we neared the water we heard a sound like the rushing of a river over rattling stones, and going to the elevation of a sandy hummock alongside the stream, an amazing and wonderful spectacle presented itself. In the clear waters of the crystal river thousands of silver fish pressed onwards with deep-set purpose.

> " And thick and fast they came at last,
> And more, and more, and more."

Over the shallows at the head of the estuary the salmon forced their way, stranding themselves momentarily very often, an unending stream of· silver, layers and layers of glittering fish, flank to flank, head to tail, close together. Over shallow reaches the salmon put on a spurt and travelled more speedily, as though to obviate the danger of being stranded. We left our vantage ground to wander up- and down-stream the better to view the piscine progress, and though we remained, fascinated, for an hour or more, the end was not when we left.

The shores of the river were strewn with the bodies of stragglers pressed out of the water by sheer weight of the multitudes forcing up in serried ranks, and the cry was "Still they come!" We gathered up a number of fish for drying, beautiful, shining salmon, of exquisite proportions, fresh run.

The salmon never jumped, only the fins and noses showed above the surface of the water. And as I gazed in interested wonderment, it seemed difficult to believe that this great swim, this stressful journey, was the last the strenuous salmon would ever take. It is, I believe, an indisputable fact that of this triumphal procession not one fish would live to return to the sea. It makes one ponder and ponder how it can be that the supply is kept up yearly. And yet it never fails.

In a land where salmon are so easily caught by simple methods, fishing with rod and line is unknown, but the lure of a spoon ensnares some monster fish, and provides some unforgetable sport. One evening, as the salmon came into the inlet in shoals, Cecily and I had out the ship's boat, and Ralph and the Leader the dory, when we had a lively two hours' trolling, fishing with spoon bait, and successfully landed some fine fish, successfully losing still finer. It was quite an education as far as the customs and manners of Alaskan salmon were concerned. The instant I threw my spoon overboard a fish seized it with such avidity that he bit the gut right through, and went off with all the hooks in his "Little Mary." How uncomfortable must that poor fish have felt that night! They were not in the least capricious, and distributed their favours very evenly. Sometimes a dog-fish, who followed in the wake of the glittering salmon, seized the bait, and was hauled to the side of the boat, turning over and over. This necessitated rowing to the other boat, that they might cut the creature off, for we had to be as careful as can be with the tackle, and such weighty fish play great havoc.

Suddenly Cecily hooked a mighty salmon, who ran off like a torpedo towards the river, but the water got into his gills and he had to stop. We saw him slashing the surface of the water, churning the sea to little wavelets. Next he ran so close inshore to the rocks we feared the line might be cut, or the weight of the fish break him loose. Cecily took in a few yards of line, and the Leader and Ralph feverishly watched the end of the ding-dong struggle. They called to Cecily to make a landing and play the fish from shore, but Cecily was paying out again, and could not for the moment alter her tactics. The salmon got behind a rock, and rested and sulked, and meditated on the problem of life and death.

I rowed the boat to the beach, and as the boat's nose touched Cecily jumped ashore with the rod in her hand.

That fish was resolved to die game, but the effort exhausted most of his waning strength, and he was hauled in almost to striking distance of the gaff, which Ralph, who had also landed, held in readiness. As if foreseeing his fate the salmon rolled over, showing all his glittering scales and perfect proportions, and then—swam out ·of reach again. The angler took to the water, wading waist-deep, and dragging her prize along the beach-line drowned him remorselessly. He was hauled in, and the gaff went through him.

How I admired that salmon, and yet there was something unsporting in the glorious sport. The shooting of pachyderms is merciful in comparison. Of course the fish has no such complex system of nerves, but his agony is so long-drawn, he has no chance from the beginning. If he did break loose, he has the hideous thing within to torture him slowly to death. I like my quarry to stand as good a chance of escaping me as I have of bagging him. In this sort of salmon fishing the chances are all against the fish, for the line is strong and the gut very short.

But the instinct of pursuit is strong in all of us, and is part of the great scheme of Nature. 'Twas but an incident, and I was as full of the lust of killing as any of them.

How magnificent the fish looked as his thirty-two pounds hung from the scales, his fins just quivering as the rigor was overtaking him !

All about us the silver creatures flicked the water, and at intervals monster fish jumped out of the smooth sea, in frolic or in fright.

L

After the salmon came the dog-fish and hair-seals. On the reaches of the river countless bald-headed eagles hovered and sat waiting.

There are several varieties of salmon on the Pacific and Bering Sea coast, but for canning purposes it is usually the king—called in British Columbia "chinook"—and the red salmon which is put up. In short seasons, when the catch seems likely to be insufficient, one or two other kinds may be pressed into the service, or rather into the cans! The dog-salmon only is *anathema*, and this only because its flesh, though firm, is white and unpleasing-looking. In all other respects the fish is "fit to stand by Cæsar," which is the king variety.

All the salmon running into this creek were of one species, but our men told us that up some rivers one or two varieties of salmon run at once. The eggs hatch out in winter, and when the ice is broken down come the small fish to the sea, a piscine army. The average king salmon when fully grown scales fifty pounds, and frequently reaches eighty. The salmon most in demand for canning purposes is the small red, for its dark crimson colour lends it an enchantment to the home-buyers of canned salmon which all the others lack.

Cecily's delight when she saw Kitchener was boundless. The little creature made no favourites, and did not bestow his favours by halves. He simply loved every one alike enthusiastically. Our cabin-boy constituted himself nurse-in-chief, and the cub seemed very contented.

NATIVE SALMON DRYING GROUND NEAR AN AMERICAN CANNERY IN THE BERING SEA

We delayed sailing again for a few hours in order that every water-keg and tank might be filled up preparatory to setting out on a quest after walrus. Our pilot promised to steer us to some islands where he confidently hoped to prove to us that it was not too early for walrus to haul out.

We anchored for the night in as sheltered a cove as we could find, a little farther up the coast than the spot where we had slain the two bears, and weighed anchor early. When I came up on deck after breakfast the atmosphere was clear, and the placidity of the sea most unusual. Strange eddies of air rushed at intervals through the shrouds, gusty and ominous. Then from the distant mountains a mighty puff of wind came singing over the sea, and the mainsail flapped with a report as of a gun going off. Far on the horizon line was a dark riband of purple, and on the now freshening breeze strange murmurous deep-toned mutterings of a brewing storm became noticeable. Vast black clouds rolled over the sky, travelling apace, and then a swinging wind lashed the sea to a seething, boiling pot. Captain Clemsen, cool as ever, gave his orders in clear tones, and in no time the *Lily* was almost bare of sail. This was a "woolly" of "woollies." The waves charged and ran in cataracts over our small craft, and it seemed to me, watching from a safe perch on the companion-ladder, that at intervals the ship heeled over down to her waterways.

Suddenly, in the squall and driving spray, a phantom-like hull arose on our lee, driving the waves before her graceful bows, tossing, eddying, falling as a sea-bird on a crest of foam. Behind her trailed a wake of snowy water. Captain Clemsen saluted by running up a small ensign, and I saw it fly out with that wave of patriotic emotion which must, I think, come to every Britisher as he stands beneath the Union Jack. I say "wave of emotion," but afterwards I was a little afraid that the feeling of tremulous excitement was much more hum-drum and prosaic than an emotion of pride of place. The way in which the *Lily* was acting just then was too much for a fair-weather sailor like myself.

From the peak of the passing vessel we saw the Stars and Stripes break and batter in the gale. An American cruiser, and a very smart ship she looked as she drove slanting by.

How I wished, in my distress, that Father Time would jump the next twenty-four hours, and then stand stock-still awhile, or give me back the glorious harmony of yesterday. No, not yesterday. Yesterdays are yesterdays, and but "light us fools the way to dusty death." A wonderful to-morrow, pray you, Father Time, to make up for this most miserable to-day.

We had to put back to the shelter of a rocky cape, where a tiny cove granted sanctuary. Here Nature had outdone the art of any engineer, and built a most effective rocky breakwater.

On the surrounding rocks countless birds resorted, in numbers almost incredible. The murres out-numbered all the others by quite ten to one. Each bird stood sentinel over an egg. If we made a sudden noise, shouted or dropped anything heavily, many birds took fright and flew into the air. The whole atmosphere was thick with murres, the water dotted with them, the rocks alive with them. The feeding of such an army would be almost impossible, one would think, to any ocean. And yet they multiply and multiply. Nothing checks the numbers save the inadequate supply of nesting-places, and of that a murre craves but three inches. The torrent of sound from this hatchery was almost deafening, and every bird seemed to contribute to the general din by uttering a weird crooning cry.

The Bering Sea is not a sea to be trifled with, and he who sails over it should have time unlimited at his disposal, for you may arrange, but the fog will disarrange, you may sail, but stress of weather forces you to anchor. Our captain appeared quite indifferent to the multitudinous dangers of the coast, and his small craft seemed to him as safe as a Cunarder.

Familiarity must kindly breed contempt in sailors more than in any other race of men, I think. Surely it must be habit which permits a sailor to be so absolutely fearless and disregardless. Captain Clemsen once told me he would be very much afraid to face an Alaskan bear, and wondered how on earth we did it. He reminded me of a comical drawing I once saw in an American journal, which depicted a workman standing on a steel shaft three hundred feet in the air, over an airy network of scaffolding and pitfalls, watching a street-cleaner in a congested thoroughfare. " Now that man," said the workman, standing nonchalantly erect, with arms folded, " must have great nerve to do such dangerous work !"

CHAPTER X

A MOVE IN SEARCH OF OTHER QUARRY

(By the Leader of the Expedition)

There ! I hit it right
Romeo and Juliet
How ill it follows after you have labour'd so hard
King Henry IV

AFTER several dreary days of sailing up the coast we could faintly distinguish a small chain of islands lying near the mainland, which Macdonald, our pilot, told us was our long-sought goal, and the haunt of mighty walrus bulls. As we approached them we saw that these islands were merely desolate barren sandbanks, between which and the mainland lay a large sheltered lagoon, where Macdonald said we should find a safe anchorage. Whilst still a mile or more from shore the look-out man reported some large animals swimming in the sea, and these, with the aid of glasses, we soon made out to be a herd of bull walruses besporting themselves in the water, their hoarse bellowing roar being audible to us whilst still a great distance from them.

As the *Lily* glided slowly in towards the lagoon the walruses evinced decided curiosity at the unwonted sight, and commenced swimming towards us, roaring, diving, and rolling over in the water, displaying the marvellous swimming powers of which these ungainly brutes are capable. As we sailed to leeward of them they approached within a hundred yards of the vessel, a performance which we afterwards discovered they would not have done had the wind been blowing in the opposite direction, since they are very keen-scenting animals, and, like most other wild beasts, are terrified by the smell of a human being.

The whole herd consisted of some fifty or sixty bulls, and Macdonald informed us that at this period of the year all the cows and young ones had gone far north through the Bering Straits on the edge of the ice.

The bloodthirsty Cecily was all for trying a long-range shot, as several of the huge brutes raised their head and shoulders high out of the water, taking a good look at the vessel. But she was at once dissuaded, since Macdonald declared that a dead walrus immediately sinks, and there was no chance of getting it ashore unless it has been killed and harpooned from a boat, and thus towed to land. He said that our best chance was to wait until the animals hauled themselves out on dry land, as they often did.

It required some skilful seamanship on the part of Captain Clemsen to sail the *Lily* safely in between the islands, as the entrance to the lagoon was very narrow, and constant shifting of these sandbanks renders all charts more or less unreliable. The wind had almost died away, but fortunately what breeze remained blew dead astern, so that we were enabled

THE LEADER'S WALRUS HEAD

to steer a straight course through the narrow entrance. Here a rising tide rushing into the lagoon caused a current swift as that of a fast-flowing river, which drifted us onwards ahead of the light wind. One sailor, standing in the bows heaving a lead-line, kept reporting a depth of four or five fathoms. This was ample water for the *Lily*, which only drew some ten feet of water. Suddenly, after the usual monotonous cry from the bows of, "By the mark four," every one was electrified by a sudden bump on the keel, and the vessel gave a lurch which nearly threw us off our feet, and then she remained stationary. It did not need Captain Clemsen's forcible language, nor hastily-shouted orders, to tell us that we were again "held up." Rushing to the wheel himself, the captain shouted—

"Hell, boys! I guess she's aground. Let go the anchor, and pull down the darned canvas."

Quick as lightning this was done, and then Agnes, who never seems to lose her *sang-froid*, but who, like all true daughters of Eve, must have her little say in all emergencies, mildly asked, "And what next, please, Captain?"

Had I been in the skipper's place I think I should have been wild enough to say things which would have hurt, but being a bluff, good-tempered soul, and also imbued with a sense of humour, he burst out laughing, and replied—

"Well, search me, marm, if I know what next; you've got me beat all right. I guess the old hooker has got her nose fixed in a mudbank, and unless

Father Neptune is pleased to send us a drop more water, you bet she'll stop there till kingdom come."

Fortunately rock is a thing which doesn't exist in these waters, and it appears that the action of the ice has in past centuries ground everything into fine sand or mud, so that there was no risk of a hole being stoved in the vessel's side.

It was impossible to say how much higher the tide might rise, and the only cheerful fact was that it still continued to do so. A boat was lowered, and it was soon found that the ship was aground on a narrow sandbank, in less than one and a half fathoms of water. On either side of the bank lay deep water, and by sounding it turned out that we were only a few yards away from the deep channel leading through the lagoon.

There was nothing in the nature of a panic amongst members of the crew; men such as these, who daily and hourly carry their lives in their hands upon these treacherous coasts, are too accustomed to look death in the face at close quarters, and therefore do not worry about such a trivial *contretemps* as grounding on a sandbank. Certain misgivings, however, came uppermost in my mind at the prospect of having to abandon our ship, and trust ourselves to the hand of fate in nothing better than small boats on these fierce Northern waters.

Meanwhile, the crew were actively engaged in rowing some distance astern, where they dropped two anchors attached to long cables, by means of which the skipper hoped to pull off the ship by hand if the

tide rose sufficiently to help us. And this proved the
method of our salvation, since in the space of an
hour the water had risen high enough to impart a
gentle heaving motion to the *Lily*. As Ralph said,
" the prognosis was favourable," all hands, including
the ladies, started hauling on the cables. Never did
tug-of-war teams struggle for an army championship
as did our two teams hang upon those ropes. Slowly
and surely, inch by inch, the ship moved backwards,
until suddenly, with a slight lurch, she glided back
into deep waters.

Little time was lost in hoisting the foresail and
regaining the deep channel. Once there, an anchor
was dropped, and the skipper sent men ahead in a
boat to take soundings in order that they might
locate a safe spot for an anchorage inside the lagoon.
It was not long ere we found ourselves riding safely
at anchor in the placid waters of the lagoon, and
rather more than a mile from its junction with the
open sea.

The situation was far from picturesque, since on
one side lay flat, uninteresting stretches of the mainland, vast undulating sand dunes quite destitute of
timber far as the eye could reach, to where they rose
in steeper contours, till they merged in the blue distance with lofty, unknown mountain heights. Looking outwards to the open sea a semicircle of low,
sandy islands lay, and formed a natural breakwater,
which closely resembled a coral reef to the eyes of
those who have seen these curious formations in
Southern seas. Beyond the reef for ever rolls that

turbulent waste of waters, the Bering Sea. Gazing northwards out across those surging billows the mind goes back over untold years, through which, for ages past, as still to-day, that fascination of the magnetic North has cast the spell of its glamour deep in the hearts of hardy mariners or world-famed explorers. Great men and bold have risked and lost their lives in quest of the unknown, but still to-day the dark and silent North retains her hidden mystery.

Since the days of Sir Hugh Willoughby, who in 1553 was the first Englishman to lead a big expedition in quest of a passage to China and the Orient, by way of the Arctic Ocean, many of our countrymen have left their mark on history by reason of their explorations in these Northern regions. The names of Cook and Franklin loom big upon the roll of honour, and their deaths are amongst the many which have paid toll to the explorers' quests. Of recent years have we not the deeds of men like Nansen and Peary, which tend to show that even in these effete days of modern luxury men may still be found who fearlessly forsake the fleshpots of Egypt and wander, for sheer love of adventure, amidst those icebound lands, in search of the great unknown? Have not I, even in my puerile way, felt the call of the wild, and the spirit of Wanderlust, gripping at my very heart-strings, bidding us be up and doing, so that ere yet it be too late we may travel along some untrodden path which leads to fame or to the grave?

I have traversed the shores of the Bering Sea from north to south, from east to west, from Kamchatka to the Arctic Ocean, and if I found myself there again to-morrow my one heartfelt cry would be, " A few miles farther north."

Since we had come out to slay walruses, why do I not get, as the Yankees say, "right down to the solid business " ?

Now, a walrus is an animal around which there clings a host of historical romance and fable. Nor is this altogether to be wondered at when we regard the almost pre-historic appearance of the Bering Sea walrus (*Odobaenus obesus*), the largest living species of its tribe, nor when we consider at what great distances remote from the haunts of ancient historians these gigantic brutes lived. Even to-day the number of our fellow-countrymen who have actually seen these animals is small, and fewer still have ever killed one. Moreover, I believe it is correct to say that a whole specimen of this particular walrus does not exist to-day in any of our leading European museums.

We read in a work, *De Animalibus*, compiled by a certain historian, Albertus Magnus, who died in 1280, that " the walrus is taken by the hunter while the sleeping animal hangs by its large tusks to a cleft in the rock. Cutting out a piece of its skin and fastening to it a strong rope, whose other end is tied to trees, posts, and large rings fixed to rocks, the hunter wakens the walrus by throwing large stones at its head. In its attempts to escape it leaves its hide behind. It perishes soon after, and is thrown up half dead on the beach."

So much for our friend Albertus Magnus. The

only thing which surprises me is the apparent fact of a walrus possessing such a strong constitution in former days that it was not thrown up *quite* dead on the beach, after this somewhat severe treatment. If any further support is required of the authenticity of this tale it is forthcoming in the shape of a drawing by one Olaus Magnus, which was published *circa* 1555, and in which the whole scene is depicted as above described.

It is the custom of these beasts to haul out on the sandbanks and lie sleeping there, often for long periods at a time. And it is upon these occasions that the natives run in and spear them ere they can regain the water. One beast always keeps a sharp look-out whilst the others sleep, and if the wind is blowing from a hunter to the walrus it is hopeless to approach within fair shooting distance.

Far out in the offing we could see the monstrous brutes rolling and splashing in the sea like gigantic porpoises. And distinctly on the gentle breeze was borne to us the hoarse, bellowing, roaring notes to which the bulls repeatedly gave utterance. Towards evening the whole herd was seen swimming in toward the shore, and finally some of them slowly hauled out on the beach of a sandspit at the entrance to our lagoon. As night was falling all hope was then abandoned of attempting to stalk them where they lay. Every one was deeply interested in watching the actions of the ungainly brutes as they laboriously hauled themselves ashore. Telescopes and glasses were directed on the sandspit, and it was seen that the herd numbered some forty-five old bulls, many of them having splendid pairs of tusks.

We noticed that they only lay up a few feet from the gently-breaking waves, and as the tide continued rising they repeatedly kept moving higher up on to the sandspit, and occupying fresh positions. Night's falling shadows soon obscured the picture from our view, and uttering fervent prayers that the morrow might reveal them still upon the sand we bade *au revoir* to our distant quarry.

The next day was ushered in by bright sunshine, and as I was dressing Captain Clemsen came below with the glad tidings that our herd of walruses were still on the sandspit.

Nothing would satisfy the ladies save a hasty breakfast and an immediate attack upon the walruses' position. Ralph and I, with true chivalry, decided that they should share alone the honour of bagging the first walrus, and with secret pangs of envy in our hearts we watched them put off in a boat and row to a point about a mile to leeward of where the herd was lying. Here they landed, and left the boat in charge of the two sailors who had rowed them to the island. In the clear light with our telescopes we watched the drama as if it were enacted on a stage at close quarters just before us.

Not a stick nor stone large enough to hide a mouse lay upon the sandy shore. Here and there a few patches of high, coarse grass were growing, but these afforded scanty covering for the stalkers to avail themselves of as they advanced. Creeping and crawling slowly the two Dianas advanced, taking advantage of every knoll and mound of sand, behind which they rested at intervals to regain their breath.

Even from our distant *coin d'avantage* it was clearly visible that one large bull was ever on the alert. At intervals he raised his head and gazed in sleepy fashion all around, and then appeared as if, like his companions, he had sunk to sleep. But such was not the case, for in a few seconds up bobbed the vast head once more, and the nose was raised, sniffing the air to see if it could detect any invisible enemy. This constant alertness on the part of the sentinel caused our friends considerable trouble, since, as they drew nearer to the sleeping herd, danger of being seen by this old bull grew greater. In consequence the play grew into a comedy for us, because the raising of the watchman's head was a signal for the two stalkers to fall flat on their faces in the sand and remain there till the head sank once more in momentary repose. During the latter interval the stalkers would scramble and crawl a few yards nearer, ere they fell prone once more. As the final stages of the stalk were reached, it is questionable as to whether the stalkers or Ralph and I were the most excited pair.

Whilst we judged them to be about one hundred yards or more away a great commotion began amongst the herd. A loud bellowing note of warning from the watchman roused his sleeping companions, and they with one accord started with strange lumbering motions to make for the water a few yards distant from them. Agnes and Cecily, realizing that all secrecy was at an end, sprang up and ran quickly forward, thus gaining a few yards more ere the walrus reached deep water. Agnes dropped on one knee— she hates to shoot standing—and by her side stood Cecily. We could distinctly see their rifles raised, and the echoes of four shots rang out across the water, wakening strange unknown sounds upon this desolate waste.

In vain we looked to see one animal collapse, and from our distant spot fruitlessly we tried to guess the cause of the disaster, for it was clear that the whole herd had taken to the water without leaving one of their number upon the beach. Still watching closely we saw the walruses swim out towards the open sea, moving very fast through the water, diving and re-appearing again at ever-increasing distances from the shore, all travelling at a great pace. Presently we noticed one animal lagging behind the rest, and then we saw Cecily running frantically along the beach, waving for the boatmen to bring up the boat. It was clear for us to see that the straggling bull was badly wounded, since he moved but slowly, and kept making shorter dives, until at last he seemed to give up swimming altogether, or spun round in small circles. Obviously the ladies hoped to get up to him with the boat before he sank, and possibly to tow his carcase ashore. And this indeed was what they had designed, but Fate was otherwise disposed. For, though the men rowed hard and both ladies jumped aboard her as she touched the beach, the boat was still a hundred yards away when the struggling walrus sank from

M

view. Although the boat was rowed for some time in circles where the animal had sunk, and a sharp look-out was kept by its occupants, nothing could be seen of the sunken beast. Ultimately it was a very doleful pair of huntresses who returned empty-handed to the ship, and each more like Niobe than Diana gave us their version of the episode.

It appeared that whilst stalking the sleeping animals they had especially singled out one bull which appeared to carry a particularly fine pair of tusks, and they had both agreed to shoot first at this one, and if it fell to try and bag another before they all took to the water, and although finally they had despatched four bullets at the animal he had managed to get away.

We questioned them closely as to where they had aimed, and they said that their fire had been directed to a spot which they believed was behind the animal's shoulder, but that in such a huge, ungainly shape it was hard to locate at a distance where the brute's heart might lie. Subsequently Macdonald told us that this was absolutely an unreliable place in which to shoot a walrus, and he regretted not having told us sooner that the correct place to kill a walrus was by placing a bullet in the back of its head, where the skull was thin. But he added that not even our powerful 450 cordite rifles would kill walruses if shot in the forehead, where, he declared, their skulls were many inches thick, and also that the vast mass of blubber and fat, which constituted their bodies, contained very few really vulnerable parts. This we found subsequently to be a fact.

Needless to remark Agnes and Cecily were exceedingly chagrined at their failure to bag a walrus in their first attempt. We were doubtful if the animals would return to the same neighbourhood for some time after being thus rudely disturbed, but Macdonald declared that it was hard to drive them away from a favourite haunt, and that, as there were no native settlements within a long distance of our lagoon, probably this particular herd of walruses had never been hunted by men, and therefore they might not be very wild, and would probably return before long to one or other of the sandbanks.

CHAPTER XI

AMONGST THE WALRUS ISLANDS

(By the Leader of the Expedition)

How many goodly creatures are there here?
The Tempest

And let us banquet royally
After this golden day of victory
King Henry VI

THE question now arose as to what form of amusement we could find to pass away the time whilst our friends the walruses were pleased to forsake us and disport themselves in the open sea. The ladies were both in favour of rowing to the mainland, and although the flat sand dunes of the shore looked very uninviting and uninteresting we all decided on the trip. Taking our largest boat we set out with two sailors, rowing a distance of a mile or more to the nearest point, which was a sandy promontory jutting out into the lagoon.

On landing we found the ground covered with a thick growth of long, coarse grass, and all along the foreshore were countless tracks of foxes, showing plainly where these animals had roamed along the beach in quest of fish, flesh, or fowl, thrown up by the tides.

We soon saw quite a number of foxes moving on the side of a sandy hill above, and nothing would content Cecily but an attempt to bag another of these animals, since, she declared, a second one was needed to make a collar arrangement to match the muff she hoped to make out of the skin she had procured on Kodiak Island. In vain we tried to dissuade her from such murderous attempts, because I knew that at this season the foxes change their coats, and the skins are worthless.

But alas! 'tis ever thus with women.

Cecily said it was a case of "seeing is believing," and off she went, rifle in hand, to stalk the nearest fox. It was a curious thing that these foxes did not seem to fear the sight of human beings, and they ran about outside their earths in full view of us, just like rabbits playing outside some big bury in a warren. And with our glasses we could see that the whole hill was honeycombed with earths.

There must have been between forty and fifty foxes moving at one time on the hillsides, and many of them permitted Cecily to approach within about a hundred yards before darting into earths. At last she singled out one more inquisitive than the rest, and raised her rifle. Slowly, very slowly and reluctantly she brought it down again. Finally she returned to us looking very cross. In answer to a query from Ralph as to what the fox was like, she replied, " Rather like a mangy rat, and hardly a hair on it." It was needless to say, " We told you so"; in any case this was a situation in which silence was golden.

Henceforth, although we saw many foxes at close

quarters, they were regarded as sacred, and not to be slain.

Along the shore we saw a number of gulls, terns, and smaller birds, such as phalaropes, small ringed plover, and several forms of waders. And of these I was enabled to make a small collection, having had the forethought to bring ashore the small 410-bore collector's gun.

Presently Agnes, who will always spend her time climbing to the highest point she can reach, shouted and beckoned me to come to her on the top of a small hill where she stood, and on arrival there she showed me a rare and wondrous find. Here the long grass ceased to grow, but in its place were masses of wild strawberries, positively acres and acres of them, larger round than a shilling piece, and all of them of the most splendid flavour. How and when this luscious fruit first happened to take root upon this barren spot it is impossible to tell, but here the strawberries grew, and probably still continue to grow, in such profusion as we had never seen, not even in the most highly cultivated English garden. Needless to remark that all hands set to eating as many of the fine berries as they could, afterwards filling handkerchiefs with quantities to take back to the ship. Nor indeed was this the last visit paid to our new-found garden, as various members of the crew made daily expeditions to the spot, armed with barrels, returning each time with the boat laden, and looking somewhat like a loaded waggon *en route* to Covent Garden in the strawberry season.

As we returned to the *Lily* a strong tide was running into the lagoon. Our thoughts were always wandering to that absent herd of walruses, wondering when, if ever, they would return once more to their accustomed haunt upon the sandbank. It was, therefore, with no small satisfaction that as we rowed slowly homewards there was borne across the waters, from the open sea, those deep, hoarse, bellowing notes to which our ears were now accustomed.

Soon we saw the herd of monstrous beasts swimming slowly, and coming in upon the rising tide. A gentle breeze was blowing towards the shore, and thus the oncoming animals could not wind us. Presently they swam right into the lagoon, and gradually approached quite close up to the boat, some of the more inquisitive members even approaching to within thirty or forty yards of us. Very imposing and fearsome did they look. Again and again one bolder than the rest would dive, and suddenly appear quite close to us, then, raising his huge head and shoulders well out of the water, would gaze intently at us ere diving again and retreating to join his companions.

Our sailors displayed unwonted energy in rowing, since they were clearly frightened by the thrilling yarns that they had heard of small boats being attacked and capsized by walruses in Arctic regions. Personally we regarded such stories as tales to be taken *cum grano salis*.

As the monsters rolled and dived around the boat bitterly I regretted the absence of my camera, which reposed in my cabin aboard the *Lily*. But now I had hopes of using it successfully before we left the place, which we had christened Walrus Bay.

Next morning it was by course of due rotation the turn of Ralph and myself to try our hand at bagging a walrus. Our hearts rejoiced when early dawn revealed to us the whole herd once more hauled out on the sandbank, and the wind still in a favourable quarter for a successful stalk.

We did not forget to take the camera on this occasion, and we set out and rowed across to the same spot where Agnes and Cecily had previously landed. As the result of tossing for it the first shot fell to my lot, but being equally keen on shooting with the camera as with a rifle I elected to stalk with the former only.

Ralph was sufficiently sportsmanlike to say he would remain behind, and allow me to stalk alone, and declared that he believed the beasts would not go far away even if disturbed by my stalking them without firing a shot.

I shall long remember that arduous crawling along the barren sandy beach. Not a stick nor stone to afford any cover, and constantly having to lie flat on my face, in cramped position minutes at a time, in order to avoid the vigilance of the look-out sentinel bull. Three times during the time I took to crawl that distance did the sentinel get tired of his duty, and roused up another one to undertake this apparently irksome task. As each fresh sentinel took up his duty the former one promptly dropped his head and went off to sleep.

A HERD OF WALRUSES ENTERING THE WATER

How long that seemingly endless squirming and crawling occupied I knew not, but Ralph told me that it lasted about two hours, during which time I had barely covered eight hundred yards. Finally, having approached by slow degrees to within about twenty-five yards of the sleeping herd, I ventured to rise on one knee in an attempt to focus the camera. Being caught in *flagrante delicto* by the sentinel's watchful eye, he gave vent to a loud grunt or roar, and the whole group of animals were on the *qui vive*. Now or never was the time for a snap-shot, and trusting to luck I " pressed the button," and devoutly prayed that the great photographic company which advertises that they will " do the rest " might in time develop a fairly successful print as the result.

The outcome was not equal to my anticipations, but it is ever thus. Life is made up of disappointments. This picture, though no exception to the rule, may still stand as a somewhat unique photograph, if only the inscription beneath it conveys to the spectator what particular scene it is intended to illustrate. And in this respect the snap-shot is not singular, for many others which we see might well be superscribed " this is a walrus," etc., etc., etc., and thereby leaves less to the imagination.

It was only a few seconds ere the whole herd had floundered clumsily into the water, and started swimming some distance away from shore. I retired backwards on hands and knees in crab-like fashion, hoping that the walruses had not all discovered the real cause of this trouble. And apparently my hopes were justified, since the animals remained swimming and diving close inshore and near the spot they had left.

Throwing myself flat on the sand, and beckoning Ralph to advance, I began to excavate a form of improvised shelter pit, using my hands to throw up a small mound of the loose sand in front of me.

Ralph had the forethought to bring with him my rifle, and after a long crawl he reached the spot where I lay, without the walruses apparently having observed him from where they swam in the water. Soon we had both well screened ourselves by piling up sand in front of us, and there we lay, determined if need be to remain till nightfall, on the chance of the herd coming ashore once more.

It was fully two hours before the bulls did finally show signs of coming to land again. From where we lay, a distance of eighty yards separated us from the spot where the walruses had been lying. And it seemed that this was their favourite haunt, because countless holes were made in the loose sand, showing where for ages past their huge bodies had reclined. At last, one by one, they came swimming in to shore, and when in shallow water again began floundering clumsily to land. It was very tempting to try a shot at them as their huge chests and foreheads were exposed to us, but profiting by former experience we decided to wait until we could get a side shot at their heads.

Gradually they hauled out on the sand, some rolling over on their sides at once and dropping asleep *instanter*.

Already we had each singled out a beast apiece, and the two chosen ones seemed to carry the largest tusks. Just as the best heads are always the hardest to acquire, these very bulls were the last of all the herd to leave the water.

Lying side by side Ralph and I were able to converse in whispers, and how very often during that momentous waiting each of us in turn restrained the other from shooting too hurriedly it would be hard to say. At last the two great brutes came rolling ashore, and for a moment they were both broadside on to us. On the word from Ralph, " Are you ready?" as pre-arranged, I replied, " Yes, fire," and simultaneously the two shots rang out. Both beasts dropped like pole-axed bullocks, and on examination of them we found that the solid bullets from our powerful ·450 cordite rifles had completely smashed to atoms the back part of the animals' skulls, thus killing them instantly.

We might easily have got in a second barrel at others of the herd before they took to the water, but as there is no great sport or danger attached to slaying them Ralph and I had previously decided that one good head apiece would satisfy our wants, and these undoubtedly we had in those two before us.

Ralph went and hailed the men to come up with the boat, and through the glasses I observed a *bidarka* put off from the *Lily's* side, shortly followed by our small dory, which contained the ladies, who obviously intended making an inspection of our trophies.

The advent of Ned and Steve in their *bidarka* was

a welcome addition to our strength, since the four men of our party were utterly unable to move either carcass, and roll the huge brutes a few feet beyond the rising tide. In fact, we found that with the united efforts of six men we barely moved each beast a few yards up the shelving sand. Hence it became a question of removing the skulls and scalp as quickly as possible. This was no easy task, as the hides were several inches thick, and so tough that a skinning-knife soon lost its edge.

Before the operation commenced I photographed the dead beasts as they lay, and then ran the tape measure over them. The largest bull measured twelve feet nine inches from nose to tail, and its companion was only an inch or two shorter. We estimated that either one weighed nearly three thousand pounds. Veritable mountains of flesh, bone, and blubber. Ugly, ungainly brutes in life, and uglier still in death, weird monsters of a pre-historic type, but still trophies which a man can proudly show and say they cost him certain hardships to procure.

Ere we had finished skinning them the water came rapidly upon us, and we all soon stood knee-deep in the breaking waves, determined at all costs to save at least the skulls.

At last the heads were severed, and we rolled the decapitated carcases into deep water, where they soon went floating into the lagoon on a rising tide. Thus leaving their favourite haunt unpolluted if the herd returned once more to the sandbank.

The weight of each head and scalp alone was just

as much as two men could lift and carry to the boats, and finally we returned triumphant to the ship. Nor were the ladies behindhand with their congratulations upon our success, in spite of their previous bad luck, and displayed the truest *camaraderie* and sportsman-like sentiments. Indeed, Agnes had ordered a banquet of banquets, and a raid was made upon the case of champagne which we reserved for emergencies and festivals.

Our natives were busily occupied for many hours in cleaning and whittling down the immense thickness of the walrus scalps, which before being pared down were almost three inches thick. It seemed almost incredible to us that any men could ever penetrate these tough hides and actually kill a walrus with spears or harpoons, as the natives still do along the Arctic coasts.

On the next day no walruses returned to the sandbank, although through our telescopes a number of them could be seen swimming far out in the open sea. Macdonald assured us that these animals could sleep upon the waters, and that on occasions natives thus approached them noiselessly in canoes and harpooned them before the animals observed their presence. Whether or no this is a sailor's yarn I cannot say, but it strikes me from observation of the animals that the performance would not be an easy one to accomplish successfully.

Whilst we were in the act of discussing this problem Macdonald, happening to glance over the vessel's bows, suddenly said, " Well, darn me, gents, if there ain't a thundering big brute bearing down on us now, and if he's not asleep, I guess he's dead, anyway."

Hastily going forward with glasses we made out the body of a walrus coming up the centre of the lagoon on the fast-rising tide, and drifting in such a direction that it must pass close by the *Lily*. At first we thought it might be one of our floating headless carcases still drifting with the tides. But a closer inspection revealed the fact that the animal's head and neck were still intact, although the former lay deep in the water, as the body lay on its side.

The animal was obviously dead, and then we realized that in all probability it was the beast at which Agnes and Cecily had fired two days before. A boat was quickly lowered, and Steve with two sailors put off to intercept the carcase as it came floating past. Steve stood in the bows holding a rope, which he soon slipped round the dead beast's head and thus towed it to the ship's side.

Steve, who apparently thought we might be in doubt as to whether he had accomplished a perform-ance equalling that described by the worthy historian Albertus Magnus, shouted out, " He dead all right, big one, you bet !" And forsooth it was a big one, since Agnes and Cecily had had first pick of the herd, and this beast was even larger than either of the others, and carried a fine pair of tusks, measuring twenty-two inches below the gums.

It was no easy matter to remove the scalp and head, as the carcase was too heavy to lift bodily on board the schooner. We found the most efficacious method to be that of pulling the head and shoulders out of the water by roping them up to the mast, and the natives getting to work on the skin by standing in two boats alongside the *Lily*. Fortunately a walrus has no hair to slip, and this huge brute's tough hide was none the worse.

As the evening tide rolled in we heard the distant bellowing of walruses. A welcome sound, foretelling the return of that absent herd once more to our lagoon. For such a prospect we were all duly thankful, as each day wasted now in waiting meant a probability of arriving late upon the grounds where we hoped to find some wild sheep, and thus far none of us could tell how long the proposed trip up the Kuskokwim might take us ere we reached the mountainous sheep country.

Early next morning I saw the walruses occupying the old haunt upon the sandbank, and soon afterwards the boat carried the ladies as before across to the desolate island. I had advised them to adopt the same tactics as used by Ralph and myself on the last occasion, and, of course, it was the intention to shoot but one walrus, as one head apiece was sufficient to take away as trophies of these harmless beasts.

A friendly squabble arose between Agnes and Cecily as to whom the first walrus belonged. We suggested tossing up for it, on the understanding that the loser took the first shot on the chance occur‑ ring. Agnes, sticking to her usual assumption of bad luck, declared that she would never win anything at tossing, and that therefore the first beast was already as good as Cecily's. Nor was she wrong in this, for Cecily won the toss, and it was in vain that we tried to point out that at last she had actually won something, because the next shot was hers by all ruling of the gods of chance.

She returned, unlike Niobe, all smiling, from the sea, triumphant in the result of a well-planned stalk, since with the first shot she bagged another fine walrus, and according to our compact Cecily, who had accompanied her throughout the long and arduous crawling process, had been obliged to come back without firing a shot. What force of will-power it required on her part to refrain from firing at another beast, as the whole herd dashed into the water, she alone can tell, but it is on record in our memory to her everlasting credit that she did so.

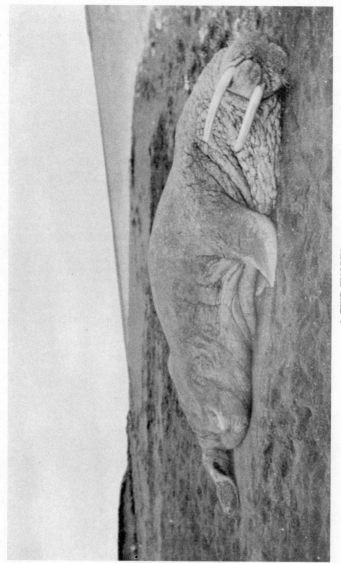

A FINE WALRUS

CHAPTER XII

THE ESTUARY OF THE KUSKOKWIM

The story shall be changed ;
Apollo flies, and Daphne holds the chase
Midsummer Night's Dream
Thus with imagin'd wing our swift scene flies
King Henry V

Do you know what it is to waken to a sense of impending disaster, to open your eyes to a cold world you confidently feel is just about to frown its blackest ?

The murky little cabin looked its worst, the ubiquitous cockroaches—have I told you of the portly cockroaches who resided in their dozens in the planks of the schooner?—appeared more objectionable than usual in mine eyes, as Tom, for the nonce a messenger of evil omen, brought in my *chota hazari*, and the news which almost outed itself ere the necessary words could be formed and spoken.

" Kitchener is dead, m'm."

I sat up. The blow had fallen. I had felt it would. How can one hope to rear a bear cub on a sealing schooner with a crew constantly offering the animal rations, ranging from inadequately cooked beans to drinks of hot, greasy cocoa?

The pretty little cub! I would he were still a

creature of the boundless wild, I would—— But Tom began, with the fell ghoulishness of the lower orders, to describe the manner of the end. This was too much. If he liked to harrow his own feelings why try to harrow mine? When we jump a stiff fence we sometimes land on a harrow, but there's no earthly need to put one there.

On deck the crew were wrangling as to which of their number killed the little bear with o'er much kindness. The cook accused a shrinking youth, a French Canadian, who seemed so likely to be blamed for the disaster, as he had not sufficient go about him to repudiate all connection with it, that Cecily and I felt we must to his rescue, albeit we were biassed. Women are very seldom impartial; their sympathies go out, rightly or wrongly, to the weaker and losing side; their desire is always to "assist the dog that is under," and have nothing to do with the cynical advice of the philosopher who advocated the system of taking the part of "the man with the largest club."

Cecily suggested that very likely the chef himself had overdone his attentions a little, a flank movement which diverted things, and left the cook stranded in a backwater of unspoken annoyance. I was glad that Cecily got in so telling a shot, for the cook paid no attention to any one save himself and his own creature comforts. In some men, as they grow older, the milk of human kindness dries up. They have no sympathy.

Ralph came upon the scene, and smoothed and

soft-soaped the crew and glossed things over. If the cook had killed the bear, which was not for a moment so much as hinted at, he probably considered that the animal would prefer death to continued life aboard a sealing schooner. If the sailor in question had assisted our pet out of this world of tears, it was done in the way of kindness. If anybody else was responsible for closing the cub's career, no doubt there were excellent reasons to be brought forward, if we only knew them. In short, the blood of the bear was on its own head, or rather on its own " Little Mary."

It was most annoying, and this backing the horse both ways, into which Ralph had suddenly launched, made Cecily and me think we must be electioneering, instead of sailing on a sealer over the Bering Sea.

Ralph explained afterwards that it was a piece of diplomacy, and very necessary, as it was useless to annoy the crew, who had it in their power to make things very unpleasant for us an' they wished. I think now, looking back, that we should have got on much better than we did if we had used a little *less* diplomacy when we were on the *Lily*. Amateurs at it always show their hand, and the one weak spot at the same time. Indeed, even in the great crises of the world I am not sure but that diplomacy should be relegated to a back seat. Is it so good perpetually to gloss over? Does it not often merely make a film over the ulcerous part, whilst rank corruption, undermining all within, spreads unseen?

Off Cape Constantine we encountered the densest

fog which had as yet barred our progress, and it was often impossible to see the bows of the ship from the stern. Creeping warily inshore we anchored in a little sheltered inlet, and there remained over-shadowed by a dreary belt of mist for two whole days.

Weighing anchor at last, we sailed by the black-looking, forbidding precipices of Hagemeister Island. Our hunters told us it was said, by men likely to know, that bears of a fierce and magnificent description inhabited the recesses of this frowning isle. We had not the time to verify the statement for ourselves, even had we the inclination. Bear pelts at this season are apt to be not worth the taking.

On the gaunt cliffs the sea-birds rested in thousands, changing the colour of the dark grim rocks to tones of white and grey. Murres there were in myriads, but gulls, cormorants, auks, and other diving birds were present in solid masses. The Aleuts call the murres " arries," a familiar, meaning word, and I should like to know the origin of it in Alaska. " 'Arrys " are very common with us at home, too common altogether. Can it be that the Aleut mind bestowed the name in a spirit of fine irony ? I think not. There be English " 'Arrys " and Alaskan " arries."

We sailed through a dense curtain of birds, dividing up their multitudes as our ship ran on. As a murre flies the feet do all the steering, for so stumpy a tail as is this bird's makes for awkwardness, and gives no guidance. When the course must be

A CALM SPOT IN THE BERING SEA

changed out go the slim red feet, and make the balance perfect.

For one evening the wraith of the mist hung on the skirts of the horizon, and no fog banks dimmed the lustre of a perfect scene. Perhaps the silence, the loneliness, the fierce, sad splendour of the chill and haunting North, had never before seemed so insistent as the sun sank, lighting up a path of glowing glory for so far as the eye could reach, and rising high beside us, sombre and grand, the great rocks of Hagemeister Island, set in a waste of desolate waters, a facetted jewel in a crownëd world.

Around Cape Newenham races the strongest tidal current of the Bering Sea, and our skipper, forewarned, took precautions accordingly, and gave the Cape a wide berth. Even so we felt the giant hands of the deep drawing us nearer, and ever nearer, to the coast. At times the strong ship turned as though she were on a fixed pivot, so little progress made she, so strong were the eddies and whirlpools around her. Captain Clemsen, or, more properly speaking, the pilot, had not miscalculated, and we cleared the fearsome place with a few hundred yards to spare.

Far out of the swirling, whirling rapids we caught a glimpse of two fur seals, the first we had seen, bobbing and curtseying on the waves. Their shrift would be short if the spirit of Wanderlust took them much closer to shore. Steve and Ned looked longingly at the *bidarkas*, and in fancy threw the deftest of deft spears, but the sea ran much too strong to permit of hunting seals.

From Cape Newenham onwards to the estuary of
the Kuskokwim one gravelly beach succeeded the
other, and going ashore was made delightfully simple,
because the water held deep right up to the tide line.
Driftwood was very plentiful, but the only growing
timber seemed to be entirely composed of belts of
attenuated dwarf willows.

Near one of the prettiest of the shingly beaches
Cecily and I landed one afternoon bent on a long
foray, and for the first time on this trip we intended
to sleep in the open, with the sky for tent. The *Lily*
lay out in the offing, a sentinel for our safety.

With our sleeping-bags strapped to our backs, and
a few eatables bestowed in our pockets, we took a
straight line from the beach, through the dense
willow scrub.

Trekking onwards, with the enthusiasm of untried
explorers, we suddenly came on the smallest little
homestead, for all the world like a settler's hut in
the Canadian backwoods, which so surprised us we
pinched our arms to see whether or no we were awake
or dreaming. There stood the shack right enough,
shakily, a rude dwelling made from the whitened
timber cast up on the beach, a stove-pipe doing duty
for chimney, and a window about the size of a handkerchief inset into the rough logs. A low door stood
open, a-swing, and on a rubbish-heap near by a
pair of bald-headed eagles fought each other for
possession of some putrid bones. No smoke arose;
the silence seemed charged with the electricity of
mystery, and burdened with weird, indescribable

imaginings. A haunted homestead. Haunted by the ghosts of the Past, Regret, and Memory.

We tip-toed across the marshy quagmire intervening, and peered inquisitively round the creaking door. In the cavern-like fireplace a dead log, charred and dull, gave the whole room the sad, forlorn aspect chill embers always bring. We ranged right inside, and through the bare room we caught a glimpse of a little lean-to, and—surely—a figure prone on the cold earth floor. This was exploring indeed. We called out to ask if we, who were already in, might enter. No reply.

A squat, untidy figure lay before us, all of a heap, and a hood of a *parka*, made from loon skins, concealed the face. Cecily drew the folds back—and with a gasp, which changed to a little cry as she saw us, an Innuit woman looked up at us. Old she was in grief, but not, I think, in years. It is very hard to guess accurately the age of native women, but we judged this one to be about twenty-four. There was nothing romantic about her, for an Innuit lacks royal grace and dignity of carriage, but there was that in her face which told of the sadness of the ages, and her eyes were wells of unshed tears. She rose to her feet in a sort of maze, and we stood, an extraordinary trio, looking inquiringly at each other.

The Innuit woman spoke to us wonderingly, questioningly, with eyes yearning. We could neither understand nor offer any comfort.

By signs she made it clear to us that she no longer lived in this small shack, she lived somewhere " over there," waving to a distant settlement; but once this had been her home. Some one else, apparently, had lived here with her, some one she loved. The Some one was drowned, for we had the drama acted in silent pantomime before us. The throwing the spear, the first success, then the *bidarka* ripping open on a treacherous rock, the sudden immersion, the swimming, and then—the end. It was all very marvellous, and most weird and heart-stirring to see.

Our new acquaintance pitifully laid the goods and chattels of the drowned before us, bringing them out from a secure hiding-place in the roof. With some surprise we realized that the Some one must have been a white man, a trapper or prospector perhaps, "gone native," as is sometimes the case. The Innuit woman probably recognized that she stood face to face with others of her man's race.

The relics were very few—a pipe, an old silver watch, a very pre-historic Winchester repeater, and two photographs, of the variety to be found in every old album—a lady with a chignon, a man with a wealth of white tie and murky apparel. They were tied together in a much-worn, much-read newspaper of ancient date. I looked at this five-year-old breath from the outer world, and found that the torn sheet emanated from Birmingham, and it recorded, in faded ink, a great speech made by Mr. Chamberlain. On the margin of the paper, written in pencil, in an educated hand, we made out, after some difficulty, the words—

" Joe loves his country. That is enough for a statesman."

And lower down the column this comment—

" There can be no decay if such a vitality exists."

This settled the matter for us. The man " gone native " was an Englishman, a patriot too, whatever else he was not. More we could not grasp, save the paper, and that we annexed, by permission, as a souvenir.

Our Innuit, putting away her treasures, by signs begged us to follow her, and, having nothing on hand but the further gratifying of our detective propensities, we decided we wished to pursue this adventure to the end. Following our guide up hill and down dale we rounded a bluff, and came on a small settlement, nestling on the banks of a small river. Our friend did the honours, and introduced us to the chief of the tribe, a crafty-looking personage of unusually small stature, and shifty, deep-set eyes.

Every one crowded close about us in a state of unfeigned surprise. They were not at all unmannerly, and seemed glad to have us there, but they could not hide the astonishment they felt at our appearance. The chief tried to detach my rifle, whether because he would relieve me of its weight or not I cannot tell. Just as gravely, just as solemnly, I held on. Dried salmon was brought to us and berries which made us feel the awkwardness of having nothing to present in return. We turned out our pockets, and found a spare box of matches. These took pride of place, and the chief condescended to accept them. We had a flask of whisky on us, but refrained from handing over. The natives of the coast line, from Cape Constantine to the Kuskokwim, are free—more or less—from the temptations of strong drink, because the conditions which govern navigation thereabouts are not attractive to the whisky trader. Therefore, why create a want? Besides, as Cecily said, we should very likely need the contents of our flask ourselves before we had done.

How glorious it was to lie in a warm sleeping-bag watching the stars twinkling in a sky of ultramarine, to listen to the desolate cry of a loon, the very tongue of the wilderness, and hear the plaintive snipe overhead. How splendid to be so independent of any camping arrangements, to require so little as to be able to say any instant, "Let us rest here," no fuss, no settling, no palaver of any kind.

After a breakfast of some of the gift salmon, toasted by the fire, we set out in another direction, and to our vexation came on another Innuit settlement. We seemed to have found a very residential part of the country. The inhabitants of the coast, from the mouth of the Yukon to Bristol Bay, are called Innuits, and they are the most numerous of any of the tribes allied to the Eskimo. Very simple-minded and kindly, it would be impossible to dislike them for anything but the absolute filth of their half-underground residences. These semi-earth houses, called baraboras, beggar all description for dirt and wretchedness. Some baraboras have square, wooden apartments raised on stilts, to be clear of the floods standing alongside, and these fish-drying and storing rooms are infinitely preferable to the Innuit living establishment. For the most part these people live on the salmon of the country, hair seals, from the outlying rocks, and an occasional delicacy in the way of walrus meat.

This newly-discovered settlement was very deserted, and appeared to be in the charge of an old patriarch, who sat in the sun chewing tobacco. The younger people of both sexes were harvesting, the men spearing hair seals, the women catching clothes for the family in some far-off range. We noticed that the *parkas* worn by the Innuit women were made much shorter in length than those worn by the men. Some of the Innuit ladies affected shapeless boots made from seal-skin, which reached half-way up to the knee.

The Innuit seldom smokes, but men and women chew, soaking the tobacco beforehand in seal-oil, and rolling it into a tight ball. Seal-oil is the everything of life to the natives of Alaska, sauce for all eatables, and no excursion is possible without a goodly store. Very often the oil is carried in an ingenious bag made from a whole seal-skin which has been skinned out from the neck. In the September berry season, when the wild raspberry, the saskatoon, and the soap berry can be gathered, the natives pick them by quarts, and putting them into a can or cauldron of sorts, squeeze the fruit through the fingers, beating it about until the whole is a frothing mass. Seal-oil plays the part of cream, and it is poured in lavishly. Then—what a banquet! We had much ado to refuse politely to sample a portion after interestedly watching its preparation.

When both Cecily and I would not have even a small helping, the disconsolate faces around told us how much our friends felt the thwarting of their hospitable intentions. A weird-looking girl handed me a salmon from a pile of dried fish heaped near a barabora. I took it and scrutinized it closely without thinking, for, of course, even in the Innuit world it is very rude to look a gift horse in the mouth. I was really trying to discover its variety, whether king salmon or salmon of lesser rank. Again a look of disappointment crossed the faces of our kindly would-be entertainers. How tactless it was of me to seem so unappreciative. A gleam of intelligence lit the eyes of an Innuit matron. Taking me by the hand, and bidding Cecily to follow, she led us to the back of a *barabora*, and there before us we saw what any one would take to be a very recently made grave. Such a large one, the tomb of a veritable giant Innuit.

Ghoulishly our friend commenced to scratch up the soil, throwing it hither and thither. Prepared as we were by that time for an exhumation of some sort, we could not help gasping with astonishment as she struck boards, and beneath the boards, which the energetic woman carefully lifted, salmon in countless dozens, decaying and rotting. The smell well-nigh overwhelmed us, but we realized that this time we must not fail to be obliged and appreciative. We stood our ground, and the Innuit lady seemed to fairly drink in the noxious odour, her nose wrinkling up like a rabbit's as it sniffs new grass. Dipping her arms deep into the mass of rapidly-decomposing fish, she brought out a specimen *sans* a good deal of itself, but quite sufficient to be exceedingly impressive. This she smilingly bestowed upon me with the air of one who feels that this time at least there can be no doubt as to the value of the gift.

My diplomacy was now to be tested. I grasped the horror by what tail it had left, and smiled and bowed my thanks. Every one seemed delighted that at last I was fixed up with something really edible, and in the end we had to take the salmon aboard the *bidarka*, which came to take us back to the *Lily*, because our friends of the settlement would not leave us, and had we remained ashore we must have been compelled to devour the fish.

I afterwards discovered that these salmon pits are to be found in many Innuit settlements, and nobody dies from the effects. The natives are like the bears, and prefer salmon with a little " bings " about it.

The skipper asked us that night if we had, by any chance, a skunk in the hold! It was the redolent whiffs of my *khaki* coat really—for the salmon had been consigned to its own element long ago—and it took days and days to go off.

Nearing the estuary of the Kuskokwim, a dull expanse of mud flats, rather like the reaches of the

Severn round about Chepstow, a great colony of
birds fished assiduously, scurrying and swirling on
the face of the waters. The quarrelling and fighting
was incessant, and the many cries rent the air in
volume of sound. On the outskirts of the noisy
throng was a solitary pure white gull, of Point
Barrow variety, most handsome of sea-birds. No
bars of black marked his spotless coat, his bright
beak of flaming yellow being the only vivid colour
about him. In slow majestic turns and twists the
beautiful bird neared our ship to settle peacefully
on the tossing waves beside a blue-black cormorant,
a contrast in colour schemes.

On the estuary numbers of brent geese paddled
about in the oozy mud, washed by the waves. Most
wary and careful of birds, they took to the open sea
at night, and when rising to fly never sailed landwards. As they flew, their wings beating the air in
great rhythmical strokes, the whole concourse of birds
called in a hoarse wild note, and given in the unison
of several hundreds of throats the noise sounded like
a clanking cough requiring a " One-day cold cure "
badly. All around the feeding grounds the sea-grass,
torn up by the roots, floated in solid masses, the most
edible bits having been eaten off.

Ralph got a lucky shot at a straggler, after stalking the bird for an hour or more. Brent geese are
really hard to bag without the paraphernalia of punt,
gun, etc., and here on the estuary of mud stalking
was a disagreeable, messy business.

We anchored in the wide mouth of the Kuskokwim

River, a bay in itself, and up stream we made out, with our glasses, a large native settlement, the Mecca of our hopes just now, since the next thing on the cards was to discover men willing to follow our fortunes after we should quit the *Lily*.

CHAPTER XIII

ON THE KUSKOKWIM RIVER

Then sit we down, and let us all consult
Titus Andronicus
I'll pluck thee berries,
I'll fish for thee, and get thee wood enough
The Tempest

NEXT morning we four, with Steve as interpreter, rowed to the settlement, nestling on the south bank, a filthy, evil-smelling collection of *baraboras*, and as we landed the women left their work and mounted the roofs the better to see the visitors. Pulling up the *bidarkas* with very willing hands, a crowd of Innuit men gave us greeting.

Decaying carcases of seals and rotten salmon dotted the trodden earth, and but for the ravens and the eagles who played the part of Health Officers, I imagine the state of that Innuit abiding place would have been even more insanitary than it was. The birds swooped down and picked up pieces of decomposing matter from under our very feet. The whole village was rather like an *abattoir*, and the most ordinary sense of smell would guide any one straight to it from a mile off.

A great catch of hair seals was in process of being converted into blubber, and everything in the vicinity was larded with the liquid, people, beach, air, houses, dogs, and *bidarkas*, a veritable orgy of oil. At intervals, down what Ralph called "the High Street," fires were burning, encircled with stones, and a strong iron kettle, somewhat like an Irish pot, simmered on the red ashes, reducing pieces of seals' fat to liquid form. An attendant handmaiden ladled out the bubbling oil as it melted into native baskets, so wonderfully woven and meshed that they were watertight. As the oil cooled it was run off again into bags made from whole seals, or primitive tubs for storing purposes.

Other women prepared the seals for the pot, lifting the carcasses off-handedly as a fishmonger seizes a salmon for cutting up. All the seal seemed of use save the head and clean-picked backbone, which was thrown on to the beach to add to the already shocking condition of things. The skilful dismemberment of the seals was accomplished by the aid of a rude stone knife of great sharpness. The split carcase was then laid, hair side down, and having removed the body of the animal almost whole, the deft worker stripped off the fat in a solid sheet clear off the skin.

Seal-oil boiling is to the Innuit matron what the domestic function of preserving is with us. They stir and watch it just as diligently. But for the smell almost one could think strawberry jam manufacture was in progress. We got so interested and muddled with memories, that Cecily said at last, very anxiously to one matron, "Oh, I'm sure it is time to skim now. The scum is rising."

O

Propped against the half-underground dwellings stood worn grey vertebræ of whales, souvenirs of the passing of the whaling fleet.

All the inhabitants of the village wore the *parka*, and here the shirt-like costume was cut much longer at the back than the front, giving a quaint tail-like effect. One could hardly make a way through the settlement for poles and crisscross thongs whereon were drying remnants of seal, salmon, and flat fish of great size. Skins full of the blubber swung from standing scaffolding, nets made from seals' skins set traps to catch the unwary feet, and all sorts of ingenious bags and baskets made from the ubiquitous universal provider to the Innuits dried in the wind and sun. The skins are made up in all kinds of ways, into useful hold-all baskets, sagging in the middle, sewn to two pieces of wood, not unlike a butcher's tray, and contrived into the fashion to which I have already alluded; bags skinned out from the neck, or into a most useful second variety cut from flipper to flipper, and then laced together.

A great many dogs were sniffing and gnawing amongst the refuse. They were large grey brutes, not unlike a coyote, fierce and wolfish-looking. Their looks bewrayed them, for they greeted us with courtesy, and made no attempt to snarl or bite.

We held a council with the chief, or headman of the tribe, explained our wants, and expressed our desires through Steve, who seemed to be able to make himself understood with most of the natives we had come across. We desired to engage six Innuits, with

bidarkas, to take us to the headwaters of the Kuskokwim, thence to trek with us across the divide
between that river and the Sushitna, and carry our
stores, trophies—when we got any!—as we hunted
the country we should traverse. On meeting the
band of natives to be sent up from Cook's Inlet by
Captain Clemsen, the men from this settlement at
the mouth of the Kuskokwim could return to their
homes.

The affair seemed most difficult to arrange. The
general impression and consternation which we
created could not have been more acute had we been
calling for volunteers to accompany us on an expedition to the North Pole. I imagine it was because
the trip was an up-stream affair, therefore a hard
nut to crack. All the Alaskan tribes look with suspicion on anything which they have not personally
seen and sampled for themselves. These men did
not know the river so far up, nor guessed the exist-
ence, so far as we could gather, of the great divide
which lay between the rivers. Unknown bits of any
world must be bad. The chief thought so, and the
men followed suit.

" Him say no good, you bet," said Steve, methodically.

Never strike sail to the fear of a native, I say,
and the Leader agreed with me. Indeed, the more
difficulties the Innuits set in the way the more resolved
seemed the Leader to overcome and overthrow them.
As a real leader should do. It always seems to me that
a man fitted by nature to lead and govern others

never complains of the idiocy of his coadjutors, of their incapability, unsuitability, and other shortcomings. A born leader sees in all these things the proof of his power, his power to meet and beat them.

At last appeared a real travelled Innuit, who was introduced to us as a veritable Stanley, with a dash of Sir Richard Burton thrown in. This dolorous-looking individual had actually hunted over the sheep ground we were aiming for only some two years before, when he convoyed an American magnate, for whom the native had not one good word to say. It is always a matter for interested amusement to me to notice the manner in which all shikáris, black and white, talk of the last sportsman whom they served. The last is very first, and referred to, and his doings quoted and dragged into the conversation at all sorts of odd moments.

According to native hunters but two varieties of sportsmen exist. The one a demi-god, a little lower than the angels, one whom it would be impossible to imagine doing aught wrong or mistaken, who never misses a shot, invariably clean kills his quarry, never swears, never loses his temper, and treats his shikári like a friend and a brother. A being almost too good for this world and most wearisome to meet, did he exist, for such self-evident worth and complacent excellence would pall inevitably. Then there's the other sportsman. Look on this picture, and on that. An imp of evil, a being brought into this vale of tears for no other reason than to make an honest shikári's life a burden, a bungler, a no sort of a shot, a cumberer of the ground, a useless, greedy creature of uncertain temper, and new original swear-words. There is no middle path. Angel of light or demon of evil must you be. It all depends on the hunter's point of view. The much-travelled one counselled that some of the men of the settlement accepted the offer made to them, and matters took a more encouraging turn. At first a dollar and a half per day was demanded for each man, and they stated that they were not moving up river for less. They were not skilled in the type of hunting we were about to engage in, and this seemed a stiff price. To our astonishment the avaricious creatures finally consented to take a dollar per diem each man. After agreeing to pay something for the hire of extra *bidarkas* we hied us back to the *Lily* to complete all arrangements.

I did wish we had a dug-out of Pacific Coast variety, for they are so excellent for poling up rivers. However, we had not, and a dory must be towed up so far as practicable to aid in the store carrying. Sorting the goods and chattels to be taken was a big business. Ample supplies had to be left on board the *Lily* for the men who were returning in her to Cook's Inlet, where more stores could be obtained, and ample supplies had to be taken for our big trek to the Sushitna. We calculated it would take us three weeks to get to the shooting-ground, and after leaving the Kuskokwim all the transport available would be the shoulders of our henchmen.

That evening, a day but one before the start, as I

was looking over the trophies in the hold, Steve stood beside me, and in his odd mixture of Americanese and English desired me to grant him a favour.

" You do this for me, you bet, I do all same for you."

Which meant, in effect, that if his wants were favourably considered, mine would receive his careful attention when the right time came.

The little native wished to remain with us, to see the trip through, to hunt with us, and be our interpreter and general factotum. We had never figured on such a stroke of luck. Ned might safely be trusted to care for the trophies, and Steve could work his way back to Kodiac from Cook's Inlet as occasion offered. I closed with the sporting offer, and, much delighted, Steve curled himself up in a maze of blankets in a corner of the hold, and set himself to sleep.

At dawn the loading up of our flotilla commenced in earnest. We conveyed everything to the mouth of the river, and then packed the *bidarkas* and a dory with a heap of stores, rifle cases, tents, and cases innumerable. Leaving all sorts of instructions, verbal and written, with Captain Clemsen, we said goodbye to our fragrant *Lily*, with not a few regrets, and, speaking personally, not a few qualms.

Now were we fairly launched into a nomadic life. I set out in a three-hatch *bidarka*, with a sinister-looking paddler, who hugged a little bag of seal-oil to his manly chest. The energetic paddler had not corked his treasure sufficiently, and presently the deck skin streamed with evil-smelling oil, and ere I discovered it I had mopped up a considerable quantity with my coat-sleeve. All the men appeared to cling like limpets to a skin full of the seal-oil, and we were glad each proprietor considered his quantum too valuable to let out of sight, for it made for the preservation of the stores. A seal-oil flavour does not commend itself to all men.

Almost as soon as our journey up river commenced we landed again to call on the missionary in charge of a Moravian Mission, which made the natives' minds wonder considerably. A flourishing trading post stood alongside, all built in a neat corral. The natives living in this centre of civilization, an Alaskan metropolis, had in some ways risen above the habits of their ancestors, and in others fallen below their standard.

The influence of a trading post always has a direct effect on the clothing of natives, and here the men and women wore immaculate trouserines showing below their *parkas*. I have to call their kit trouserines, because the garments were not trousers, nor short enough for knickerbockers, but a sort of compromise between the two, a sartorial half-way house. I wondered if the missionary had set the fashion in this attire. Or had the primitive savages evolved it from their inner consciousness?

> " Fashions that are now called new
> Have been worn by more than you ;
> Elder times have worn the same,
> Though the new ones got the name."

Up stream, away from the benign influence, savagery came to hand grips with extreme punctiliousness of costume, ousted it, and fairly ran amok. In some of the temporary residences of nomadic natives we came on Innuits of all ages, more or less, usually more, in "the altogether."

The *bidarkas* which carried the stores naturally made slower progress than the ones less encumbered, and as for the manœuvres of the men in charge of the dory they were strenuous in the extreme. Very often we settled on a spot for camp long before the necessary camp kit hove in sight, meanwhile we foraged around for anything we could get in the way of waterfowl to fill the pot. Teal delighted us with their unsuspicious ways. They so readily allowed us the easiest of shots, and were so amiably willing to fall into the snares of the fowler. No crouching or grovelling is required here, just a straight walk to the place where the birds settled, and with any luck a right and left chance was the inevitable reward. You need quick eyes and a ready finger, for the teal quits the land or water with a springing dart, an arrow-like movement, with no sort of a warning such as an upraised head, or hurried quack of alarm.

Wood was scarce at first, and all along the banks for many days we came on small settlements whose inhabitants fished and hunted the little world around them, making it difficult for us to keep our larder filled. Tobacco was the "open sesame" to most things, and procured us the granting of our simple desires much more expeditiously than the proffering of the brightest silver half-dollar ever minted. Here, in this back of beyond, fifty cents was the standard trading amount, not the dollar, as in so many other parts of North America. This is a great economy.

The daily vista was uninteresting enough at first, but as we progressed the river banks became more entrancing, the bird life more amazing. Save for the presence of the ferocious mosquitoes our days would have been cloudless. The little pests were the source of the greatest annoyance, and necessitated the wearing of veils and gloves.

Our daily programme varied but little, and our custom was to start after breakfast in any kind of weather, and do as much travelling as strength permitted, then to halt, rest awhile, cook a good meal, and go on again until late evening, when we camped for the night.

I wish I could tell of hairbreadth 'scapes, of battling against rapids, and running into rocks, for such things would seem to be an indispensable part of the exploration of a comparatively unknown river in the wilds of Alaska, and inseparable from the mysterious whole. There were rapids, there were rocks, but truth compels me to say that neither were dangerous. The Kuskokwim has no big rapids, some swiftly running water, racing apace over sandy bars, but the finesse of our little navigators was never at fault, and they propelled the light *bidarkas* gallantly over the tossing ripples. The slow, tortoise-like dory hugged the bank, usually in tow from the shore ahead.

The greatest hardship on the voyage was the

cramp in our limbs, a natural result from the awkward position a *bidarka* mariner must take up. The same little sinister Innuit paddled my craft daily, and at first I thought he was the ugliest living creature I had ever come across, but after glueing my eyes for days to the nape of his short neck, ringed round with creases, and catching a glimpse of his countenance as he half turned to the paddle, I got so used to this vision of hideousness that almost he seemed to climb to a pinnacle of ugliness, and tumble over to a Looking-Glass topsy-turvy world which returned him revivified and passable. Have you ever noticed that queer-looking people are like ugly photographs—they grow on one? At first you think " Dear me, I cannot bear this caricature near me." Next you get to, "It is really not so bad, after all," and, lastly, a sort of pleasant toleration comes.

Sometimes a great log came rolling by, continuing its weary journey from the heart of Alaska to the sea. Our men would dash after the treasure-trove, lasso it, broncho fashion, and haul the baulk ashore. A big fire would follow, and much drying of camp kit, indiscriminate roasting of fish, flesh, and fowl also. Not often flesh, just occasionally. I bagged a small black bear one night as he feasted upon berries, his jaws dyed red in the juices of the fruit. His paws were stuck full of porcupine quills, a prickly hint of sorts for Bruin evidently. The men feasted merrily on this addition to their rations. We kept to the birds of the air. Bear meat is really only possible when one is next door to starving.

At one of our camps we called a longer halt, and
Cecily and I had a washing day, making a fire by
the unlimited water supply, and requisitioning the
constant services of the camp kettle. As we rinsed
the clothes in the river my boot struck against something hard beneath the sand, and I stooped down
to redeem the treasure trove of a mastodon tooth
in excellent preservation. We thought that this rem-
nant of a pre-historic monster had been washed down
from the river banks during the floods of spring, or
snow-falls of winter. Our natives told us that they
often came on many large bones buried in the shale-
like bluffs along the sides of the Kuskokwim. We
saw no game of any kind, and save for a musk-rat
or two swimming away from us for dear life, and the
wildfowl who had their haunts in the quiet slopes
fringing the stream, this world of ours was solemn in
its desolation.

On and on we went, a round of days very much
alike, rain and storm and shine, strenuous days
enough, crammed to overflowing with the manifold
interests of the trip. So at last to wilder waters,
broken country, split up into many channels, with
infinitesimal islands and streams branching forth from
the mighty mother. Mountains loomed on our
horizon, and above all rose the dominating peak of
Mount MacKinley, the highest on the North American
continent. Chains and networks of water intersected
the land and spread into lagoons, where mallard, teal,
and the common snipe abounded.

On the other side of Fort Kalmakoff, established in

1832, now a dreary native encampment, we steered
right into the midst of the Upper Kuskokwim
Indians, of whom we had heard from our friend
the missionary at the mouth of the river. A large
flotilla of *bidarkas*, and some graceful birch-bark
canoes, lay hauled up on the banks above water-line.
The chief came down to the edge of the river to
receive us, and every other inhabitant of the settlement left work, if they ever did any, to come and
look at us.

The headman wore a very superior *parka* made
from Siberian reindeer skin, and some of the belles
had on *parkas* composed of loon skins stitched together, and these garments were in a pitiable condition of moulting, and dropped feathers as the wearers
moved.

We could have run the blockade of this encampment without going ashore if the pilot in the first
bidarka had not made the welkin ring with impossible-to-understand messages announcing our
approach. We presented a little tobacco and a pen-
knife or two, which seemed to please the people. The
chief, oddly enough, spoke a Russian patois, and
began a persuasive argument in varying tones, trying
first a high key, then, as no answering light of understanding shone in our eyes, dropped his remarks to
a lower register, and finally, as he saw that his
rhetorical efforts stood an excellent chance of being
entirely wasted, came out with a basso-profundo
sentence which made us jump with surprise. Obviously a reply was expected. Naturally we looked

to the Leader to do the right thing. All he said
was—

" Oh—er—really, hang it ! Where's Steve ?"

Steve could not help here either, and finally we
discovered a minion who translated to Steve in a
lingo understood by him, and the message gradually
filtered through to us. The chief would like some
" hootchinoo." A diabolical form of whisky. We
explained, again by the complicated form of word
transmission, that we were anti-hootchinooers, and
proffered a small bottle of lime juice instead. A
woman seized it, somewhat roughly certainly, and
the outraged chief caught her a terrific blow on her
shoulders, and annexed the trophy himself.

The women of this camp struck us as being a
frightfully put-upon lot, and even in the short time
we were there we saw one or two incidents which
made our blood boil. Perhaps it would be too much
to ask that savages should not push and cuff their
women-kind in a scrimmage of get-there-first variety,
but at least they need not treat the harmless feminines
as though they were militant suffragettes. Juvenal
asked, " Who shall guard the guards themselves ?"
Cecily and I paraphrased this query and inquired,
" Who shall guard the Indian women from the
Indians ?" But there was no reply. However, this
tribe, whatever they might be called, could not be
regarded as pure Indians. A strain of Indian hung
about them, showed in their cheekbones, in hands
and skull conformation, but the infusion of other
blood was stifling the characteristics of the Redskin.

Slowly and surely the bad attributes of all the amal-gamated tribes were coming to light.

They did not use *baraboras,* and thereby differed from the Innuit. Rude, worse-for-wear tents made up their residences for the time being. Steve said that as winter approached the tribe would move to more permanent quarters. In the chief's tent lay a pile of half-dried caribou skins and moose antlers of last season. He offered us our pick for a bottle of the much-demanded " hootchinoo," just as though we went about loaded up with the stuff. " Get thee behind me, Satan !" murmured Ralph, for really the heads *were* tempting. Such magnificent antlers, with a span of anything up to seventy-two inches ! We admired, and passed on.

I shall never forget the filth of that settlement. The eagles and the crows descended and ascended steadily, but for these scavengers the health of the community must have suffered considerably. Children rolled about in piles of rotting fish, unwanted skins putre-fied on heaps, fearsome scraps slid beneath our boots —nuff sed ! We fled to our canoes thankful to start off again on our journey. This camp being passed, every sign of human occupation in this remote corner of the world faded.

On these quiet waters, where the trappers ceased from troubling, for the reason that as yet no trapper had found them out, the beavers were unmolested, and could be seen in great numbers all along the banks. One or two daring spirits swam out to us and investigated thoroughly the great trespassers, lifting rounded noses clear of the water, sniffing, and gazing at us with beady, interested eyes. Then, satisfied that there really was something very unto- ward afoot, the investigator dived quickly, and in turning over the strong wide tail hit the water with a smack, a *sauve qui peut* signal, which sent every beaver scuttling. They are wondrous little animals, with their endless schemes and plots and plans.

It is difficult to see a beaver actually at work on tree-felling, because the little creatures are only busy at night, but the result of the labour is very apparent. For the most part the trees felled are of small girth, cottonwoods and poplars, but here and there we came on a few really large trees cut through by the sharp teeth. The provender for winter is then dragged— just the top branches—to the river's edge, and thence to the beaver pantry down below their houses.

Cecily and I overhauled one beaver residence, un- doing it from the top, for there is no ingress save by diving down into the river, and coming up the narrow channel leading to the marvellously planned little house nestling upon the bank. Quite imposing miniature residences, domed, and made of logs and sticks, all plastered together with river mud and clay. In the centre of this bee-hive apartment we found everywhere exquisitely coated with grass and more mud, every interstice snugly lined, making a warm nest for the facing of the Northern winter. Though the river be frozen for miles around, the food, tightly packed away deep below the surface, is always get- at-able, and needs but a dive to bring back a succulent bit of bark from the supply. Mr. and Mrs. Beaver alone dwell in these houses, no mother-in-law or sisters, or cousins, or aunts. Just Mr. and Mrs. Beaver and the youngsters of one season.

On two of the backwaters of the Kuskokwim River we found beaver dams of great size, amazingly planned. One was in the course of construction, the other—alas—useless now, and all its little engineers and contractors were dead and gone. The hand of the trapper is over the land, and where for generations the beavers have worked unmolested the day inevitably comes for their whereabouts to be discovered.

The life of the trapper is a terribly hard one, working as he usually does all alone through the bitter winter that he may catch the fur-bearing creatures when their pelts are at the best. He has a string of residences dotted about his district, for his traps are laid over a great tract of country and each trap is visited once a week or so, if possible. With the aid of his snow-shoes the trapper can put a girdle round his little world.

The sky was intensely blue and almost always cloudless, only the jagged peaks of the mountain monarchs round us were swathed about the summits with white vapour.

In one desolate ravine we found the former home of some energetic trapper, the abode of him, I suspect, who had put an end to the engineering works of the beaver colony near by. The tiny hut was of tree stems, laboriously garnered. It stood there, looking so out of place—man's handiwork—in a

A CAMP IN THE CARIBOU COUNTRY

region in which every element of wild nature reigned sovereign in magnificent desolation.

I have often wondered if our men, on their return journey back to their homes at the mouth of the Kuskokwim, ended the lives of the little beavers whose home we came on by chance. I fear so! The native knows too well the value of every pelt.

Along the shores the wild raspberry and the soapberry, the latter a small red fruit with a very bitter taste, grew luxuriantly, and Cecily and I stewed them in quantities for ourselves and the men. We had to eat the fruit without sugar, because the supply was not equal to any undue demands. Sugar in one's tea is a necessity—to the sweetest of us. The men tackled their portions of the stewed berries with a plentiful bespreading of the seal-oil, a shocking looking feast, but a great favourite with them.

At last the day arrived when it was considered we might vacate the *bidarkas* for good. We found suitable places to cache the small craft, far beyond the possibility of a flood, ready for the returning Innuits as they harked back to the Kuskokwim to make their homeward trip. The dory we hauled to safety, placing it high and dry on a grassy hummock.

We formed camp near by the while we carefully thought out the best line to take, for it was our desire to get some good caribou heads on the divide before we climbed to the roof of the world above the Sushitna. With the map before us we decided on a route, leading us in a fairly even line to the mountains, and then carefully and methodically we divided

P

up the whole of the stores into packs such as men could carry. Women too, for we meant to do our share. It is rather extraordinary how little seems so much, and how much seems so little when it comes to carrying one's all in an expedition like ours.

For two days we rested by the river, dawdling away the time, prospecting around for points and things of interest, until we all felt thoroughly fit and ready to take on the big trek before us. I found a shed antler of a caribou, very old, in a hollow near the stream, which was encouraging as a precursor of the hoped for hunting.

Our little band set out into the wilderness, crawling laboriously up hill and down dale, for all the world like a small colony of loaded giant ants. The ground was very heavy going, the small stones hurt the feet so, even through shooting-boots. They were rubber-soled, and may be that made all the difference. Big journeys are wearisome enough when accomplished with unladen shoulders, but impeded by multitudinous packs we found the task of " getting there " a trying affair enough. It was always a very joyful moment when one might lay one's burden down, and remember that holiday was the order of the hour—until to-morrow.

To save trouble Cecily and I shared one tent between us, and the Leader and Ralph slept in the open. They seemed to think that until rain fell, or necessity demanded, it was such a nuisance to have to undo the carefully made up packages. We had enough open as it was.

The first day we covered ten miles, the next a little more, and the third twelve. A prodigious feat, all encumbered as we were.

On the third evening Ralph sighted four caribou as they crossed a bit of plateau ground, and all about us grew the sort of herbage beloved of the tribe.

In the keen air, and as a result of the exercise, our appetites became enormous, and we began to fear a shortage of provisions. The inroads on the stores were already great. We had no fresh meat, and but a few tins of beef for use in emergencies. Except for flour, tea, coffee, and a few impossible-to-get-along-without necessaries our supplies were not overwhelming in quantity. We were rather alarmed at the prospect of depending entirely on our rifles for a living. The problem of " How to live on nothing a year" was as great a poser to us as it becomes annually at home during the "silly season" correspondence-era. Our men, too, were a ravenous horde, and needed some providing for. Meat simply must be forthcoming, and we planned out a regular campaign for the next day. If possible all four of us must return to camp with a caribou, bull or cow, and some of the surplus meat could be dried. Immediate necessities being provided for, we should be able to take our own time to pick and choose our heads.

We planned and arranged as though a thousand head of caribou waited our pleasure on the grassy, snow-patched slopes. I walked and walked from early morning to late afternoon, until I was thoroughly wearied out, with a hungry henchman walking behind, carrying my rifle. Never a sign of a caribou had I sighted all day. Save for nothing but a red fox, and the marmots—all I suppose unpalatable—my beat was very lonely.

I wandered up the bed of a river, dried up by reason of a natural dam of stones fallen from the mountain, which had deflected the flow of water, climbed upwards towards a rounded bluff, and curving round the moss and snow-covered slopes I espied on the shoulder of a high escarpment, high above me, away to my left, something which looked like a very excellent imitation of a caribou lying down. My glasses told me more. It was a caribou, but the haunches of the animal were towards me, and the head was held so low I could not tell whether it carried decent horns or not. I quite forgot in my excitement and interest that I was not out head-hunting, but larder-filling.

I signed to my man to remain where he was, for the position was too open to allow of his following me. He handed me my rifle with a world of entreaty in his eyes. "I am hungry," they said eloquently, "get me meat." I prepared for a most careful stalk, thinking out the best course to take, and making a big circuit, commenced to climb the hill on the other side to that upon which my quarry lay. I intended climbing until I was level with the animal, and then to creep round the edge of the bluff, when, if Providence had any consideration for me at all, matters would be so arranged that I merely had to shoot to win.

A small brown bird twittered ahead of me, always keeping just in front, rising sometimes with a blithe air of abandon to settle again on the stones before me. He had a slender song, with a silvery ring about it, not many notes, but very alluring and joyous.

I put up a ptarmigan, then another, and another. They flew off with a flurried whirr of wings and chuckles of dismay, swooping down to the river bed below. In summer the mottled coat of the Alaskan ptarmigan blends with the rocks they love to sun themselves upon, and in winter their snowy plumage is one with the whitened landscape.

A few stones rolled from beneath my feet, and I waited in silent trepidation. The caribou was apparently still ignorant of my proximity, though I could not see the creature. We should not meet until I had ringed the summit, but I should have heard any attempt at breaking away.

I reached the altitude which I judged would be the required height, and next instant realized that my plans were well laid indeed, for the cause of all my trouble lay just below me, not more than fifty feet away. I grew quite indifferent then. I knew that I held the trump card. I stood upright, and prepared for action. With a start my quarry awoke from sound sleep. She was a graceful cow, with prettily turned horns, though so small, and well-formed shoulders.

Turning round, paralyzed with sudden terror, she faced me, her limbs rigid, her stiffened legs immovable. Never before have I seen deadly fear so strongly expressed by any wild creature. The scent of a human being, so terrifying to all the deer tribe, reached her nostrils, the sight of the intruder filled her with unnameable horror and dread.

We stood looking at each other, and so interested was I that I made no attempt to get up my rifle, and my position was by no means the comfortable thing I could so easily have made it. The great, soft, round, appealing eyes of the beautiful deer looked full into mine, as though she would read her doom, asking—begging—entreating—praying.

She asked life of me, and I gave her life, even at the cost of mine hunger.

"Pass, Agnes Herbert's caribou, and all's well," I said, laying my Mannlicher down, and subsiding myself.

The creature gathered herself together, and with a rush and an arrow-like dart she cleft the hillside in mighty bounds, disappearing for ever from my ken.

Ah, well! I like not to war with feminine things. They have enough to contend with as it is. Let her go, and my blessing with her.

As to my man, who had seen his certain chops and steaks vanish on the horizon, he met me with a look which should have withered me entirely.

Fortune, tricksy dame, next half-hour rewarded me full measure, running over. A splendid caribou crossed my line, going strong with a little harem of cows about him. They did not see me, as I dropped in my tracks, and I counted on the chance I ought to have should the animals get the wind,

as it seemed likely they would, of my hunter, who
roamed a hillside gathering berries, and eating them
in reproachful mouthfuls. So carefully I watched
every moment of the little group; there were eight
of them, counting the bull I craved, and presently,
sure enough, they halted, pulled together, and with
little tails erect, as is the way with caribou when
startled, trotted back over the path by which they
had come.

Going easily, they passed within a hundred and
fifty yards of me, as I waited a chance to get the
sights on my bull. A cow suddenly sorted me out as
something untoward, and in her amazement cannon-
aded violently against the following animal, thus
disorganizing and jumbling up the party. The bull
was, by this manœuvre, well in range, outlined like
a target, and I speedily took advantage of the excellent opportunity, drew a bead on his heart, and fired.
The caribou ran on for some paces, and getting in
another bullet well behind the shoulder-blade, I saw
the animal's nose touch the earth, and he fell forward
all of a heap.

Circling round in wondering amazement, the cows
with fearless interest pondered on the disaster which
had overtaken their lord. With sniffing noses and
extended necks the beautiful animals ventured very
close to me. A strange contrast to the conduct of
their sister of the mountain top. As my hunter came
up, into the midst of this *embarras de richesses* in
the way of meals for days ahead, the cows trotted
silently away.

Could anything be more exquisite than this head

of my first caribou! The horns were of great length, and measured fifty-four inches over the curves and the spread came out at forty-nine inches. The whole effect was wonderfully symmetrical, with thirty-eight points. From the base to the tops the glorious horns were most gracefully palmated, and the brow antlers matched one another exactly, thus rendering the head unusually valuable. I knew that I had been lucky enough to obtain an extraordinarily fine trophy, even without the "Oh's" and "Ah's," expressed in an unknown tongue, with which my hunter greeted me. Some of his delight was very personal, no doubt, but apart from selfish considerations his congratulations were genuine.

We were about six miles from camp, and it was then getting ominously towards late evening. The larder question was forgotten by me, the distance from camp troubled me not at all. Everything was lost in the wonders of contemplation. The marvels and the splendours of my caribou filled all my thoughts.

A shout from the top of the hill, and in giant strides Ralph came down the side of the bluff, with Steve hurrying after him.

"I've been watching that herd for twenty minutes or more, and was just contemplating rushing down the slopes to meet them. Aren't you lucky? This is a topping head!"

Ralph had not been within shooting distance of a caribou all day, which was rather convenient now, as he was completely unloaded, and could well help to transport portions of my beast to camp. The

"A FAIRLY DECENT ANIMAL."

men accomplished the dismemberment process, and then we all loaded ourselves up, carrying as much as we could. Personally, I hauled along more than I bargained for, and the leg of caribou, which I changed from my right hand to my left, seemed a terribly out-sized and over-weighty affair ere I put it down triumphantly in camp.

The Leader had bagged a fairly decent animal, and Cecily a two-year-old bull, so the wolf was not as yet to howl discordantly at our door.

I may as well say right here that caribou shooting has no sort of interest for me, and the whole thing to do with stalking these animals, if one can call it stalking, is what one would imagine a battue among cows at home might be like. The caribou in the district we shot over having been so little hunted knew no fear, and would just as soon join the hunter as not. In fact one animal did keep Ralph company whilst he skinned her dead lord. It made him feel so small and impertinent for having rudely broken into so friendly a domestic circle he said he could not apologize enough.

The veriest tyro could procure two good heads in three days in the region we trekked across, and as soon as we had totalled that number apiece, shooting no more and no less, we set gaily off for the heart of the mountains. Before climbing much higher we buried our caribou heads in an accessible tomb, to be retrieved later. The head-skins had to be taken with our party, so that the curing process might have no cessation.

CHAPTER XIV

HUNTING THE WHITE SHEEP

Now for our mountain sport
Cymbeline

Here's the place ; stand still !
How fearful
And dizzy 'tis to cast one's eyes so low
King Lear

WE marched each day into more and more exquisite scenes, with only the scenery to interest us, for shikár of any moment was not, and all the signs of big game we discovered for five days was the very old spoor of caribou. We came on it as we crossed a clay tract, which held the impress like a mould.

Giant mountains towered on every side, miles on miles of snowy peaks, great gorges, narrow valleys, hemmed in by precipitous cliffs, were on our line of route. It seemed to me, wearied and often considerably overtaxed, that we should never reach the summit. The place of our desire was always just beyond, like the jam to-morrow, jam yesterday, but never jam to-day of Alice.

Clouds of vapour-like mist enveloped us each day as the sun gained power, a veil of obscurity which looked like being as difficult for us to combat as it would be helpful to the sheep. Through tortuous purple-black gorges whose walls at times excluded the light, and only a jagged line of blue told us that the day was ours to hold a little longer.   Over a shining glacier, a frozen Niagara, emerald tinted and opalescent, to an autumn valley, afire with myriad glowing tints.

The scheme of colouring was Nature's own, and therefore perfect.   Everlasting mountains pressing close about one adumbrate the spirits, it becomes wearisome to be perpetually overshadowed.   This was the smiling valley.   There was nothing wanting.

Here we camped, and knocking over four ptarmigan had a supper worth remembering.   All around us these beautiful birds were forming into packs, in autumn habit, the cock ptarmigan crowing in mournful tones the requiem of the short summer, so different to the laughing chuckle with which he salutes the spring.

The brilliancy of the stars at this altitude was a revelation, and the transparency of the atmosphere imparted a very clear-cut effect to all the surrounding country.   The tiniest crevasse in any mountain limned clear its slopes in magical array.   It was as though one perpetually viewed the landscape through a powerful field-glass.

If *Ovis dalli* had minds like ordinary sheep such a spot as we were camping in would be their Mecca, but, then, they are not common uneducated specimens of the genus, and take up positions at a great altitude with the deep-set purpose of obtaining a clear view of all on-coming enemies.   We were supposed, if

Nature granted us the strength, to be going on climbing and climbing until we climbed even higher than our quarry.

On the mountainous slopes of a range lying to our westward we hoped to be able to take our pick of heads, and divided up the country into blocks in order that there should be no overlapping or poaching on each other's preserves, with the possible result of spoiling chances. Needs having to be fined down to the barest necessities, we decided to form a comfortable base camp where we were, and then go off on expeditions from it which should last as long as possible.

Cecily and I rose betimes, and taking as much and as little as we could, set off for the sheep ground, accompanied by two of the least complaining of our retinue. We climbed steadily all the morning hours, but climbing is very exhilarating if one is in the mood. For there's the wonder, and the interest, the expectation and the mystery, and that indefinite feeling of something new which urges one on and on.

In the distance we saw many sheep dotting the hillsides, but all of them were quite out of our proposed path, and we thought it better to hold on and not be tempted from the straight, if narrow, way.

At last—ideal sheep country. The face of a precipice with tiny dark riband-like bands across its surface, ledges whereon the sheep could find a foothold and keep the balance. Camp was formed here, an insignificant camp enough, on a terraced plateau, with the roar of mighty torrents sweeping down from the snow-fields to sing us to sleep o' nights.

The ridge poles for the tents, one for ourselves and another to shelter the men, took some procuring, and we did not get them pitched until night fell. All our wood had to be carried for a great distance, and the two hunters spent most of the hours hauling it, and the rest sitting practically in the glowing embers of the fire. We could only permit ourselves a small one; hard lines this, as the snow lay patchily all about us and at night the cold was painfully acute. The men never gave over grumbling, and were the most egotistical couple any sportsman was ever burdened with.

Ovis dalli feed in the early morning and late evening, and spend the rest of the day lying down, spying out the land.

We got up on our first morning in this mountain camp in blue-black darkness, a pair of miserable feminines, in shivering distress. But the cup that cheers, which we had to prepare for ourselves, even to lighting the fire, as neither of our men were up and about, soon helped us to a happier state of things. Presently one of the men, a sad-eyed individual, with never a smile for anything, condescended to put in an appearance. Cecily and I christened him Mrs. Gummidge. He simply could not look on the bright side of things, and admired nothing that anybody else admired (*Nil admirari*, etc.) and wet-blanketed everything.

Gummidge knew the country, and had hunted it once before with an American, who got some fine rams hereabouts. Very likely, Gummidge said, all the best ones were shot then. Just as though the sheep world stood still! Below us, miles below, we saw a mass of vapour waiting to encompass all our little world, so it behoved us to hurry. The blue-black light gave place to grey, the faintly outlined precipices took on clearer pencillings, the sun arose in majesty, and it was full day.

Off we started, Cecily, Gummidge and I, striking up the bed of a small frozen water course towards a steep ascent, leading Heaven knows where. After a considerable amount of climbing had been done, involving no small amount of stress on our clothes—Cecily is an ascetic in all but her *khaki* suit—we came on a distinct path, trodden down and clear, the path of sheep for centuries. Following its course we were led to a fearsome corner of the world, a jutting promontory, round which we craned our interested heads. Precipice on precipice met our eyes, going down, down, to a foaming torrent beneath.

Gummidge said he saw some sheep, but though we looked and looked we could make out nothing alive. It is very difficult to see white on white, even with glasses.

Then—yes, yes! Three-quarters of a mile away some goat-like specks, in single file, leaping the terrible ridges, nonchalantly, easily. We retraced our steps for a little way, then climbed again, watching the while the ever-nearing bank of cloud that crept insidiously towards us. Over a spiky ridge, down the slopes of another ravine, and there, round another bit of jutting rock, we saw bands of sheep, many ewes, and, in lofty isolation, groups of rams, in threes and fours. All completely out of range. Gummidge, in unusually hopeful mood, said that the way of the wind did not matter in the least, that sheep could not scent a human being at a greater distance than a hundred yards or so. I afterwards found that this fallacy was held by a great many natives. We did not stop to argue the point, but laid our plans without consulting our hunter. We thought out the ways and means of a careful stalk, a really masterly stroke.

Cecily was to get much higher, and then, by creeping to the very edge of the place, cover as much as she could with her rifle, whilst I did a big detour down a water course, and come up, a Nemesis in *khaki*, just below the feeding sheep. We proposed, but the elements disposed. I dived down and climbed up as carefully and silently as I could, but I took an unconscionable time over it, and by the time my quarry should have been at my mercy the clouds had crept like a protective barrier around them. I could hear the stones falling in showers as the agile feet disturbed them, hear the moving, hear the bleating; and, oh, how I prayed that the mist would lift for one instant, just one little instant!

I sat ever so still on a boulder waiting and hoping, for I did not dare to move, and perhaps spoil the possibility of a shot. I grew numb with cold. A sheep at very close quarters would have been fairly safe with me just then. Rain began to fall, indeed, the mist itself seemed a heavy drizzle of most wetting variety.

I shouted, and all the echoes took it up and bandied my voice from one ravine to another. Then Cecily's ringing treble, and the throaty bass of Hunter Gummidge.

A fog on these Alaskan slopes can be as dense in its own way as a " London particular," and this one illustrated the fact effectively. We all met at last after bumps and falls innumerable, and together tried to negotiate the return to camp. We had completely lost our bearings, if we ever had any. " This way," said Gummidge, dolorously, but a torrent, dull sounding under its coverlet of ice, surged before, and in another instant we should have all been waist deep. This is no game, with waterfalls, ravines and precipices on every side. Hither and thither we wandered, falling and scrambling, until I suggested we should call out the other man from camp by firing three times in quick succession. No help arrived, I expect our henchman was asleep over the fire. There was nothing for it but to stay where we were for the time being. We crowded close together the better to withstand the cold. The minutes dragged by somehow, lengthened into hours, when, even as we meditated on the horrible possibility of being out on the slopes all night, the mist lifted slightly, then rolled down to the valleys below.

That night was hideously cold, even in the valued shelter of our sleeping bags, and the ever useful *parka* on top. We wakened to a clear bright atmosphere, and the very sunrise heralded a Red Letter occasion. As the glinting rays smote the lofty peaks with lances of gold the snow reflected back, heliograph-wise, the message of the dawn of a perfect day. Underfoot the snow patches, overhead the sky of wondrous blue, and so—to the sheep ground.

We took a new direction this time, and as we climbed the rarefied air told on us, and our senses seemed awhirl. Rounding a corner, on a ledge of a precipice, a small black bear, shambling and shy, met us face to face. He fled, wise animal, to a fastness of rock in his rear. We had no designs on his simple life, because our sole quest was the wily sheep, and our watchword was silence.

Outlined on the giant slopes we made out many feeding groups of rams and ewes, but to get within range seemed beyond our powers of limited endurance. On peeping round a rocky wall I saw, perched on a ridge of a black-looking crevasse, a lordly patriarch, whose head seemed to me the most to be desired in all the world. He had got beyond even his powers of climbing, and looked more than a little puzzled as to his next move.

Cecily was behind me, Gummidge behind her, and a long way off, like a klipspringer on a pinnacle of rock, sat our other man, with a coil of emergency rope round about his shoulders. I alone could peer round the frowning fortress, and that only by leaning carefully against the wall of the precipice above us, with due regard to the drop below, a yawning abyss that stretched in unbroken lines down to the glacier beneath.

He was still there, my ram—I called him mine

Q

already. For what chance had he now, unless he contested the path whereon I played Horatius? There was no escape else that I could see. Beyond him a row of upright spurs stood sentinel. Below my cornered prize yawned a crevasse, below again shale-like terraced plateaus, which made feeding ground for many sheep, then the glacier country.

I carefully got up my rifle. The slightest mistake now and I should pay a heavy price. A whisper to Cecily, and she braced herself against the cliff, pressing me with her as tightly as she could. I levered myself carefully against the spur, saw my quarry in one dazzling moment square on, a chance which would have delighted the heart of the veriest amateur, sighted for the shoulder, and pressed the trigger, instantly seizing with a now tremulous hand a piece of rock which seemed to speak of safety. My ram, oh, where was he? He took a header into space, alighted again, bowled over and over, and then in an avalanche of dislodged stones fell smack over the crevasse.

We all got ourselves round the point of the dangerously jutting cliff, in such a fever of excited interest that the difficulties and awkwardnesses of the trip did not worry us in the least. To have hit the splendid ram, and to have lost him!

"Look!" from the hunter, who was lying down, flat on his face, peering over the edge of the crevasse. I crept alongside him. Ah, there! My ram! A crumpled mass, pinned behind a boulder.

Then began a discussion as to how to retrieve him.

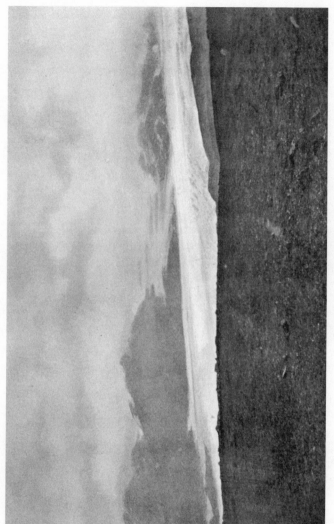

A GLACIER IN THE SHEEP COUNTRY

It does not, I think, really require much strength to do things, but it almost always requires great strength to know just *what* to do. Finally we decided that, as there was no other way of getting at the sheep, one of us must go over the ravine after the trophy. Being the lightest weight the onus of the business fell on me.

A shout for the other hunter, and that tattered person hurried up, taking a considerable time to edge himself round the jutting spur. Alas! his rope failed to reach the depths, a distance of some forty-five feet down. Then began a weary wait in an icy blast the while we sent back to camp for every available scrap of rope. In worried trepidation we watched the ubiquitous white vapour gathering, gathering on our horizon, rolling nearer, ever nearer.

The rope came at last, and it was firmly knotted to our inadequate supply. Gummidge made a noose, and we adjusted it underneath my arms, gave the rope a turn round a convenient promontory, padding the parts where it rubbed; the two men and Cecily took hold of the line, taking up as firm positions as could be found, and with a tremor in my heart and a hope that it did not show outwardly, I crept to the edge of the crevasse, holding the rope in my hands. For a sickening second it seemed to me that I swung clear, the next I crept spider-wise against the face of the cliff, and all the while the rope paid out slowly and evenly.

Not for nothing had I birds' nested in the days of my youth on the great gaunt cliffs of Hall Caine's island. Barring a few rasps to hands and knees I reached *terra firma* safely, when, releasing myself from the cutting rope, I made my way to the sheep, and discovered him, wonder of wonders, more or less intact. Less as to body, more as regards horns. After this bit of amazing luck nothing else mattered.

Fitting the rope around the carcase I gave the word to haul up. My shout was called from rock to rock until all the air commanded. The heavy body dragged over the shale surface, but I held the wondrous head out of the way of harm until up and up he whirled, sometimes coming in hideous contact with outstanding rocks, sometimes catching on needle points, until at last he was hauled to the surface safe and sound. I could see Cecily's excitement from my depths below.

My ladder to safety alighted at my very feet, and the ascent proved a much easier business than the swift coming down, or else it was that the thoughts of my reward at the top made the fearsome journey easier.

The white sheep of Alaska, *Ovis dalli*, takes its name from Professor Dall, who was one of Alaska's earliest explorers. It has its habitat in very inaccessible fastnesses (unless in a region rarely hunted), and has a wide radius, from within the Arctic circle to the Liard River. White in the coat, every hair is tipped as though slightly singed by fire, and in summer the back takes on a darker shade.

Always residing far above the timber line, beyond man's footsteps, the stalking of this *Ovis dalli* tribe, wary and agile as they are, makes excellent sport, and calls into play every quality of finesse and endurance

A MAGNIFICENT HEAD

a hunter of any worth possesses. When dotted about the mountains, away from the snow patches, sheep can be very plainly seen, and in the wonderful atmosphere it was often the simplest thing in the world to judge accurately from a great distance whether or no a head was worth the trouble involved in the taking of it.

The Indians have it that by the rings on the horns you can tell the age of a sheep. A dreadful give-away this for the ladies of the genus! They only carry small, graceful horns, curving backwards, which rarely exceed eleven or twelve inches. The sheep in the locality we hunted over are considered to boast much finer heads than the rams of the Kenai Peninsula country and nearer the coast. A circumference of fifteen inches at the base of the horn would be a very splendid trophy from most of the get-at-able sheep districts. One of mine from this Sushitna River region came out at sixteen and a quarter inches base measurement, and forty and a quarter inches on the curves. A magnificent and wonderful head. One of our other trophies topped fifteen and a half, another fifteen, so that we grew exceedingly uppish, and regarded anything under fifteen as too beggarly for words.

I think it is quite accurate to say that the rings around the horns do tell the age of the carrier, for it is easy to estimate the years of a sheep by the teeth, and almost always the teeth and the rings, taken in conjunction, gave the same evidence.

We had mutton chops for supper the night we

killed our first ram, indeed, we lived on mutton for days afterwards, the supply seemed inexhaustible. Two days of drenching rain followed, a real distress in so exposed a spot. Then hail and icy winds, which blew our meagre fire this way and that. We moved to a sheltered cave, an ideal camp, which had passed unnoticed before, and had a real drying of everything.

We planned a great campaign, and agreed to separate for the day, taking a man each, leaving the tents to see after themselves. My route lay over vast pyramids of Titanic rocks, down gigantic masses of contorted glacier country, and so at last to a series of terraced plateaus over which I could keep watch and ward. Hours I waited, silent and inert, numbed by the cold, hoping that the bunch of sheep I had in view might give me just the smallest chance. So wary were they that I had not been able to approach within striking distance. In a clatter of stones a fresh lot of sheep suddenly rushed joyously towards me. Down the terrible gorges they clattered, easily, out of range as yet. Ah, they have winded me! They rush downwards, change their minds; they come, they come—*towards* me! Now, now or never! Phut! The bullet told. Over went the foremost ram, and for an instant I thought he would die where he fell. Gaining an impetus he rolled over and over, poised for a second on the edge of a mighty ravine his silhouetted form hung for the fraction of a second, and then was gone.

Afire with eagerness I slid and pushed and tumbled my way to the depths below, where I searched and searched, investigating each cranny and every seam. And as I forgot the flight of time the vapour clouds descended into my little world, which caused my hunter much concern. He advocated giving up the search for the day. I espied an escarpment, high above our heads. " The ram will be there," I confidently remarked. But my hunter would have none of it. Impossible, he said, the sheep did not fall in that direction. Why should I be so convinced that it did?

> " I have no other but a woman's reason.
> I think him so because I think him so."

This puzzled him more than ever. He was like an Englishman in requiring a woman always to have an adequate reason. And why should she? A reasonable woman is always stealing something from man's prerogative. I hate a silly woman, but I like a woman to be natural, as God made them, and if He happened to make a few of them reasonable I am sure He never meant them to air this freakish faculty. Perhaps my hunter thought that if I had no plain-to-be-seen reason it must just be a caprice, which does not, in a woman, by any means follow All men, black and white, hate a capricious woman. She so often hurts their *amour-propre*.

I wasted no more words, but commenced to ascend the cliff, the man perforce following me. There, wedged in between Titanic rocks, lay a broken heap of white. I raised the head. Alas! the beauteous horns were smashed beyond all hope of mending, and the handsome head was a thing of beauty and a joy for nevermore.

The man loaded himself up with scraps of mutton, and hid the rest until he could return for it. We had more than a sufficiency as it was, for Cecily returned from her expedition with a fine ram and a small black bear.

The management of natives in any country is always a difficult affair for women to tackle, but with such low-class half-breeds as we had in camp it became a real annoyance. Generations of looking down on femininity, and familiarity with the ways of some white men had made an impression impossible to erase. The contamination of race mixings had worked the inevitable havoc. We tried always to be very fair in our dealings, never requiring anything done which we would not do ourselves; but fairness our men took for weakness, kindness for fear. It was often a puzzle what line to take. Women are not given the same amount of power, in its wider aspects, as men, and they like to use what they have. If not used with fairness, the softer is often as harmful as the rougher.

Matters reached a climax one afternoon when Gummidge entered our tent, without a "by your leave," or "with your leave," and nonchalantly, with all the assurance of a friend of standing, sat himself down on a box of provisions. He commenced to say something, but the words died in his throat as I ordered him out. My fingers had jumped to my belt, and half instinctively I had pulled my shikár pistol out. I frightened my man all right. Familiarities were off henceforward. I thought I should never get over it, never be won over, but—every man has his price, Talleyrand said. I expect he included women. My price was an *Ovis dalli* ram, and when Gummidge brought me the propitiatory news, an hour or so later, I forgot and forgave like a good Christian.

The ram, he said, was a ram of rams, and the span of its horns was wide as this—spreading out his arms. It lay asleep on a hillside. Following my guide I crossed the narrow end of a shining snow-field on to a shale slope, across a small ravine to another valley. There, sure enough, as I could see by my glasses, lay a very fine sheep indeed, motionless, and his head looked topping. I commenced to climb above him, and threw a bit of grass into the air to see the way of the wind. The Fates were kind, and what air there was blew in a favourable direction for me. The little grey marmots scattered to right and left as I disturbed them, in long shrill whistles giving warning of our approach. Sentinels for the sheep these small rodents, often signalling to the ewes the presence of a predatory eagle bent on annexing a lamb for dinner.

I crept on as silently as I could, but sometimes a stone would rattle down the slopes. I waited for the ram to rise and break away. I came within splendid range. How well I'd stalked. How clever it was of me! What a really excellent plan I must have laid.

I gained a still nearer vantage ground, but hated the idea of murdering my quarry in his sleep, it was not sporting. Let him have his chance. "Shout," I said to my man, who was close up with me. He yelled until the echoes rang, and all the distant white

dots that peppered the surrounding hillsides started
in amaze. No movement of any kind from my sleeping beauty, and then I realized that there must be
something untoward. He slept indeed. Death, in
kindly fashion, had stricken him, and he lay, as yet
untouched by eagles and carrion hawks, a gem of his
kind. His perfect head in an attitude of repose, his
splendid horns catching the rays of the setting sun.
A patriarch by the rings, and this easily come-by
trophy was our record head, we never matched it in
beauty or inches.

I could not help feeling amused at the praise I had
so generously given myself for my masterly stalk!
Things one takes are seldom deserved. We take
credit to ourselves to bolster up hope, to counterbalance our liabilities. Unfortunately we are not our
own auditors, and the recording angel only accepts
items that pass muster.

We were on the verge of a grocery famine, having
worked through our small stores of tea and sugar, etc.,
so decided to trek next day to the base camp and refit.
Setting out very early we marched ahead of our men,
and all suddenly came on a path of sheep, the tracks
looking very new. On down another ridge, and
there, right on the sky line, silhouetted on a topmost
pinnacle, stood a fine ram listening. He faced the
other way, and clearly had not winded us. I dropped
into a sitting position, and prayed that the men would
have the sense to keep quiet and not spoil it all.
Nearly two hundred and thirty yards separated me—
for I paced it afterwards—from the sheep, and I

telegraphed with my eyes a message to Cecily to ask her if she would take on the job to add to our bag. I felt I would much rather she missed the creature than I. She smiled, and shook her head.

I sent up silent prayers that it might be written in my Kismet book that I should bring off the somewhat difficult shot. I fixed the two hundred yards' sight, and aimed for the side, the most vital part in my line of vision. Then my nerves began to play me false, and my rifle came down a trifle. This irritating " buck-fever " is not unknown to quite experienced shikáris, and comes, I think, from long inaction. In these minor shoots there is so much tracking with so little real excitement to become used to. At any rate, I, personally, find it very different from shooting, or trying for dangerous game, and I ascribe it to the fact that in stalking game more than able to defend itself the rigour of the chase is continuous, steady, and uniform in daily excitements. All the same I did not spare myself to myself, and the result was a moment of supreme courage and confidence, and I dropped my ram " in one."

Before we made the smiling valley Cecily had added a remarkably fine specimen of the black bear tribe, a quaint-looking little creature, whose coat was in excellent condition considering the time of year, though it was very short, but a good black. Cecily shot it just as we entered the timber belt which had provided us with firewood.

At the base camp we found that Ralph and the Leader had just come in too, as they were all but out of provisions also. We gloated over all the trophies, and my patriarch, whom I had found dead upon the hillside, kept his pride of place, none of the other heads could touch his.

We reorganized things, and fitted out two more expeditions, this time arranging that Cecily should hunt with Ralph and I with the Leader. I was very glad of this new position of affairs, because now the Leader would have to boss the men, and I was heartily sick of them. I expressly begged that Gummidge should be allotted to Ralph, who was in such a state of happiness at being with Cecily again I thought that no amount of dolorousness could affect the idyllic situation.

CHAPTER XV

THE SPIRIT OF THE MOUNTAIN

Nay, how absolute she's in't,
Not minding whether I dislike or no!
Pericles

Lay not your blame on me if you have lost him ;
Why, I have lost him too.
Othello

THE Leader and I made for quite a different part of the ranges, not nearly so difficult as the ground shot over by Cecily and myself. The peaks were much lower, and though there were some difficult bits to daunt us, the place was not a sort of miniature Himalayas.

We chose a delightful spot for camping, a green strip of ground, backed by a rocky escarpment, on which dozens of ptarmigan thoughtfully roosted o' nights. A river ran almost at our very feet.

The first evening led us down the ravines and up again to the hillsides, which were dotted all over with bands of sheep. Sometimes we needed both hands to help us keep the balance, and rifles had to be carried in slings. The men had a holiday, and we tried our luck alone. Half-way up a shale slope, fissured with small dry water courses, we heard a great commotion. Crash! Crash! A noise like a heavy bale of goods falling with a thud as the something struck *terra-firma*, a sound of showers of stones rattling, then—silence. Far up the precipitous sides of the opposite valley we saw a lonely sheep, rushing along post-haste to tell the others to be warned in time. It must have got our wind, and decided to make a bold bid for safety by taking a header down the steep incline.

Clinging spider-like to the ridges we worked our way to a fearsome bit of country, beyond which many worth-having rams grazed in bunches of three and four. To get to the fairly open ground within range it was shorter to cross a natural bridge to the spot, a narrow track leading round the side of the crevasse.

The Leader said he did not think it advisable to travel by this route, as the path appeared to him to have no real ending round the corner, and we should probably have to retrace our steps and so have all the excursion for nothing. I gave it as my opinion that the track continued for some way beyond our line of vision along the side of the ravine. I was not stubborn about this, because I am open to conviction on any point. I am ready at a moment's notice to change completely round if I can see I was wrong at first. I pride myself on being able to say, " I have made a mistake." There are some men, and many women, who think it a sign of strong-mindedness to stick to a thing when once they have said it. I count it greater and more magnanimous to confess an error and redeem it.

We never stopped to convince or think it out, but essayed the bridge of Nature's building. Crossing it, with the cliff on our left, the drop down into the ravine on our right, we covered a few hundred yards only to find that the path was barred as the Leader had feared, by a sheer drop leading down to nothingness. He only smiled at me, and being a man there was no triumphant, "Told you so."

Turning to go back again, we luckily delayed our return for a moment that we might watch the flight of two golden eagles circling far above us in blue ether. Suddenly a mighty dismemberment sounded through all the ravine, a splitting, tearing noise which wakened the very echoes, and the path, our road to safety, receded from our very feet, leaving us with but a scanty foothold. The stones and earthworks of centuries caved in, loosened by the chance passing over. The Leader said I must be very heavy! The gap widened to an impassable gulf, and for some minutes little rivulets of earth and stones chased each other down the chasm just created. We had now got ourselves into a really awkward situation. With the cracking away of the path behind us the way we had come was effectually closed, to climb upwards was unthinkable, for the face of the cliff curved, prow-like, over our heads. Below was the steep shale slope, then a drop, and the dried water course, in the bed of which a few stunted alders struggled to grow.

The Leader looked at me. "You are not frightened?" he asked. And I was not annoyed at such a question as I surely would have been at any other time, for there was that in his voice which said plainer than any words that he would build me a wide path to safety, if he could.

Does not tenderness sit more sweetly on rough men when it deigns to settle there at all? Tenderness should come, I think, in little flashes, illuminating everything. It should not be incessant. If it were it might become obtrusive. Nature has ordained, with her marvellous wisdom, that there should be nothing in the world of which we cannot have enough.

My brains grew like dice in a box, ever so rattled, but I said nothing. I watched the Leader's face, the while he thought out the ways and means. Then— action was needed, he said, instant action, for night would fall presently, and our men would never trouble to come and look for us, and if they did, what could they do? Our only way was to take hands, set our heels firmly, and go sliding down the face of the precipice to the bottom. A bad fall only would result, perhaps not even that. Would I do this thing?

Would I not, for such a Leader? How I loved his recklessness, and yet I never like headlong insane recklessness. Give me the man who weighs the ways, and then regardless of self chooses the one best suited to the end in view. That is noblest. Calm self-reliance, not over-confidence, just collected presence of mind. That is why, I think, that I admire Marlborough more than Wellington, as I cannot help doing. Wellington was admittedly lucky, though wise. His enemies so often gave him victory. But Marlborough foresaw as no other man,

THE LEADER OF THE EXPEDITION IN NATIVE PARKA DRESS

there was no element of gambling in his schemes, and they always seemed to come out as he had calculated. He would chance very little, and was a positivist, and yet when chances had to be taken he took them boldly and fearlessly. There was no half-hearted element in his nature. I would ever take a leaf out of his book; not all the leaves, for some of them won't bear translating.

When my Marlborough asked "Ready?" I clicked my heels together, stood rigid, and waited—if only we had never come along the treacherous path. "Now!" With a sickening rush we slid right over the edge of the kloof, the shaley stones following us in a little shower, and in a sort of mazed shock I realized that the sheer drop was before us to be jumped, or fallen over, somehow.

"Jump!" came a clear, commanding voice. I jumped obediently. A friendly clump of alders broke my fall, and I was not really hurt, save for the knock my rifle gave me as it jerked in its sling, just dazed, and shaken and very much astonished.

"Not hurt?" he asked gently.

"No, Marlborough, not at all."

We went back to camp through the weird silences of the black ravines, with an occasional bleat of a startled sheep to break the stillness, or a shrill whistle of a disturbed marmot as he sped over the ground ahead.

After supper we sat on our terraced plateau, dwarfed by mountain giants, enfiladed on all sides by mighty ravines, marvelling at the wealth of beautiful stars.

R

Never before had they seemed so lustrous, so dazzling in brilliance.   Marguerites in a sea of blue.
Little filmy clouds, shadow-like, flitted across the face
of the heavens.   The stage was set for a drama.

I had turned in for the night, but at the Leader's
call I turned out again to see that wonder of wonders,
the Aurora Borealis.   Contrasted with the inky blackness of the ravines about us, the desolate wastes of
mountain, glacier, and stream, over which the marvel
cast the brilliance of its forked spears, the light
seemed extraordinary, awe-inspiring, and intense.
Right over the heavens from end to end the silver
glory shimmered, an emperor's diadem, and from
the glowing mass sudden flashes and tongues of white
flame quivered across the sky, putting the stars out.
The ravines gave up the secrets of the night, the
mountains, silver-tipped, limned clear their slopes
in the wondrous Polar lights.   Marvel of the world,
how exquisite!   Never still, moving hither and
thither, tongues and forks and darts and spears of
molten silver.   It seemed to me, watching, that from
such a vision of splendour a Jupiter must arise,
radiant, glorious, transfixing Phaëthon in chariot of
gold.

Contracting, spreading wide again the silver arrow
shafts, in even waves and billows of flame the lights
died out, suddenly as they came.   Then again from
out the high blue arc the marguerite-like stars
twinkled and shone.   For some seconds, to my delighted eyes, the wondrous Aurora still glowed,
unforgetable, and with a brilliancy which seemed to

exist in my retina long after the magnificence had paled and fled away.

With the dawn came a silver mist of rain, light, but most penetrating, and it was not possible to see clearly for more than fifty yards ahead. We played patience in more ways than one, and I understand that there are some ninety ways of doing it.

We were really anxious to bag a ram to fill our larder, for we were trenching on the stores again. The men were exceedingly anxious to be allowed to try and shoot a ewe, as a native is permitted to do at all times and seasons, but we managed to stave the thing off by saying confidently that we hoped to return from the next stalk with a quantity of meat.

The following morning dawned bright and clear, and it did not need our glasses to tell us that the hillside opposite our camp was dotted with myriad moving sheep. It was a " hen " party though, for counting up to one hundred and ten we could not spot a decent head among the number.

We set off along our side of the river, Steve following in our wake, and commenced the ascent of the cañon, whose slopes were some 1,500 feet high, and fairly sheer, in places really precipitous. At the summit, crossing an undulating bit of plateau country a fine ram got up from nowhere, and standing a moment in terror-stricken amazement, actually bolted straight towards us. At sixty paces off it pulled up in a great slide, with fore-feet planted well together, head slightly lowered, a formidable looking creature.

Place aux dames, in our shoot, anyhow.

I fired, and missed ignominiously. It seems a ridiculous thing to clean miss so large a mark as an *Ovis dalli* ram at sixty paces. But when winded, after a long, hard climb the hands are apt to be very unsteady, and an odd trembling of the limbs affects a certain number of us.

I felt very small as the Leader raised his rifle to mend matters. All this takes a long time to tell, but it happened in the fraction of a moment really. The ram, not moved by my fusillade, presented a most desirable chance, standing broadside now, quivering; he seemed almost magnetized with terror.

Bang!

The bullet passed over the back of the sheep, and for that animal the spell was broken, and he bolted incontinently, slipping and sliding down the slopes.

"You might say it for me too, will you?" I said to the Leader, who was saying things to his rifle, as he regarded it closely, as though wondering if he might portion some part of the blame to the weapon.

Steve was heartbroken. Why not kill a ewe, and have done with it? We could get any quantity, he said, without travelling so far. Just as though our object on the trip was to keep these natives going with unlimited provender!

At that moment a bullet hit the ground about four paces from us, another fell ominously close to Steve, who ran round and round in a circle in a most ridiculous manner, as though by keeping moving he might avoid the hail of lead. Another and another bullet struck the rocks near us, and we were just about to fly on the wings of terror to some likely bit of cover when suddenly, on the peak above us, a tatterdemalion figure appeared on the sky line, and slowly sauntered down to us. He showed no surprise at seeing us, expressed no regret for making targets of us, and he did not seem in the least inquisitive as to whence we came or why. He stood leaning nonchalantly on his rifle, and let us admire him; he knew we were doing so, and indeed we could not help it. A great sombrero curved on the red-grey hair, which fell to his shoulders, a wavy beard grew to his waist, and in the interregnum between it and the top of his trousers was a band of red leather stuck full of cartridges. A scarf of red was knotted about his throat, and ever and again we caught a glimpse of a lump of Cassiar gold, big as a pigeon's egg, doing duty as tie-pin. This romantic figure of the mountains, who had been doing his best to send us out of this world, said he guessed his bullets had fallen " kinder close." He was real mad at missing a fine ram, so blazed away anyhow.

" Rather a waste of cartridges," I said, thoughtfully.

" Say so, ma'am," our friend answered, " but you waste them or words these times."

He invited us to lunch with him upon the mountains, striding on ahead the instant the invitation was given, as though he were a Pied Piper we must fain follow. So he was to Steve, for at the first mention of food, that worthy practically ran the trail at the heels of our host-to-be. Round the green slopes, climbing still at an easy gradient. And set in a little cleft of an overhanging rock, a Titanic mass of granite, with three sides of the walls ready made, stood a crude, stern homestead, with frontage of the grey, grim rocks. It had all the appearance of Druidic remains. It was Alaskan beginnings really, or perhaps endings. I don't know. No window, an entrance for a door, a pile of wood ashes where a fire had been, a roof of alder branches, banked outside with earth. There was no furniture whatsoever, a heap of blankets lay in dishevelment in a dim corner.

The forequarter of a sheep hung on an outstanding point of rock, most convenient walls had this small domicile, with hat stands and pegs ready made.

Presently strips of mutton frizzled on the stones before a small wood fire. Help from on high to Steve, who scarce waited for the flesh to warm through ere he seized it with greedy fingers and devoured it *au naturel*. This was the simple life if ever it was lived.

"Guess you are speculating what I'm doing here?" said our host, in between moments of gnawing a mutton chop. We had no bread or biscuit.

"I confess to a slight feeling of curiosity," replied the Leader, "but of course——"

Slight feeling of curiosity! I nudged him furtively. I did hope he would not pretend we were not consumed with inquisitiveness. The detective-like propensities which lie dormant, unless they are active, in every woman, were all alert in me now, and I judged, and considered, and decided the case every five minutes.

A GOOD RAM

" 'Twas a game of poker." The red-grey head nodded towards the Pacific Coast, as though locating the scene of the catastrophe. " *He* cheated, and— wal, I shot him dead!"

We went on eating, to all appearance quite uncon- cernedly, though I remember being thankful that Steve sat out of earshot.

" You'll not give me away," said the great rugged creature, with a kind of certain confidence. " I'm glad I told you, guess it's kind of lonesome up here."

" How long must you remain?" I asked, a wave of pity for the broken man surging in me. " Surely you will not winter at this altitude?"

" No," he said, dully, " when winter comes I'll turn trapper, and take to the woods."

A group of four rams passed below, pulling up to graze; the Leader picked up his rifle, handling it as though he was glad to be recalled to the present, sighted carefully, and bang! Another try. The rams raced off, but one lagged behind, going with difficulty. A well-planted bullet finished the busi- ness, and the sheep jumped clean into the air, an expiring effort, then fell a-heap.

As the Leader ran forward down the hill to in- vestigate he put his foot into a pitfall that waited for the unwary, and fell heavily. He was in great pain, too great to bear sympathy just then. I have always found that the axiom about a woman being such a ministering angel rather vague and indefinite. Cer- tainly it says, " When pain and anguish wring the brow, a ministering angel thou." It all depends upon how long the pain and anguish have lasted. At the first shock of anything of the kind the instinct of a man in pain is to creep away like an animal and hug his wounds in silence. The woman who attempts to offer sympathy at the first onslaught of the anguish which is sufficient to wring a man's brow, stands a very good chance of hearing—*sotto voce*, of course—desires expressed that some beneficent being or other would take her away and wring the ministering angel's neck!

Very rude, but—my advice to ministering angels is, don't commence to minister until the psychological moment. Then bring up the sympathy in cartloads, and you cannot overdo it.

The big romantic murderer helped to carry the fallen Leader to the Druidic cottage, and most unlike a murderer—I have really very little experience of the genus, this was the first murderer I have met in society—helped to ascertain the damage. He diagnosed the case as a sprained ankle, and put his country seat at the Leader's disposal.

Steve went back to camp with orders to bring up my tent and some stores to this roof of the world, where we had to sojourn awhile whether we would or no, as the Leader could not put his foot to the ground.

It was a land flowing with milk and honey for our men. This spirit of the mountain had but to wave his wand, and lo! a sheep, ram, or ewe, it mattered not, fell before it.

I made some bread from hops, and cooked the dough in the ground in a tin pan, with glowing wood

ashes set around and over it. The poor murderer
had not tasted bread since he fled up here, a month
ago. He had mixed up flour with water, and cooked
it over the fire. My bread was to him what a lump
of cake would have been to me.

Below the Druidic cottage, on a rock platform,
guarded on all sides by forbidding precipices, a
pair of golden eagles had an eyrie. The friendly
murderer told me of it, thinking I might like to see
it. He called the eagle residence "a nest." Somehow it seems to me that such a word, the simplicity
of which strikes home to all of us, is out of place
in connection with the egg-home of the King and
Queen of the air. Eyrie is much higher sounding,
therefore more suitable. Nest is almost *lèse majesté*.
A King would be out of place in a nest. He might
possibly condescend to inhabit an eyrie. Then
there's the old world meaning to add lustre to the
word. Eyrie came, I think, from the Saxon "eghe,"
with the g sounded like y. Modern English would
get that to eggery, and old English would make it
eyrie. Chaucer, too, wrote of egg as "ey."

Leaning over the edge of the cliff, with my obliging friend the murderer hanging on to my coat with
a good firm grip, I could see the great heap of nest,
four feet or more across, and with my glasses two
young birds, fully plumaged, sitting dolorously inside. A second family, perhaps. I don't know.
But it was late in the season for young birds to keep
to their breeding place, unless indeed the youthful
eagles go on using the eyrie until they are quite

big, and able to fend for themselves under any conditions.

I watched the parent birds for hours, as with mighty sweeps they cleft the air, circling with scarcely moving pinions over infinite space, magnificent creatures of the rugged cliffs. I never saw the young ones make any attempt to fly. They simply sat there, Micawber-like, and waited for something to turn up.

The second evening after the accident as we sat by a small wood fire—it had to be small because the men grumbled so at hauling wood such a distance—overlooking a scene of grandeur which baffles description, our host suggested a game of cards. Poker! I fairly trembled. I frequently cheat at cards, either to end the game, or from sheer lack of interest, and almost invariably revoke. If it is possible to revoke at poker I should do so, without a doubt. It really was not safe. Whatever might not the consequences be!

I said very firmly but politely that unfortunately I do not play cards, and as for the Leader, it was a standing joke that he did not know one card from another.

"Read, then," commanded this extraordinary being, "read out of that book you carry in your pocket."

I drew out my Shakespeare, and obediently set to work on *Julius Cæsar*. My audience said that Julius Cæsar " fairly beat the band," whatever that might mean. It was appreciative though, for presently he would know if " Julius," as he called him, ever lived; Shakespeare, too, was he anybody? Did I suppose that Julius Cæsar was as great a soldier as General Howe of Bunkers Hill—it was easy to read the hero worship in the haggard eyes —and this Shakespeare, would he be as handy with his pen as Mrs. Beecher Stowe?

It was an odd quartet. Julius Cæsar, Shakespeare, General Howe, and Mrs. Beecher Stowe. Never mind, different as they are, each name rings for ever down the corridors of time.

As soon as the Leader could move—four days afterwards—we trekked away, for we had so much to do in a very given time, Cecily and Ralph to meet, the moose hunting, and the locating of our new men who were to come up from Cook's Inlet.

We left our friend of the Druidic cottage as much of our stores as we could possibly spare, and the last we saw of his solitary figure was the red-grey hair waving in the breeze, and the glint of his fiery tie. Cecily and Ralph waited for us impatiently in the base camp, and having loaded ourselves up with all the new trophies we trekked for the moose country.

At last the fringe of a mighty forest belt, a mass of greens on greens, and wonderfully timbered glades. We prospected carefully round as we gained the Sushitna for signs of our servants to be, but the great silences were unbroken. Our servants from the Kuskokwim settlement kindly agreed to remain with us until the new followers arrived to take over, and the four of us settled down to the most enjoyable sport of the trip.

CHAPTER XVI

IN THE PRIMEVAL FOREST

By honour, truth, and everything, I love thee so
Twelfth Night

She'll not be hit with Cupid's arrow ; she hath Dian's wit
Romeo and Juliet

And I myself will see his burial
King Henry VI

Now began the times of times in the moose world. Every Jack was seeking a Jill, rushing through the vast forests to find her, roaring out his love troubles, calling defiance to rivals, thrashing the trees with vigorous antlers. All around we heard them, in the tense silent nights, and our world seemed a-hum with weird sounds, which carried on the new frosty air with great distinctness.

From the early days of September the bull moose, monarch of all the deer tribe, travels rapidly, from the low-lying swamps and rivers where he sought, after the last of the snows, the sweetest willow shoots, to the higher grounds, after the cows sequestered in the sheltered forests and secluded timbered glades. The calves are born early in the June days, and here, in the primeval forest they all remain until the heavy snows drive them to lower grounds.

In Alaska the primitive birch-bark horn is not used

252

as a lure to attract the bull by imitating the "Come hither" call of the cow moose. In the New Brunswick backwoods many gallant beasts are lured to slaughter through answering this alien call of the wild. The Mic-Macs, too, are past masters at it. There are very few men in Alaska who make a success out of moose calling at all, and the ones who are adepts use, instead of the counterfeit mating cry, the challenge of the bull. Both forms of "sport" are very low down ways of procuring splendid heads, for used successfully there is no difficulty in getting a choice and to spare. To my mind this calling is the antithesis of sport, since it is not argued, I suppose, that there is any overwhelming difficulty in shooting so large a bulk as a called-up moose, standing like a target. If one is not allowed the pleasure, and the interest, of still-hunting him, I would forgo the delight of possessing the finest moose head in all the world if it came to me by the mere luring of the noble creature into my very presence by an artificial cry. There is something rotten in the state of Denmark here.

I know that this system of calling is acceptedly installed, is held in honour among most sportsmen, and who am I that I should judge; but I am proud to say that what moose we got we worked hard for, and they had their fighting chance. We certainly were not tempted at first, for none of our Bering Sea men could counterfeit the war challenge at all, and attempts at imitating Mr. Moose on our parts, with the idea of making observations, were much more reminiscent of a person in the throes of *mal-de-mer* than anything else. Steve had a way of hitting the trees with a stick, which he said was in imitation of the noise a bull moose makes as he thrashes the willows with his antlers, preparatory to going for a hated rival.

Any sort of noise will bring up moose in this strenuous season, and they have been known to come right into camp, attracted by wood chopping. Still-hunting for moose in the primeval forest, requiring as it does knowledge of the habits of the quarry, skill, finesse, endurance, and scheming, is surely one of the most heart-gripping forms of stalking. I loved it, and played the game to the top of my ability.

I saw my first bull moose when out early with Steve for guide. The forest seemed possessed, and as we crept through it, in moccasined feet, eerie sounds of moving moose met my listening ears. But I saw nothing. Thrash! Thrash! A moose, with sharp rattling noise, polishing his antlers. He gave a coughing, panting roar, and it sang through the woods. I crept on warily, praying that the wind might be favourable. Alas! the unkind breezes carried the warning, and I heard a crashing of the undergrowth, a rush of galloping hooves striking the dry ground. I moved on, and a short tour round some fallen forest giants brought me to a bit of thickly timbered country. A bull roared close to me, so close indeed that we must be practically in each other's presence. I could hear his quietest grunts distinctly, and located him to a nicety by them. I feared to move, for now that the frosts were so sharp at nights the recesses of the forest did not thaw out much in the sunny hours, and every twig and branch snapped sharply as one trod upon it.

Into my line of vision strode the giant deer, a king of his kind. I could see his great bell hanging, see too the glimmer of his brown antlers with their whiter shining tips. It appeared to be a fine head, but through the intervening trees it was difficult to make absolutely certain. I did not wait, but took my chance, not a particularly good one, I am glad to think, for I missed ignominiously, and the big bull rushed away in the thick fastness in front of him, going as easily as though he were negotiating park land.

I followed on his tracks as quickly as I could, a hopeless and useless task, and encumbered as I was with a rifle and shod in moccasins, the going was rather difficult. A piece of alder struck me across the face, a stinging blow, and stopped my progress for a moment. A cow moose crossed my path, at some distance, and after her raced a love-lorn swain, a two-year-old with indifferent head, and stubby antlers of small span.

The most noticeable thing to me in this tracking out of the large deer of the Northern wilds is their immense indifference to danger. Not exactly indifference, for they see after themselves to a certain extent, but compared with the alertness of the African antelopes, with their sentinels and outposts, every muscle taut for their instant flight, these denizens of the Alaskan forests seem absolutely lethargic, and lymphatic. Of course, on the constant watchfulness of the antelopes of Africa depend their every hour of life, menaced as they are on every side by beasts of prey. The moose and his kind has little to fear from any enemy save man, and but for the country he chooses to inhabit the stalking of moose would not be a matter of tremendous difficulty. Possibly if they lived in the open they might adopt different methods and modes of precaution.

Back to camp after a blank morning, and yet not entirely blank, for the sight of one's first moose is a Red Letter day of a kind. Perhaps, too, the head might not have turned out nearly so splendid as it looked to my excited imagination. So I consoled myself and hoped for "Better luck to-morrow."

In a world of love-making it was perhaps fitting that Ralph should come to me with his amatory confidences. He loved Cecily; oh, how much he loved Cecily! To think of it, that a jungle man, more used to bloodshed than to tenderness, should come to play Romeo!

All his trouble—no love affair is happy if there's no trouble in it—lay in the fact that, being comparatively a poor man, he could not ask a rich woman to marry him. Why not, I wanted to know? Love should not be confounded with money.

"Sometimes money confounds love," said Ralph. "What then?"

The dear fellow propounded a scheme of schemes to me. How would it be if he asked Cecily to make over her fortune to a fund for the Alleviation of the Sufferings of the Cree Indians, or a Mission to Distressed Dervishes? Anyway, something like that, and then they could both live on his small income, his very own to ask her to share. I smiled at his earnestness, and tried to be duly serious.

"That would be silly," I said sententiously. We used to hear that President and Mrs. Kruger lived on the extra allowance called "the coffee money," but history never said, because they were able to do this, that they were foolish enough to return the Presidential salary. "Cecily is grovelling in the river for salmon," I added; "go you and grovel too."

I was in the confidence of both the lovers, for Cecily was a lover too all right, though she was so full of doubts and fears. Being a sensible woman, and a thinker, she knew that marriage often proves a terrible destroyer. One of the saddest things in life is that love is destructible. Would not this affection of theirs, which was an anachronism, and should have belonged to the days of chivalry, succumb to marriage? Better not to force fate.

I do love the beauties of Nature, and Nature too for her bounty and forethought, but she kills everything. She will not let you *keep*. It is the one thing that she strikes at. It seems so cruel. I who love her so much should not call her cruel, but—doesn't it seem hard? "Here you are," she says, "take anything you want. *You can have it to play with for a time.*" And she appears to let you have love for a shorter space than anything else. What is the

S

reason, for she has an admirable reason for everything? Oh, never mind the reason! Drink the red wine! *Carpe diem!*

"Don't you hope they get engaged at last?" I asked the Leader, as I watched him cleaning his big moose head.

"Yes, I do," he answered, with enthusiasm for such a misogynist. "We must have a disaster of some magnitude before we can find an adequate excuse to open the last of the bottles of emergency champagne."

Then—what a squabble royal! I don't know which of us enjoyed it the most. We were not capable of paying each other off, for there was no antagonism between us. We fought with our wits, not with our hearts. Are we human beings capable of hurting what we love in our inmost hearts? Do you not think that to inflict a smart by way of retaliation argues that the heart does not really love? To be piqued is one thing, to seek revenge is another. Sometimes little hurts are given by accident, they are trifles and soon heal. There is no wound so deadly as one given by design.

We opened the champagne that night. Cecily had met her Waterloo.

A woman's devotion is a wonderful thing, perhaps the most beautiful thing in this world. She seems to play with love for a time, then gives a little, then takes it back, then she pretends, then she won't give any, then from pity spares a particle, then she is sorry, then she doesn't know her own mind, and at last she gives, not half, or some with reservations, but all, everything on earth she possesses, and if she had her soul to bestow she would add that without a thought.

The forest scenery around our camp was exquisitely beautiful, but there was a chilling solemnity in these Northern woods absent in those of sunnier countries. Perhaps the frequent finds of skeletons of trees, burnt, or decayed to the heart, turned the woodlands to a charnel house, or it may be that such deep, unfathomable tangles overshadow one, being so entirely different to the calm uniformity of the horizons in our English forest glades.

In the heart of a wanton maze of green, by a mighty shaft of granite, Ralph and I, hot on the track of a never-to-be-come-up-with-moose, discovered the whitened bones of a man, mouldering at the base of the wild monument. By the shape of the skull we saw that this was no Indian, Aleut, or member of countless other tribes, but some one of our own race, fallen by the way—some one, perchance, whose love for the lode had been his death, or lonely trapper, overtaken by the cold of the chill solitudes wherein he hunted. It was a saddening moment in our day. I am as easily made sad as glad, I cannot go humdrum through life. I must take things intensely or not at all.

I wanted the piteous bones buried, far from the tearing winter winds, or hurtling forest branches. Ralph, too, might read a few words from the Burial Service, because " it " was a white man.

" I haven't got a Prayer-book in my kit," confessed Ralph shamefacedly. " I—er—I don't think I ever carry one."

" Then you ought to ?" I said sternly. " And why haven't you got one ?"

" If it comes to that," he returned, rallying a little, " why haven't you ?"

We dispensed with play-acting a service, and tenderly placed the poor bleached bones in a grave made by the granite mass, an everlasting monument, silent witness of the sad beginning, silent guardian of the piteous end.

Next day we left the vicinity of our gruesome find, and, at the Leader's command, moved to another stretch of forest country. Not until then did my spirits recover their balance. Sorrow is like a fish that seizes my hook and drags my float right down, but it cannot stay down, my tendency is always to come up. But for the fishes I should always be up. When he saw my float below, in countless ways the Leader sought a landing-net, took the fish and flung it far away.

The mosquitoes hereabouts had entirely disappeared, and in place of these wretched little pests we had the moose-fly, a small round atom, black in colour, with a venomous bite. The first result of an attack is a small round red spot, which presently swells up, and causes great pain. The face can be protected from all the onslaughts, but gloved hands in still hunting do not make for stillness at all.

Around our new camp, which was situated on a

backwater of the Sushitna, the profusion of shed
antlers told us that this spot was a wintering ground
beloved of numerous moose. Our men reported many
recent tracks leading to the river, and in the evening
Cecily and I investigated for some miles along the
reaches. Steve led us to a ford where obviously moose
crossed to the opposite bank, too deep for us to tackle,
and we planned an excursion thither on the morrow.
Making a wide detour, into the forest belt we turned
our steps campwards, and had hardly covered more
than half-a-mile before we suddenly jumped a bull
moose, who rushed away, his antlers striking the trees
in resounding whacks. When going off, startled, a
moose crashes through all obstacles, anyhow; but
given their own time, they can pass through the
forest like wraiths, travelling silently as any panther.
Here and there we crossed trails of great distinctness
and width, evidence of the passing of numerous moose
to the river extending over a period of many years.

Following up one trail in desultory fashion, all suddenly I realized that walking leisurely along, the
same way as we ourselves were travelling, was a fine
upstanding moose. He browsed as he went, or
sniffed the ground, and I caught the gleam of antlers
as he stooped. I could get in a shot which would
rake through to the off-shoulder, so, signing to our
man, who was now beginning to prance about in his
excitement lest I should fail to see so splendid a chance,
to keep quiet and give over signalling to me—just as
though a moose at seventy yards' distance in open
ground could be easily overlooked—I aimed clear of

the hindquarters to the most vital part in my line of vision beyond the hip, and fired.

I saw no effect of any kind, save that, half-turning, the great moose looked at me, fair and square. Like some prehistoric monster he stood, his wondrous head outlined by the greens of the forest around him. Seizing the short opportunity I put the ivory foresight on his forehead, beneath the antler nearest to me, and—in a maze of excitement—pulled the trigger. The bullet told, and the giant deer staggered to the shot, ran on for a few paces with lurching gait, fell to his knees, then raised himself to career on for a few yards further, when, overtaking him, I ran in, and at thirty paces distant got in a heart shot which was instantly effective, and my first moose crashed to the ground. The massive antlers struck the earth so heavily I almost feared for their safety, forgetting the terrific blows they are constantly called upon to sustain.

Cecily and I examined the head with interest and delight; it was particularly finely formed, and the points, instead of being the stubby affairs one so often gets on moose antlers, were quite sharp and tapering. When measured it came out at sixty-five inches span, and was somewhat white in colour, owing to the fact that it had not long been out of velvet. Indeed, tiny shreds still adhered in places from the tips. Our men had it that the larger the moose the longer it took to get the horns clean. The bell, or growth of hair, which hangs from beneath the throat, was not long and thick in this specimen which

I shot, as it was on two or three other moose bagged by members of our party. My beast, being a mature animal, had the adornment in so bedraggled and hairless a condition that the appendage ceased to be a thing of beauty and became a mere bit of loose skin. We measured the bell of a younger moose which Cecily shot, and it came out at fourteen inches long, and the hair was very coarse, anl shaded from brown to grey black.

Steve set about taking the head-skin, which was going to be such a lengthy business we persuaded him to decapitate the great deer and struggle to camp with the whole head. He wanted some of the meat, but couldn't manage to carry more than he was already burdened with, so we comforted him by saying he could return for another load to-morrow. We helped to carry the weighty head by tying it on to a stalwart tree stem, taking one end, the man the other, and the great trophy swung in the centre. On the walk home the weather broke suddenly, and drizzling rain fell, which was the precursor of a storm which raged all night. A terrifying affair enough, and as the tearing wind whistled through the forest I couldn't help thinking what a chance there was of our being flattened out by some tree going down before the wrath of the tempest. All around us the branches crashed to the earth, the tents were blown this way and that, and our occupation during the midnight hours was to hang on to our canvas residences that we might have them for another night. With the morning the fury of the gale had passed, but it took us some little time to collect our scattered belongings, and ascertain the damage done.

After breakfasting on the everlasting salmon, Cecily and I made our way to the spot where we left the meat on the previous evening. I rather wanted to retrieve the feet of my moose in order that they might be set up somehow. We travelled very softly, as it behoves a hunter to do in a part of the world in which the most unexpected things happen at any moment. We stopped to pick and eat a few salmon berries which grew in profusion near the place where the headless moose lay.

Suddenly, with very little parting of the under-brush, a hunched, cat-like form streaked along, a piece of thieved meat between its jaws. Cecily, quicker than I can set it down, had her rifle up, and the quick bullet caught the retreating animal in the hindquarter. It was a lynx, and a very well set up specimen too. On being hit the poor creature gave the most piercing shriek, a concentrated essence of cat-calling, and bowled over and over. Cecily, worried at her failure to kill her beast outright, and grieving for its pain, ran forward, and the cat, with amazing dexterity, turned with flattened ears and vicious, snarling face, and shot towards my cousin with arrow-like swiftness. It flew straight at the calf of Cecily's leg, and its teeth struck in, through gaiters and all, and clung there, tooth and nail.

Impeded by the gripping terror the victim could do but little to free herself, and I ran in, laying my rifle down. I seized a stout gnarled stick which lay conveniently adjacent and brought it down with a swinging smash on to the shoulders of our enemy. The blow was at such close quarters Cecily almost fell with the impact, but the cat, fortunately, let go suddenly, turned a half somersault, and to my immense surprise dropped dead in its tracks. We afterwards found that Cecily's bullet had penetrated farther than we had at first thought. I carried the remains to camp. It was such a beautifully marked beast, with enormous length of whisker, and thick, glossy coat.

Cleaning the wound on Cecily's leg I found that the incisor teeth had made considerable havoc, so I iodoformed and bandaged.

When Ralph returned to camp with a wonderful story of a moose that was missed, he was terribly upset over the lynx episode. If Cecily had been gnawed by a tiger he could not have fussed more. All his regret was that he had not been with us. In that case the accident could never have happened. Isn't it odd, the way in which men consider themselves such lighthouses and pillars of strength?

"And how could you have prevented the lynx biting me, I should like to know?" said Cecily, concluding that her reputation as a capable huntress was seriously impugned. "Besides, I suppose I can be bitten if I like."

For three days we feared blood-poisoning, and things looked quite nasty, but matters took a turn for the better, and bar a few days of absolute lameness, Cecily got off all right. She and Ralph pottered about the camp, collecting birds and a musk rat or two from a little colony who dwelt on the river bank, near to us. We could hear them snorting in the water at night, when all was very still, and the faint aroma which clings about them was distinctly notice-able if the wind happened to be our way. Rabbits, which were very plentiful in these woods, had been warned off the commissariat department. Our natives told us of some unknown and terrible scourge that had visited the rabbit genus, a scourge that had killed them off in dozens. That this plague had not entirely passed was evidenced by the fact that once or twice we came on newly-dead carcasses, and the rabbits had not come to a violent end by the efforts of eagles, lynxes, wolves, or other preying creatures. It seemed safer to abjure rabbit altogether, and nobody fancied it. The ubiquitous spruce grouse abode with us to fill the pot, and dried salmon formed a really valuable stand-by.

Nikolai finally brought home the remains of the moose I shot for the men to gorge upon. The eagles as well as the lynx had found it out, and one way and another it did not look inviting. The men seemed to find no fault with it, and roasted it in strips for every meal.

The cleaning of a moose head is a really big busi-ness, and we had to do a lot of the drying of skins by the fires. The heat of the sun at this time was nothing very great.

On an estuary of the river Ralph was fortunate enough to bag an otter by a very sporting shot. He hit the animal fair and square just as it slid from its holt, quite a marvellous performance when one considers the lightning movements of an otter about to take the water. The rush of the river carried it to a deep-set pool, and we had some difficulty in retrieving the treasure, which we accomplished finally by the aid of a salmon net. Of course, Ralph's otter was only the otter of the Alaskan rivers, not its valuable cousin of the sea, now almost extinct through such persistent hunting. Still, the pelt is a good one, and much in demand by fur traders.

The Innuits were very much upset when they heard of the incident, because they have a quaint superstition against shooting otters, which does not seem to apply to trapping the creatures. They believe that an otter haunts the man who shot it by coming to life again within the murderer's " Little Mary," which naturally causes the greatest annoyance and inconvenience. In fact, there intrenched the otter stays, unless you happen to have some milk or other delicacy to hand, when the revengeful creature may be tempted —but no reliance can be placed upon its actions—to jump back to *terra firma* out of the victim's throat !

Ralph, by extraordinary chance, was knocked up the day following the death of the otter, and, though the temporary indisposition was nothing in the world but a bilious attack, our men regarded the matter very seriously. The skin of the otter swung in the breeze, from the branches of an adjacent cottonwood, but this indisputable evidence appeared to carry no weight at all, forebodings dire were in the mind of each little hunter.

The Innuits are very full of weird superstitions, and all believe in evil spirits who live far inland from the coast, spirits who descend from the Nunataks, or peaks, which are to be seen in the heart of the glaciers. The special function of the Nunataks, so far as I could gather, is to work havoc to the Innuit hunter—to steal the fish from the drying ground, cut the skins of the canoes, drive away the seals to other waters, and generally make themselves all round disagreeable.

At nights around the camp fires I would try and engage the men in such conversation as we could muster, but I could never discover that there were any good fairies in the country to counterbalance all the evil sprites. The goblins of Grimm alone hold sway. Oberon and Titania could not live in the frozen ways of the Arctic regions, needing the suns of the South to gild their revelries.

Much of the folk-lore gleaned by the way from the natives, more especially from the Aleuts, is extraordinarily interesting and weird, but unfortunately very many of the stories are not printable in these days of High Moral Tone, Nonconformist Consciences, and the rest. The older natives yarn away these strange romances, full of fierce sad glamour, loves and hates, and feuds and factions. Alas! that the majority of the legends must remain locked in the memory of the hearer. The " bowdlerizing " of them for books is an almost impossible task. There is one, less lurid than many, which is very firmly fixed in my mind, perhaps because it has for its *raison d'être* the accounting for the creation and appearance at some long-ago period of that priceless creature, now almost extinct, the sea-otter.

A strange old Aleut told me the story as we sat by a flickering fire, beneath a sky of deepest blue, dotted with a wealth of silver stars, wreathed here and there in a veil of gossamer mist. And as the native wove his romance into the silence of the night the witchery of the scene and the hour lent a thrill of enchantment and imparted a sentimental feeling of poesy which, perhaps, the story lacks when told again in England, in plain, bald fashion.

A mighty chief of the Aleuts had a beautiful daughter, and, by another wife, an equally handsome son. Nobody could hunt the creatures of the wild like this young Aleut; nobody flung a spear so accurately, or sought the earliest walrus with such success. These two young people, who lived but the breadth of a river apart, had somehow never chanced to meet until they were about seventeen and eighteen years old, and when at last Fate brought them together she decreed that the ill-starred girl and boy should not know that their relationship was such as to preclude the great burning affection which instantaneously arose between them. When the Aleut chief heard of the desire of the lovers to marry each other his horror knew no bounds, his rage no limits; for the Aleuts regard a thing of that kind as deadly sin, contrary to one or two other nations and tribes we wot of. He came as a Daniel to judge. His commands were issued, and they were to the effect that the young people must never meet again, nevermore hold con-

versation together, on pain of instant death, and that
the sentence should be carried out effectively the boy
and girl were imprisoned in *baraboras* built at some
distance from each other. Love laughs at locksmiths,
and perhaps Alaskan locks are easier picked than
most. The youth escaped, and straight as an arrow
from a bow sped to the prison-house where lived his
father's daughter. Even as they met they were
caught, and so read their death warrant in the fierce,
stern eyes of the offended chieftain.

From the top of a great cliff, down the face of a
precipice, the lovers were hurled to the sea below,
striking the cruel rocks ere the bodies fell into the
water. The spray shot up incarnadined, then—stillness. Next morning, round and round the scene of
the death agony, in ever-widening circles, swam two
strange creatures, otter-like, but more beautiful and
wonderful than the otter of the rivers. The Aleuts,
wise and learned in all animals of their sea and land,
had never before known anything like these agile
swimmers, who remained in the vicinity for some
hours, and then headed to sea to return no more.

The spirits of the lovers had not died, so said Aleut
superstition. They lived on in a new form of life,
lonely creatures of the deep, and from these two sea-
otters sprang the race of the most scarce, much hunted,
exquisite animal of the Northern Seas.

Many more strange, weird tales come to my mind,
but it is so hard to make them readable. Told in the
heart of the mysterious and wonderful solitudes the
barbaric plainspokenness of each legend is, by the

very breath of the wilderness, freed of aught that is— in civilization—counted as unspeakable.

One fine evening I shot a porcupine. I slew him as he made a meal of a piece of bark gnawed from off a cottonwood-tree. My quarry made no attempt to get away, or to conceal itself, trusting to its deadly quills, I conclude, for protection. They were very much in evidence, and their serrated edges were ready and waiting for immediate reprisals. The natives told me that as winter approaches the porcupine in these regions acquires a long growth of hair, which conceals the quills entirely.

Ned carried my trophy back to camp by fastening it to a stout bough, which he carried across his shoulder, and the prickly porcupine swung to and fro a few inches from my henchman's back. All the way home I thought how best to make an appetizing meal of this innovation in our larder. One always hears of this Northern porcupine as being such a delicacy, especially in autumn and winter when they are very fat.

I was like Brillat-Savarin and his first wild turkey-cock.

" I," said he, " was lost in profound reflection, and I thought of how I should cook my turkey-cock."

I wrestled with a similar problem with regard to my trophy, and went on puzzling as to the most reasonable manner of cooking it, until it was time to introduce it to the fire somehow or other. Finally the animal was stewed to a condition resembling leather, and it was a mass of little sinews of the toughest variety. It must have been a patriarch porcupine, and the oldest inhabitant of the forest. None of us liked it at all, and I suspect that the travellers who say that the flesh of this creature is so very appetizing have really eaten something else instead and didn't know it, or, most probable of all, were so hungry as not to care.

CHAPTER XVII

MOOSE HUNTING

(By the Leader of the Expedition)

Well, in that hit you miss
Romeo and Juliet

How mightily sometimes we make us comforts of our losses !
And how mightily some other times we drown our gains in tears
All's Well that Ends Well

AGNES has asked me to describe the hunting of
moose, and instance any particular stalk which still
lingers in my mind. Although a spell of time and
many thousand miles lie now between me and the
scenes herein discussed, yet ever and anon there
comes a gleam of vivid light travelling back across
that bridge of memory which spans all time and
space to help me live once more through never forgotten days.

Looking over cherished diaries of halcyon hours,
there comes a picture of those distant lands, a picture
fresh and bright, as if the artist's colours still lay
moist upon its canvas. Once more I see those distant snow-clad mountains towering aloft in silent
grandeur, whilst from out of hidden ice-bound clefts,
far up among the peaks, a host of foaming torrents
spring, awakening strange echoes with the laughing

music of their bubbling waters. Far below the vast primeval forests lie, as yet scarcely trodden by the feet of men, and still immune from devastations wrought by their destroying axes. Here is the land of mournful solitudes, where oft " the air a solemn stillness holds," and where, when Nature shows her fierce moods, chill blasts sweep down from barren wastes to work destruction 'midst the fading summer leaves.

Who is there amongst us that can listen unmoved in mountain lonelinesses or forest solitudes, to the wild, weird cadence of rushing waters mingled with the sighing of the winds?

Long since I read the words of an unknown writer who was gifted with that golden talent, the glory of words. Time has doubtless dimmed my memory, but I venture to attempt a repetition of the lines, since none which my feeble pen can create will so aptly describe the feelings of a wanderer in the wilds of Northern climes.

" When the wan fires of twilight are dying to a weird and ghostly light, and the woods look lone and spectral against a fading sky, when the silence dares not breathe for dread, and the wind wails once and dies, it is as though some great magician had laid the world under a spell. For the feelings excited by twilight's phantom gloom are restless, fevered, morbid. An hour ago, looking on the ineffable glories of sunset, the soul was touched by a divine longing, raised to invisible heights, set above the reach of Time, with the angelic host in the eternal

DISTANT SNOW-CLAD MOUNTAINS TOWERING ALOFT

places. And then—this spell of twilight, ghostly, vague, elusive, stirring the heart with fearful long-forgotten dreams of evil, of wild despair, and death. It is the fascination that the secret, the unknown, the terrible, have always exercised over the heart of man —a survival, may be, of the primeval belief in the cruelty of Nature, and of the unseen spirits who do her will."

The writer of those lines was surely one who in youthful dreams had wandered through the land of Faëry, and whose thoughts perchance still roam out beyond the great divide to that shore where the waves of Time lie tideless, " soft by the walls of that fair city whose foundations are builded in Eternity." For him, for such of us who feel its spell, the glamour of the wild still murmurs softly through the silent wastes, or beckons with out-spreading arms of beauty, luring us onwards to those Elysian 'fields 'midst enchanted solitudes of far-distant lands.

What is it, this undefined sensation, this indescribable fascination of the magnetic North, wakening in men's hearts such weird feelings as they gaze from lofty heights across boundless unknown regions, where fathomless waters and vast, silent spaces rest peacefully beneath the Arctic sun ?

All the air is laden with perfumes, as countless soft, subtle scents are wafted upwards, borne on the breath of gentle breezes as yet untainted by smoke and dust of cities. Here we stand face to face with Nature in her every mood. Thoughts drift back unknown ages, as we wonder if in bygone years these desolate wastes were fertile regions in which gigantic mammoths roamed amidst luxurious forests, where now for centuries untold their huge bones have lain deep buried beneath the soil. What sudden spell was cast upon the face of Nature? What fierce agency conspired to sweep from off the earth these prehistoric giants?

Over dreary wastes, where once huge pachyderms roamed, the traveller now may journey countless miles whilst death-like silence reigns supreme. They loom insistent still, those weird and long-lost memories, finding responsive notes deep down in our hearts, awakening some forgotten cry, drawing us back across some visionless bridge of dark ages to the time of our primeval ancestors, rousing an unspeakable yearning to pierce oblivion's dark shroud, and live once more in scenes now dead and gone for ever. This, this is the Call of the Wild, and it speaks loudest to those who in childhood were dreamers, who, ever enthralled by elusive charms of unknown mysticism, sought to grasp the intangible, lived in a world of fancy, peopled with a host of unknown sprites.

Ralph and I had been encamped for two days upon the western slope of the great mountain range which forms a divide between the valleys of the Kuskokwim and Sushitna rivers. Our tents were pitched in a sequestered nook overlooking a diminutive lake, from which a tiny stream emerged and flowed onwards to join the mighty Kuskokwim.

Although none of them attained any considerable

size in height or girth, a profusion of forest trees grew around us, and these consisted chiefly of firs, cottonwood and silver birches, which in places were most densely packed, since the region had escaped all forest fires, which in more frequented parts of Alaska have wrought havoc over countless acres of the woods.

Not far from camp the timber line abruptly ended, and beyond there lay an open track of tundra, which sloped upwards till it reached the grassy mountain sides. From this point a climb of some three thousand feet led to the summit of a commanding peak, which we had christened Beacon Hill. On its topmost point our natives collected heaps of wood, and each night a brilliant fire was kindled there, to act as a guiding light and beacon for the natives whom we daily expected from the Sushitna.

From the top of the hill on a clear day the climber was rewarded with a view which baffles description. Far below, on either side, lay the great basins of the Sushitna and Kuskokwim rivers. Gazing out towards the north-east, although some eighty miles away, the vast perennial snow-clad peak of Mount McKinley reared its towering height, a veritable giant amongst giants, the highest and grandest of Alaskan mountains, whose topmost pinnacle has still defied the foot of man to reach it. A lonely watcher on this Beacon Hill, looking upon the boundless panorama of great mountains, wide open valleys leading downwards to the ocean, vast forests dotted here and there with countless lakes, and intersected by winding, silvery streams, might dream that he stood upon the roof of the world. At his feet on every side lay some of the sublimest works which that great Craftsman, Nature, has devised.

At the end of the second day, although we had seen a number of small bulls, we had only succeeded in bagging one animal, since we had firmly decided not to shoot at any heads which we thought did not attain a measurement of at least sixty-five inches span of horns. This standard may sound rather high to sportsmen accustomed to moose hunting in the Canadian forests, where a sixty-five inch head would be regarded as the trophy of a lifetime. Heads of seventy inches and over are by no means rare in the Alaskan forests, and the writer to-day possesses one head which he brought from the forests of Alaska, and when killed the antlers exceeded the gigantic spread of seventy-seven inches.

One evening Ralph and I had wandered far from camp in quest of spruce grouse, commonly known as fool hens, which we shot for the pot with a small ·22 Winchester rifle. These silly birds will fly up into a tree, and the whole brood, including young and old birds, sit calmly a few feet overhead whilst they are picked off one by one with a small-bore rifle. By this means a good dinner may be assured if the hunter is fortunate enough to encounter a few of these birds in his day's wandering. Moreover, the use of a noiseless rifle has the advantage that its small report does not scarce the game in the vicinity, as the use of a big shot-gun will do.

I was walking slowly in front carrying a small rifle, whilst Ralph brought up the rear with a Mannlicher slung across his back. Suddenly we emerged into one of the numerous open glades of the forest which are bare of trees, where nothing save tundra and dwarf bog-myrtle flourish, and there, standing in full view, at less than a hundred paces, on the opposite side of the clearing, a noble bull moose was apparently listening intently, possibly having heard our distant footsteps.

It required but a second for me to hold up a finger to warn Ralph that there was game afoot, and gently stepping backwards I bade him advance to where he could get a good view of the animal.

In moving slightly forward, intent on unslinging his rifle, Ralph unfortunately trod upon a small stick, which broke with a resounding crack. This noise immediately disturbed the moose, since it is seldom that a wild animal thus breaks a twig when moving at its leisure through the Alaskan forests, and this fact is all the more remarkable when we consider the enormous weight of such huge beasts as the moose and bears which inhabit those regions. Although I have watched for hours the movements of these creatures of the wild, even at close quarters, I have seldom heard them crack a twig unless scared into moving at a high rate of speed owing to the approach of danger.

As soon as this old bull heard the snapping of that stick he commenced walking slowly towards the cover of the trees, and Ralph, realizing that he must shoot now or never, began to cover him with the foresight, in hopes of getting one chance of a crossing shot. For a second the great beast stood, and half turned towards us, affording a good chance of putting in a shoulder shot. As Ralph instinctively pressed the trigger, ere the bullet reached its mark, the bull turned diagonally away from us. Before he had put down his foremost foot the bullet struck him somewhere, and giving a convulsive spring sideways, he dashed into the trees and disappeared from sight.

What Ralph said may be better imagined than described, as we hastened across the open glade with but faint hopes of being able to come up with the wounded beast, which seemed to be only slightly hit. After following his tracks a mile or more we found that he had not broken out of a long striding gallop, and scarcely a blood spot was visible, as is often the case from a wound inflicted with the small-bore rifles, such as a Mannlicher, which, in my humble opinion, is the chief drawback to these handy little weapons.

After deciding that our pursuit was hopeless we resolved to retrace our steps, which proved to be by no means an easy undertaking. For during the quest of the spruce grouse, and in tracking the moose, neither of us had taken notice of our bearings, and night was rapidly closing in upon us. In addition to which Ralph had lost our only compass, which he carried on a chain that had snapped without his noticing the event, probably as we forced our

way through some of the dense underwood whilst
tracking the moose.

To make matters worse it commenced snowing
sharply, and in the cool evening the flakes lying
thick on trees and ground helped to disguise any
distinctive trees or landmarks which we had passed,
and might under different circumstances have recognized again.

After wandering somewhat aimlessly for some time
Ralph sat down on a fallen tree, and began to revile
his fate and luck, etc., etc. As he tersely put it,
" to miss the largest moose we had yet seen was bad
enough, but to get wet through, and have to spend
the night out cold and hungry in an Alaskan forest
was the utmost limit which his patience could en-
dure." This was rather amusing, since Ralph prides
himself on being somewhat of a philosopher even
under the most trying conditions. There came to
my memory some old lines which I had seen in-
scribed on the wall of a hunter's hut in the backwoods of western America, and quoting them as near
as my memory could recall the words, I said—

> " It is easy enough to look pleasant
> When life goes along like a song,
> But the man that's worth while,
> Is the man with a smile,
> When everything goes dead wrong."

Had we not got three brace of grouse in our
pockets? Had we not plenty of matches, fuel galore?
If the worst came to the worst we could roast a
grouse on a stick, which is food for the gods any

day. But Ralph would not be comforted. Suddenly he reminded me that on this very evening Agnes and Cecily had promiséd to come over from their camp three or four miles away to have supper with us, and compare notes. Then, and not till then, did I discover the cause of all Ralph's bitterness of spirit! Realizing that something must be done to relieve the present state of tension, I set my mind to work, and at last I said, "Well, as near as I can figure it out we have been moving due north most of the day, since the wind has been from the north, and we have travelled all the time with our faces to the wind."

"True," said Ralph, "but how in this infernal snowstorm when the wind is always shifting, and blows from all four quarters of the globe at once, and in this cursed darkness, how, I ask you, can we tell which is north and which is south?"

My reply was that if he had not been temporarily off his mental balance he could have solved the problem at once, since we both knew that lichen and moss only grew on the boles of trees on the side which was sheltered from the icy northern winds in these Arctic regions. And thus, if we kept walking with the bare boles of trees facing us we must be travelling due south. Suiting my actions to the words I set out, keeping a careful eye upon the bare tree stems, and followed by Ralph in moody discontent.

After walking for nearly an hour we came across a small stream, and trusting it might prove to be the one which flowed from the lake near our camp, we decided to follow its course up stream. Now, as a rule, there is nothing more confusing to a lost man who finds himself at the bank of a forest stream near which his camp is situated; for unless he can recognize some familiar landmark, he may be either above or below his camp, and possibly may decide to follow the river in a wrong direction for considerable distances before discovering his error.

In this case we were more fortunate, since we knew that if indeed this was the particular stream which we sought, our only plan was to follow it up to its source in the lake. Soon as we travelled along the banks we came across familiar spots where fallen trees blocked the watercourse, and just then if we had needed further assurance that we headed straight for home it was forthcoming. At no great distance off a shot rang out, showing that our natives in the camp were firing signals to guide us in the dark. This was a welcome sound, and Ralph cheered up amazingly, as he fired an answering shot to satisfy the watchers. The cheerful gleams of firelight broke upon us through the clustering tree stems, and as we advanced Cecily and Agnes were easily discerned as they stood before the fires.

Soon we all gathered to discuss an excellent meal of moose steaks and grouse stew, dished up for us by our men, and which tasted as good as if it had been served in one of London's greatest restaurants, although our cook was no *cordon bleu.*

The ladies decided to stay the night, and the store tent was made ready, where fortunately there was ample room and a supply of spare blankets. After a long chat over our doings, we turned in for the night to waken to a clear, fine morning, with that crisp invigorating feeling in the air which so often heralds the day in Northern lands. A slight covering of snow still lay upon the ground and trees, its glaring whiteness shimmering in the morning sun, and standing out in sharp contrast to a dark background of the sombre-garbed pine-trees. During the night another foreboding of approaching winter had cast its spell upon us, and a sharp touch of frost had made the snow firm and crackling, in which our footsteps left sharp imprints. On seeing this, at breakfast-time Agnes suggested that they remained yet another day with us, in order that we might together try to track a bull moose in the snow.

Cecily and Ralph set off in one direction, whilst Agnes and I started out on the opposite side of camp, and for reasons best known to ourselves each party decided to dispense with the services of any natives. We had not proceeded really far from camp ere we came upon the tracks of moose, where a band of three or four cows had crossed a well-worn moose trail; but here we failed to see the track of any bull. Once we struck the trail of a lynx, but the track was partly covered up with snow, showing that the beast had passed here early in the night, ere the snow had ceased to fall. Towards noon we came across the hoof-marks of a single bull moose, their size was such, and the snow seemed so recently broken, that we straightway elected to follow up this trail.

As we threaded our way onwards, here and there passing through dense patches of dwarf underwood, and moving noiselessly over the yielding snow, ever and again we came on places where the moose had stopped to browse upon the willow twigs, showing that he was not travelling very fast. Suddenly, during one of the occasional halts which we made to stop and listen for a while, there broke upon the still air the hoarse, deep, grunting note of an angry bull moose. Shortly afterwards it was answered by another bull, which seemed to be even closer to us than the first one. Standing motionless we listened, and could plainly hear the nearest bull thrashing the brushwood with his antlers, a certain sign that he was angry, and that a fight was impending. The nearest bull was barely then a hundred yards away, but so thick were the trees and underbrush that we could not catch a glimpse of him. Gradually the two animals sounded to be drawing nearer, until we heard the rushing of a heavy body through the bushes, and then a mighty crash of horns as the two monarchs met. Again and again there came to us the sound of the clashing horns, and whispering to Agnes that we must not miss this splendid sight we set off quietly in the direction of the sound. It appeared as if one bull was having rather the best of matters, and was driving the other further away, since we soon came on the spot where the combat had commenced, as was clearly evinced by the trampled snow and broken bushes. Following up the noise of battle we came on a small clearing, or forest glade, in which a wondrous sight met our gaze. There, with the furious light of battle in their eyes, one hundred yards away, stood two magnificent bull moose, glaring at each other a few paces distant with lowered horns, heaving flanks, and steaming nostrils. Scarce a moment they stood thus, and then again in a mighty rush they met with fast-locked horns, the shock of their impact being terrific. Each beast, in crouching attitude, fore-legs close together and hind-legs widely spread, endeavoured by the huge muscles of his hind-quarters to force the other backwards. A fatal moment would it be for either if for an instant he exposed his side to the deadly horns of his opponent. So intent were they upon the combat that for a time they had thrown caution to the winds, and neither animal seemed to heed a greater danger than that which stood immediately in front of him. Both bulls were magnificent specimens of their race, but one carried a pair of horns which were gigantic in size, and far overlapping the spread of the other's. I whispered to Agnes, asking if she would take my rifle, and have a shot, since she had come out without her own. She was firm in her refusal to do this, declaring that she had already killed two moose, and I had only one. I proceeded to advance cautiously towards the edge of the clearing, fearing to trust a shot from where we stood, lest the bullet should glance off some of the numerous twigs which screened us from view. I felt sure that the vast bull, which carried by far the largest horns I ever saw, was then as good as mine, for it seemed impossible to miss so large a beast at such shore range. But alas! I was counting my chickens! Just as I was nearing the edge of the glade I came almost face to face with a cow moose, which had been screened from view by a patch of thick bushes, and had been probably an interested spectator of the combat, considering the fact that the whole trouble doubtless arose over a dispute about her ladyship's favours.

Almost before I caught sight of her she was off at a gallop across the open ground, uttering a loud startled cry as she went, which gave the warning.

Now, as our friend Livy states, " Mars is fickle, and the fortunes of war are contrary," and thus it was that although this *contretemps* was the means of saving the old bull's life from my rifle, it almost caused his death at the horns of his adversary. As I ran forward a few paces to get an open space for shooting, the big bull, warned by the cry, turned slightly towards us, and in that moment the other bull, taking advantage of the exposed side, smote the big beast between the joints of his harness, and struck him such a terrible blow on the shoulder that he almost lifted the huge animal off his legs. He, poor brute, taken at a disadvantage, and threatened by a known and unknown danger, was forced to save himself by momentarily seeking the shelter of the neighbouring wood. No sooner had he recovered himself from the other's attack than he swung round quickly and dashed out of sight into the brushwood.

So quickly had the whole thing happened that I had no chance to get a shot at him ere the big bull disappeared, and realizing that he was off on a big stampede, I thought my best chance lay in shooting at the other bull. He seemed pleased to think that victory rested with him, and once more loudly blared his challenge note, little dreaming then the answer it would bring, for ere he could move, like a cunning general following up the routed enemy, the deadly bullet from my Mannlicher had reached its billet. Reeling like a storm-struck ship he stood a moment, shot clean through the heart, and his great fore-legs collapsed as he crashed heavily on his side, never to rise again.

At this moment Agnes ran up, exclaiming, " Why, oh why, did you not shoot at the other beast?" To which I could only retort that she need not add to my chagrin at having lost the finest trophy of my life, and that it was impossible to get a shot at the animal from where I stood when he dashed into cover. It was in no enviable frame of mind that I inspected the fallen beast, but we were both surprised at the size and remarkable symmetry of the horns. Producing a tape I found they measured exactly seventy inches. Then only did I dare conjecture what the other bull's horns must have spanned, for beside his these great antlers looked small. Till my dying day I shall always believe that I have seen a living moose whose horns exceeded eighty inches spread.

Agnes volunteered to return to camp and send back the men to skin and bring in the head, and taking my rifle lest she should encounter any big game *en route* she started, leaving me alone beside the dead beast. There was no need to give the men instructions how to find me, nor for Agnes to trouble how she should regain camp, for by following the trail of our footsteps in the snow these were both simple matters.

Seated on a fallen log, silently watching the curling smoke arise from my pipe in the still air of a glorious autumn afternoon, I fell to moralizing. Looking at the huge recumbent form of the noble beast beside me, there came a sense of revulsion when it seemed that the slaying of such splendid creatures was a deadly sin. What, I asked myself, wonderingly, had this poor animal done in his whole life to deserve his fate? There lay the wondrous head, for ever still, no more would beat that gallant heart which knew not fear whilst still the owner roamed the wilds, lord of the forest, proud of his fleetness and strength, defying all foes in the kingdom of his kind. Unlucky moose, that you should stray in this lonely spot across the path of the wanderer who came on slaughter bent! Though your slayer looks with pride on those vast horns, which he hopes may long adorn his ancestral halls, had he the power to heal and undo, for very pity he would give back thy life.

Perhaps these thoughts come to many men, but for my part, although admitting that I love the noble trophies, the destruction of some cruel beast has given me more genuine delight than the slaying of moose or wapiti, those noblest, yet harmless, speci-

U

mens of the deer tribe. They say—the all-knowing mysterious " they "—that Outram never killed any but dangerous game. A fine hand to play, if the cards were always obtainable.

My thoughts went wandering back across the many lands where formerly I roamed rifle in hand. I trod upon the burning sands of Africa, climbed again in fur-clad garb the vast snowy steeps of North-east Siberia, sought the keen-eyed sheep in his mountain fastness, or once more matched my wits against those lurking denizens of dense jungles. I saw a gallant salmon leap as he strove hard for dear life, and I went stumbling on with straining rod, over the rock-strewn banks of some fair river on Norway's wooded coast or Iceland's barren shores.

The sound of voices. Two natives upon the scene. Fortunately they brought my camera, which enabled me to procure a picture of the moose as he lay. The removal of the scalp and head was not a lengthy matter when all three of us set to work upon the task, and soon we set off homewards, the two natives taking turns at carrying the head and horns, whilst I packed home the scalp. Dragging a huge pair of moose horns through the dense underwood is by no means an easy task, and it has always been a mystery to me why these denizens of the thick Alaskan forests should have developed such immense antlers, re-sembling those of prehistoric beasts, which must be more of an impediment than assistance to them in their daily life.

On return to camp I found Cecily and Ralph there,

THERE LAY THE WONDROUS HEAD, FOR EVER STILL.

the latter having bagged a fine timber wolf, the skin of which already adorned a pole outside the tents, and which Ralph had skinned and brought into camp himself, a job not altogether pleasing to his rather fastidious taste.

Once more over the gleaming pine-logs Agnes and I stalked again the mighty bulls, bitterly bewailing the losing of the giant moose. In the world of sport it is ever so. Still we shall continue to lose those record heads, and countless are the forty pounders which we cannot land. It is the great uncertainty which lends the nameless charm to a wandering sportsman's life.

CHAPTER XVIII

A SCHOLAR OF THE WILDERNESS

No temple but the wood,
No assembly but the horn-beasts
As You Like It

Cheated of feature by dissembling nature,
Deform'd, unfinish'd
King Richard III

He was furnished like a hunter
As You Like It

THE moose of Alaska, *Alces gigas,* is an even finer beast than his relative *Alces americanus,* and the antlers obtained in the Kenai Peninsula of late years have surpassed in size, spread, and splendour the best trophies Canada has ever produced. *Alces americanus* is a glorious creature, but the Alaskan cousin carries off the palm.

The record moose head of the world came from the Kenai district, and was taken by a native from an animal discovered drowned in the river, caught in some scrub alders overhanging the banks. The span of antlers of this wondrous find came out at eighty-one inches, and the trophy eventually found its way to a New York club. All moose heads shrink a little in the drying, even when the antlers are wedged out with bits of wood betwixt them and the skull. Very often a head loses as much as two inches in the drying process.

One exquisite evening, when the moon was nearly full, Cecily and I wandered along the shores of the near by lagoon, a tiny lake, formed by the river overflowing to lower ground. Standing in the lush green grasses on the verge of the shimmering pool, up to her knees in water, a cow moose faced up, not more than forty paces off. The silver moonlight flashed on her huge ears, limning in clear-cut strokes her square wet nose, silhouetting cameo-like the stalwart figure. Two calves breathed on the water in inquiring sniffs, as though to discover what this wealth of liquid was composed of. One calf was much younger than the other, and would be, of course, an adopted child. A real mother, that moose evidently. A " let them all come " type of matron as rare, I expect, in Alaska as in Albion.

With a start the ungainly cow winded us—I think a cow moose is the plainest of any of the deer tribe, if a creature of the wild, with its mysterious charm of environment, and manifold allurements, can be called downright plain—and the water splashed to her shoulders as she made a bid for safety, gaining the bank in excited rush. The surprised calves tumbled after her in flurried desire to follow on the trail. Into the sombre blue-black forest glided the hurrying forms, disappearing, like grey wraiths, into the heart of the silence.

When the horns are growing the strain on the constitution of a moose is great, and often when seen carrying a head in the velvet a really fine animal looks lean and cadaverous of appearance. Once the antlers are hard, however, the bull puts on flesh at a tremendous pace, and gains in contour and weight daily.

One mighty moose crossed our path frequently, and his head carried no horns whatever. In size, bulk and general appearance he was a giant of his kind, but Fortune had docked him of his chief beauty. By some mischance, wound, or accident of sorts, his horns had ceased to grow; but there he was, a gay Lothario for a' that, with a heart for many a fair lady of the moose world. It was most strange, but this uncrowned monarch held undisputed sway over his range of forest kingdom, and his triumphal battle cry rang through the woods at night. Lying concealed in the underbrush one day, I saw our hornless friend drive before him a stalwart young moose, fitted out with antlers of most business-like appearance. A lunge of the great bull neck, a fierce drive from the razor fore-feet, and the deer fled before the battering onslaughts of his hornless foe.

This particular animal appeared to keep to the same stretch of forest country, undeterred by our presence, for we frequently caught a glimpse of the rushing bulk; but, as a rule, when suddenly frightened, particularly when crossing a trail and getting the scent of a human being, or sighting so fearsome a vision as a man in the precincts of the timber belt, a moose simply goes for all he is worth, sometimes covering ten miles at a stretch without drawing up.

The early morning we found to be the best time for tracking, before the animals lay down for the day, and also the evening, as they fed before nightfall. Of course, in such dense forest it is very hard to determine how best to avoid giving a moose the scent which is at once his dread and, often, his deliverance. On straight ground the wind blows evenly, but in forested glades, up hills and down dales, the breeze circles, eddies, and varies ten times in an hour. We likewise found it difficult to judge distances, but fortunately we usually overestimated this. The great hollows and depths of the dingles and grassy expanses accounted, in part, for the many strange errors of judgment made in some of our stalks. We all came to the conclusion that stiff-handed shooting was useless with these rushing giants, and found that to aim well in front of the quarry, following the beast with the rifle, at his own pace, in the lightning dash a moose almost invariably made as he sighted us, gave the best results.

We changed our camps in the moose country often, for the sake of novelty, but they varied little. Each one had some points of beauty, some unusual charms. Our last was pitched facing east, and situated just at the junction of two small streams, tributaries to the Sushitna, which flowed onwards into a lagoon of sufficient size as to allow its being dignified by the name of lake. On the north and south high alders formed a screen from the treacherous winds, which at times conspired to transform this paradise into an Inferno. Looking at the peaceful unruffled waters, scarcely shimmering beneath the evening breeze, it seemed hard to picture what it would be like in early spring as the fierce breath of the mountains rushed down from the snow-clad heights, lashing the lake to a seething, boiling turmoil.

The witching scene was accentuated by an ethereal splendour. From our very feet, on the one side, rose the hills, first in gentle slopes, extending for a long way, till they mounted tier upon tier, towering aloft to altitudes of many thousands of feet. Between each mighty peak vast cañons and gorges lay, deep in snow, beneath which the roaring torrents hurled their icy waters downwards to the river. The hillsides were densely clad with cloaks of alder, willow, birch, and mountain ash, whilst here and there bright patches of green carpeted a glade from which the snow had gone.

Higher still lay the vast fields of perennial snow, which defiant alike to sun and rain formed a background in vivid contrast to the foliage around. The sun climbed over a gleaming white cone, most lofty and noble of all the noble peaks, and the rays reflected a thousand tints with a brilliancy only to be seen in the rarefied atmosphere of these Northern climes. The light danced and flickered on the highest snow-clad tops, and fell slowly athwart a dark green patch of alder, outlining the vivid clumps of mountain ash, gleaming on the boles of the silver birch. The gold and silver glory of the streams rippled over the tiny boulders at our feet, falling in a sparkling chain of cascades, clear as the snow from which they sprung, adding endless music to the scene. And over all the mid-evening silence rang the trilling " Good-night "

A TIMBER WOLF

of the hermit thrush, and the lightsome touch of our chatter and plans.

It is on a night like this that one thanks God for the wild, for thinking it, for making it, for keeping it. He made the wild, as man the town, and the devil Suburbia. The nights were vibrant with the weird sounds of the wilderness. The forlorn cry of a loon, matchless diver of lake and sea, his note an epitome of indescribable desolation of solitude, the whirr of wings from myriad ducks winging their way to warmer countries—" Summer has passed, summer has passed!" sang in the musical rustle—the furious clash of horns as Greek met Greek in deadly forest combat, the soft alluring call of the cause of all the trouble, and once or twice on the cold night winds came the prolonged discordant hunting yell of a wolf. Few and far between are the wolves in the Alaskan woods, the trapper and the native hunter have seen to that.

In this forest of Arden one early morning I came on the smoking embers of a fire, evidences of a just moved camp, and a chill foreboding came to me that our little world was our very own no more. The outfit of another hunter, perhaps. But—our men from Cook's Inlet. An investigation of the river, a walk up stream, and a moving figure glided from between the tree stems and hailed me. Sure enough, a straggler from our expected servants, the others, having pulled up the *bidarkas*, were wandering about haphazard on the looking for a needle in a haystack principle. So absurd, when we had provided strict injunctions that the party should persevere to the head of the river, where we would keep a lookout for them.

It was full time that our little henchmen from the Bering Sea coast returned to their homes, ere the weather broke up and rendered the journey almost impossible of negotiation.   They set off at once, after the arrival of our new men, and we saw the little band set forth, equipped with an ample supply of provisions from the supplies brought up to us from the Inlet. Gummidge waved a dreary farewell.   He held out no hopes to his companions that any of them would ever see their happy homes again.

Letters and newspapers, forerunners of civilization, greeted us, and a sort of comprehensive log of the *Lily*, compiled by Captain Clemsen—good man—who specially commended for favourable notice one of the newly-arrived acquisitions, whose fame as a hunter was a growing one.   It was confidently said, reported the conscientious skipper, that our man rivalled the celebrated Andrew Berg, most renowned of Alaskan hunters, in successful moose calling.   We sorted out our servant and inquired his name.

" Pitka," he answered solemnly.

" Only Pitka ?" said Cecily.

" Pitka Charley, sometimes Charley Pitka," replied the odd creature, with obliging differentiation.

His personality at once arrested attention, individuality surrounded him like an aura.   He was a hunchback, almost a dwarf, with an alert, perceptive mind which seemed the more astonishing as one regarded the poor mite of a creature controlling the whole.   A

quick intuitive soul is so often housed in a deformed,
misshapen body. It is as though Nature, one hand
behind her back, withholding much, feels pity, and
in part repents, bestowing with the other gifts of
gold and pearls of price.

The hunchback was a master of forest lore, he
knew the name of every bird, whence it came, and
went, and when, and why. The trees, the herbage,
the grasses and rushes of the river side were all an
interest to the small Aleut. It was sheer delight to
track with him, for if we drew blank the hours were
spent as profitably as though we had slain the fairest
forest monarch of them all. The history of the wild
was ours, the habits of the giant deer explained, his
best loved trees pointed out, his sleeping places, his
road to the river, a mine of knowledge. Now did we
guess within an inch or so the span of horn of a
rushing moose, tell his length of years by antlers,
bell, and coat. 'Twas a liberal education. We loved
to hear this scholar of the wilderness unfold the secrets
of his realm.

Pitka was, by far, the best hunter we met in Alaska,
and in his methods of attack, natural common sense,
highly developed cunning, and powers of endurance
came nearer to the standard of an African shikári
than any other native of Alaska whom we met, hunted
with, or even heard of. The eagle owls talked to
Pitka o' nights, giving back answer for answer,
screech for screech. When I tried to imitate the hoot
of an owl no response came. Ralph said that I
paralyzed the birds with astonishment. Charmed I

never so wisely, trying every inflection and modulation of voice at my command—no reply. Let Pitka try again, and at once came the hooting answer of the bird of night.

Pitka was very clever at making the moose call with mouth and hands, but, of course, this method did not carry very far. We were very anxious to see whether or no a moose would come to the call of our hunter, and persuaded him to hold a séance the very night of his joining us.

"Me call up big horns, you shoot um, I guess," the man said, confidently. Early morning and late evening are the times most chosen for calling up moose, but Pitka would none of either, and waited until the night had fallen.

I shall never forget the weirdness of the scene, the wonder of it, the witchery of the night, the perfect moon, lighting the open glades with shafts of silver glory, the slanting shadows falling athwart the eerie spaces, the great trees, the curve of the river, the shimmer of the water, and the silence that could be felt as with a touch.

We took up positions allotted to us by our henchman, a mile or more away from camp, and I lay behind a fallen log, not far from Pitka, and so could watch his every action. Instead of giving the call in the open, as I had expected, and as one always sees it in pictures, the hunchback set himself about four feet away from the largest tree in his neighbourhood, and as the grunting, sighing, coughing roar struck against the tree stem, the sound broke up and rang

through the woods, broken, realistic, the actual inso-
lent challenge of a forest monarch spoiling for a
fight. Again and again the ringing call, full of
pulsating life, an imperious summons, afire with
furious throbbing passion.

A little space of time, and then on the still air came
the sound of a heavy body crashing through all im-
pediments, a smashing of the undergrowth. My very
blood tingled with excitement, little shivers ran up
and down my spine.

Straight as an arrow, from the depths of the forest,
a moose broke into the open, coming at a quick pur-
poseful trot, his rounded nose held high in the air,
his beautiful antlers lying along his flanks. The
moon shone full on the gleaming horns, and outlined every contour of the massive body. A splendid
tassel of hair hung from beneath the swelling throat,
and every swinging movement was a perfection of
royal grace.

Up went the weighty head, and then in bellowing
resonant tones came the answering battle cry, sobbing
and panting over the silence. "To arms! To
arms!"

The great creature stood listening, tense and rigid,
then, of a sudden, knowledge of the presence of the
unseen people around him came to his inflamed brain.
The wind carried the dread human scent to the sniffing nostrils, and I saw distinctly a visible tremor of
alarm strike the moose as he stood so near to me
that I could count the points of his antlers easily.
Gathering himself together the frightened animal

turned in a flurried circle, then fled pell-mell into the
embracing underbrush, away and away from the zone
of danger.

Next evening Cecily and I, with Pitka in attendance, took an excursion around the lake, keeping to
the banks, often crossing tracts of ground which gave
way beneath us, and precipitated us over our knees
in water. Here and there green rushes, undisturbed
in all the centuries, formed great ramparts across our
way, necessitating a big detour. The lagoon was
wreathed in the white gossamer mists of autumn,
through which the busy ducks sped and winged their
flight to and fro, hither and thither, in chattering
concert arranging for the exodus to other shores. Such
activity presaged bad weather. When ducks are unusually conversational the barometer is falling.

In the soft hush of the evening, and the clean, sweet
smell of the wilderness, we climbed a mossy bank and
lay down, overlooking a piece of water to which ran
many recent moose trails. The creatures seek the
lakes and rivers to get away from the persistent flies
and myriad biting gnats, and stand for long minutes
in deep water for protection. The moose flies were
present with us in force, even Pitka was troubled by
the onslaughts, and cast his much tattered coat from
him as though it were a shirt of Nessus. The insects
got beneath it, he said, and made matters unbearable.
Suddenly, everything happens suddenly in big game
shooting, a cow moose loomed on our limited horizon,
some three hundred yards away, unwieldy and inelegant, a tiny calf, with huge ears for so small a

thing, sauntering alongside. Then—wonderful, and yet again most wonderful—a few steps behind came a grand old bull. He walked to the edge of the lake and pushed into it, deep, deep, until the water almost covered him. " Big horns," whispered Pitka laconically.

Big ! They seemed to us the most magnificent specimens we had ever gazed upon. Excited imagination did much, but calm reason told us that the antlers were unusually fine.

Anything more sinuous than the movements of our hunter as we prepared to get within fair range of our quarry cannot well be imagined. He passed between low-lying bushes, through rushes, over hummocks of grass with feline grace. The very undergrowth held buoyant beneath his agile feet, instead of giving way with resounding cracks as it was so often wont to do with Cecily and me.

We crept along in as faithful an imitation of our henchman as we could muster. Ever and again we dropped and lay still awhile to disarm suspicion. Once for nearly ten minutes we lay thus, and raising myself carefully my survey told me that the cow, the calf with her, had gone, perhaps to lie down in the forest behind. We could hear the bull grunting with pleasure, breathing deeply as he pushed his nose into the cool waters. As we lay prone, waiting for the chance King Circumstance might deign to accord us, the giant deer emerged from the water We could not see, but we could hear him. Breathlessly we waited, and across the flume of open country ahead of us, some hundred and fifty yards away, the dripping bulk walked at a slow pace, head carried low, and great swelling shoulders hunched. The moose stopped and shook himself vigorously, such a great prolonged shake, tossing his crowned head.

It was a shot which would have delighted the heart of a child in arms.

My cousin fired simultaneously with me, and the animal staggered sideways, lurched forward, but did not fall. With a great effort of strength he made for the timber line. All pretence at scientific stalking was abandoned, and we simply rushed after our moose with the speed of Atalanta. We were using our 12-bores, so that tracking was easy, a heavy blood trail led us through the dense forest. After a heavy chase we came up with the wounded moose, very sick, in a clump of alders. Out he jumped, and off he went, game to the last; but Cecily got in two successful shots which finished the business. With a gigantic leap into the air, a last expiring effort, the wonderful creature fell to rise no more.

This was our record head of the trip. No other matched it in grandeur, or grace. It was a noble trophy, with twenty-eight points, and a spread of seventy-four inches. In the subsequent drying this measurement reduced itself two inches, but enough antlers remained to make our head an unusually valuable, picked specimen of its genus.

This piece of luck closed the most lucky trip, so far as shooting was concerned. It was now well into October, and the weather showed signs of breaking

THE RECORD HEAD

up. There is often a fly in the best bit of amber, and perhaps the saddest moment in life is the end of something which we would, oh, so earnestly, desire to keep for ever as our own. This wild of ours, this what Goethe called, "the living visible garment of God," must be left behind, for we were not primeval hunters. The chill, fierce winter would soon hold our glades and dingles in icy grip; the face of Nature would frown; the raving of the tempest drown the murmurous hum of the small, sweet sounds of the forest people; the snow invest the wilderness of green in cloak of cruelty. The great transition was at hand. Would that we might be there when the world Mother, chameleon-like, took on once more the colours and the grace of spring.

Our hunt was over. Well, I had made the most of it, and drank my fill without wasting a drop, and had taken Omar's advice, for one never knows what lies ahead. I have known disappointments before.

Sorrowfully we broke up camp for the last time— for our little makeshifts on the banks of the Sushitna were too insignificant to be termed camps at all—said farewell to the much-loved haunts, prosaically cooking a terrific meal to set us well upon the way, and, having packed the heads and skins aboard a couple of dories, betook ourselves to *bidarkas* and the bosom of the river. Our trophies made a rare show. Black bear, caribou, *Ovis dalli*, and moose antlers of the most magnificent description, filled our hearts with pride and pleasure.

It is one thing to fag up a river, against the stream,

x

quite another to flash down, meteor-like; and all too soon the uneventful journey was over, and the third day found us paddling past the Sushitna settlement out into the Inlet, where the black hull of the *Lily* waited us at Hope.

We paid off the men, all save Steve, who desired to sail down the Inlet to Saldovia with us. Ned had left the ship at Kodiac, and since his departure Tom, the cabin boy, had seen to the trophies, and all of them, bear, walruses, and birds, were in perfect condition.

THE TROPHIES ON THE SUSHITNA RIVER

CHAPTER XIX

THE PRECIPICE MATRIMONIAL

And I must lose
Two of the sweetest companions in the world
Cymbeline

I'll be an auditor,
An actor too, perhaps, if I see cause
Midsummer Night's Dream

Therefore a health to all that shot and missed
Taming of the Shrew

IT was October the fourteenth when we reached
Saldovia in the *Lily*, and the last steamer from the
Inlet was due to sail for Seattle next day. The rush
for berths was enormous, and if we meant to travel
on her our minds had to be made up at once. Cecily
and Ralph were anxious now to make civilization
as soon as possible; for they had planned a honey-
moon shoot to the interior of Mexico after *Ovis
nelsoni*, a variety of bighorn carrying even finer
heads than *Ovis dalli*. Of course the matrimonial
preliminaries would need some arranging.

All things considered, therefore, we considered it
better for Captain Clemsen to sail the schooner, with
the trophies on board, to Seattle, and we, travelling
by the just-about-to-sail steamer, would be waiting at
the Sound port, ready to receive and pack the
treasures.

The little ship was not a patch upon the *Nome City*, and she was crowded up like the steerage of an emigrant ship—even the hold was requisitioned for sleeping accommodation. I don't think any one paid more than his neighbour; it was first come, first served.

Leaning over the gunwale, watching the interesting scene, to our immense surprise we discovered a friend in the person of a well-known English shikári, a noted shot, returning home after a hunt in the Kenai Peninsula and Sheep Creek district. A distinct acquisition to the passenger list. The sombre peak of Redoubt vanished into the scurrying mists, the *mélange* of passengers, almost entirely of the masculine persuasion, dawdled about the grubby decks in unsettled confusion, and disjointed scraps of conversation floated to me on the freshening breeze.

" It panned out seventy per cent.——"

That everlasting seventy per cent. !

A rough-looking prospector leaned against a deck-house near me.

" If I can divorce my wife——" drifted on the air. *Cetera desunt.*

But what a peep behind the scenes !

Two small American boys ran about the ship, precocious children of a manager of a salmon can-nery, now closed down for the season.

"Now, Hiram, sit there!" said the harassed mother. " Cyrus, if you hang over the side you'll get yourself drowned. Hiram, give over crying, you can't be sick yet. Cyrus, let go of that there rope. Hiram, quit cutting your name on the deck. Poppa, help me scare these 'ere boys! Ain't the selfishness of men turrible? I can't tell what in the wide world women get married for!"

We shared a stuffy cabin, furnished with three bunks a-heap with dark-coloured blankets, with a well-meaning woman, who was unfortunately very deaf. A great conversationalist too, which complicated matters.

" I," she said proudly, introducing herself, " I am the professional gambler's wife."

I do not know what a professional gambler may be, but he is evidently a personage of sorts.

" Who are you?" the lady questioned.

We bawled out humbly that we had no real reason to be in the world at all. We were just Englishwomen, back from hunting different varieties of Alaskan game.

" You walk very lame? I didn't notice it."

" I'm afraid we're going to have it rough," said Cecily, trying not to smile.

" Had about enough? I should think so. I had long ago. We're packed like herrings in a barrel."

Then dinner, or rather a cross between dinner, tea, and breakfast. Every one could not sit down at once, and the meal came off in sections. The captain, a bluff American, served out portions of a centipede chicken, a bird run entirely to leg. The prospectors, miners, loggers, and indiscriminate race mixings wielded knives with the dexterity of jugglers, balancing bits of fowl on the tips, and throwing the food into the waiting caverns in an abandon of relish. A leaky lamp swung over the table, lighting up the unwashed cloth and table cutlery of serviceable design.

The English shikári had allowed himself, in an unguarded moment, to be dragged into politics, and was giving his opinion forcibly on the question of American rule in the Philippines.

" I advocate freedom of speech and action," he said, upsetting a carafe of water over his immediate part of the table in his excitement. " The country is going to the dogs, to the dogs! The policy of the American Government is disastrous! Presently a blow will fall, a blow will fall——" Here the roping of a tin box hanging on a nail behind the sportsman gave way, and fell with a resounding crash to the floor.

It was a meal! I did enjoy it.

The professional gambler's wife greeted us as we reached the deck. The clouds were banking up, and little spurts of wind sped ominously through the rigging.

" I fancy it is going to rain," said Cecily politely, as our cabin mate took a seat in our midst.

" Got a bad pain? I don't wonder. Guess that there chicken came to Alaska with the first prospector."

A crowded, uncomfortable trip enough, but the elements were on the whole good to us, and we made Seattle in excellent time.

We found that we had a few days' necessary residence to put in, and this suited us admirably, as the *Lily* could not be expected to arrive for a week at the earliest.

We thought of the Episcopalian padre to do the splicing business, our friend of the journey North on board the *Nome City*, and Ralph looked him up. The Episcopalians were very glad to see us, and most kindly asked us all to supper. I am sure she did not mean it, but really madam, she of the one-pin method of dressing herself, had a most comprehensive way of keeping the guests off the food.

" Did this duck die of pneumonia, Lee?" she inquired of the Chinaman, " or is it the one I said you were to kill because its leg was broken?"

Then, later, toying thoughtfully with the milk-pudding, she murmured, *à propos* of nothing in particular, " Our cow is threatened with tuberculosis. Such a grief to us. She is a real friend of the family."

Ralph said, when we got home, that he was starving. But when once the door of an American coffee-room is closed nothing will open it again until the scheduled meal hour.

The days passed too quickly, invitations to all sorts of festivities rained in. Our kindly American cousins welcomed us royally.

Seattle society—and it was most hospitable to us —was all agog with a story of " Vanity Fair " variety, and as we knew all the actors in the little drama we took the same furious interest as the rest of the circle, and waited inquisitively for the *dénoue-ment*, which was not, when we left. The whole thing leaked out because it had been made a secret of, and as such been confided to an intimate friend.

Mrs. A., the wife of a prominent Seattle banker, was a flighty, vain little personage, and had an ardent admirer in a certain Mr. B., a well-known real estate agent. The acquaintance was absolutely platonic. Mrs. A. said so, and naturally she would be in the know. Mr. B., as a faithful cavalier should do, escorted his ladye here, there, and everywhere, and one day, in the course of their perambulations among the shops, they came on a beautiful thing in sealskin coats, a perfect dream of a garment, priced at $500.

Pretty Mrs. A. expressed her heartfelt admiration, and her great desire to own and wear such a certain incentive to feminine envy. Mr. B. said that if he could see his way to giving her the coat without arousing any undue astonishment on the part of Mr. A., such an opportunity should be at once seized upon with gusto and delight.

But—alas!—*c'est impossible!* So handsome a coat would take some buying, any one would know that. Mrs. A.'s allowance could not be held responsible for such an outlay.

Then—happy thought—Mr. B. had an idea. He was not frightened, he often had them, but rarely such a brilliant gem as this scintillating affair which paved the way to the furriers, and, incidentally, of course, confusion dire.

"Aha!" said the erudite young man, "I have it! We will buy the coat, put it in pawn, and you, *you* shall hold the ticket."

Mrs. A., puzzled by such lightning *finesse*, said that she did not see how the pawning of the longed-for coat would help the situation at all. She never had any occasion to pawn anything, and her husband would know quite well that she never had such a garment to pawn.

Mr. B., with airy confidence, gave it as his opinion that when thoroughly grasped the carrying out of his idea would be found to be as easy of accomplishment as falling off a log, if not easier.

The coat was purchased, and duly put in pawn for the sum of twenty-five dollars, and taking the ticket Mrs. A. would explain to her worser half that she had acquired it from Mrs. X., a lady who had fallen on evil days, when Mr. A., if he had any idea of the duty of a husband at all, would at once rush to the pawn shop and please his wife by redeeming the coat of coats. The plan, worthy of a better fate, radiant with genius, worked like a charm at first. Next morning Mrs. A. launched herself on a sea of explanations, and mentioned the fact that she had come across, on the previous day, poor Mrs. X., whose husband was killed in the train smash at 'Frisco. "You remember," said Delilah, "we met them on the train going to Spokane?"

Mr. A. could not recall the fact, try as he would, which was a mere detail, for one meets so many people going to Spokane. That section of the

Northern Pacific pays very well, and the cars are always crowded.

On went Mrs. A. romancing about the pitiable condition of Mrs. X., who upon an urgent message from Chicago left Seattle hurriedly, finding herself so short of money that she came to sell the pawn ticket on a beautiful coat, a coat worth quite $250, which could be redeemed for the trifling sum of $25.

Mr. A., being a business man, wondered how it seemed so certain that the coat was worth even so much as $25, but the artful Mrs. A. had seen the treasure in the window. Of course she herself could not enter a pawn shop, would John—dear John—attend to the matter for her? Here she handed over the $25, which she was just able to scratch together out of her allowance. John dutifully promised to "fix it up," and everything seemed to herald a successful ending to the difficulty.

On his return from the bank that evening Mr. A. had regretfully to admit that he had clean forgotten the whole thing, and his wife, in a decidedly anxious condition, wrung a promise from her lord that he would without fail hie him to the pawnbrokers the very first thing on the morrow. Arrival of Mr. A. next evening, who produced for his agitated wife's inspection a small diamond ring, which when new might have cost $30.

"I guess there's some darned error about that coat, anyhow," he said. "This is what I got on ticket No. 20579."

Tableau! Collapse of Mrs. A., who foresaw some

terrible blunder, and the possible loss of the desired coat.

The minute Mr. A. took his departure on the following morning out dashed Mrs. A. to seek Mr. B., and send him post haste to investigate matters at the pawn shop. Hurrying along she took a short cut to the Real Estate Office, and skirted the granite premises of the bank. Coming jauntily down the steps, in full sail, tripped Mr. A.'s stenographer, a very pretty girl. And she was wearing the sealskin coat!

Hinc illæ lacrimæ.

The Seattle papers got hold of the story, and dished it up under thinly-disguised names. The head-lines were very thrilling.

HOIST WITH HER OWN PETARD
THE HUSBAND MARKED THE GAME
WHAT SHOULD THE LADY DO?

I wonder myself. What could a woman do under such circumstances? It is a problem. I cannot answer it.

At last the day of the wedding. We had kept it a great secret so that it might be very quiet and to ourselves. The Leader did groomsman, and I gave the bride away. The wife of the padre was got up in a truly magnificent creation for the occasion, so heavy and massive that pins were useless and a bodkin of strength and girth had to be requisitioned. Captain Clemsen was present, by special invitation.

And Cecily? Well, she did not wear a *parka*, nor yet a *khaki* suit, but she looked every inch a beautiful Diana all the same.

It was all over—they had gone! I had waved "Good-bye" to the ship which took the bride and bridegroom to San Francisco.

The bizarre hotel room looked hideously forsaken. A pair of Cecily's gloves lay on the table, a half-smoked cigar of Ralph's hung on the edge of the mantelpiece. Heavens! What a dreary hotel! What a great city full of unknown people! What a crowd of uninterested busy creatures! Why had I ever come? Were the most wondrous trophies in all the world worth the price of so great a loneliness?

The handle of the door turned, and the Leader of the expedition that was stood in the doorway. His eyes were smiling, smiling.

Perhaps, perhaps, I'm not so very lonely after all.

THE END